African Philosophy and the Otherness of Albinism

Albinism is one of the foremost disabilities and public health issues in Africa today. It often makes headlines in local, national and international media and forms the basis for intense advocacy at all levels. This is primarily due to the harmful representations of persons with albinism that are deeply entrenched in African traditions. These deeply rooted ideologies about albinism in African thought have largely promoted the continuous discrimination, stigmatisation, harming, killing, commodification and violation of the human rights of persons with albinism in African places.

How has albinism emerged as a thick concept in African traditions? What are these deeply entrenched ideas about the ontology of albinism in African thought? What epistemic injustice has been done to persons with albinism in Africa places? Why do harmful beliefs about albinism still persist in modern African societies? How does the African communalistic ethic justify the harm done against persons with albinism? What is the duty to, and burden of, care for persons with albinism? What peculiar existential challenges do persons with albinism in general and females with albinism in particular face in African societies and how can they be overcome? What can be learned from the education philosophy of reconstructionism and genetic engineering in improving the well-being of persons with albinism? *African Philosophy and the Otherness of Albinism: White Skin, Black Race* digs deep into these philosophical questions, revealing fascinating but latent aspects of how albinism is understood in African places as a necessary step to take in improving the well-being and integrity of persons with albinism in Africa today.

This book will be of interest to scholars and students of African philosophy, sociology, African studies and disability studies.

Elvis Imafidon is a lecturer in the Department of Philosophy at Ambrose Alli University, Nigeria, and Fellow of the Johannesburg Institute for Advanced Study (JIAS). He is the editor of *Ontologized Ethics: New Essays in African Meta-ethics* (2013) and *The Ethics of Subjectivity: Perspective since the Dawn of Modernity* (2015). He is also the author of *The Question of the Rationality of African Traditional Thought: An Introduction* (2013).

Routledge Studies in African Philosophy

1. **African Philosophy and the Otherness of Albinism**
   White Skin, Black Race
   Elvis Imafidon

African Philosophy and the Otherness of Albinism
White Skin, Black Race

Elvis Imafidon

Routledge
Taylor & Francis Group

LONDON AND NEW YORK

First published 2019
by Routledge
2 Park Square, Milton Park, Abingdon, Oxon OX14 4RN

and by Routledge
52 Vanderbilt Avenue, New York, NY 10017

First issued in paperback 2020

Routledge is an imprint of the Taylor & Francis Group, an informa business

© 2019 Elvis Imafidon

The right of Elvis Imafidon to be identified as author of this work has been asserted by him in accordance with sections 77 and 78 of the Copyright, Designs and Patents Act 1988.

All rights reserved. No part of this book may be reprinted or reproduced or utilised in any form or by any electronic, mechanical, or other means, now known or hereafter invented, including photocopying and recording, or in any information storage or retrieval system, without permission in writing from the publishers.

Trademark notice: Product or corporate names may be trademarks or registered trademarks, and are used only for identification and explanation without intent to infringe.

British Library Cataloguing-in-Publication Data
A catalogue record for this book is available from the British Library

Library of Congress Cataloging-in-Publication Data
A catalog record has been requested for this book

ISBN 13: 978-0-367-66471-8 (pbk)
ISBN 13: 978-1-138-33540-0 (hbk)

Typeset in Times NR MT Pro
by Cenveo® Publisher Services

For Elliott, for mostly being away in those first few months of life.

Contents

Preface	ix
Acknowledgements	xii
Foreword	xiv

Introduction: Albinism, difference and the philosophical turn   1

1   Albinism and African thick conceptualisations   8

The biological understanding of albinism in persons 9
Albinism as a disability 14
Albinism as a thick and contested concept in African thought 17
Peculiarities of albinism in Africa 23

2   The ontology of albinism in African traditions   28

An African theory of being 29
Categories of being in African ontology 33
Persons with albinism as queer beings 39
Questioning the ontological asumptions about albinism 44
The linguistic turn: albinism and linguistic ableism 46

3   The epistemology of albinism in African traditions   52

African theory of knowledge I: Knowledge as first-hand
    information 53
African theory of knowledge II: Knowledge as consistency
    with established beliefs 56
African theory of knowledge III: Knowledge as shared
    knowledge 60
Processes of knowing 63
Why do (false) beliefs persist? 66
Ignorance and systemically produced falsehood 69

viii   *Contents*

4   The ethics of albinism in African traditions   73

An African theory of the good 74
Does African moral theory justify harming persons with
   albinism? 80
The duty to, and burden of, care 83
Social justice, dignity and easing of the burden of care 87
The challenge of an elitist virtue ethic 91

5   Albinism in Africa: Some existential issues   95

Fear and dread 97
Alienation, suicide contemplation and authentic living 101
Peculiar feminine experience of albinism 106

6   Overcoming the violent othering of albinism in Africa today   111

Reconstructive and awareness education and training for key
   social institutions 113
Reconstructive and awareness education for persons with
   albinism 120
Establishment of social structures and institutions 123
Gene research and therapy: Implications and prospects for
   albinism 128

Bibliography   133
Index   141

Preface

A subject matter that has increasingly been of interest to philosophers since the twentieth century is difference or alterity. The works of notable philosophers in the twentieth century such as Derrida, Deleuze, Foucault, Levinas, Lacan and Beauvoir gained much prominence because they made the philosophical discourse of difference and the other in comparison with the identity of the self a major focal point of their works. One practical area that the philosophy of alterity or difference has been applied to is the philosophy of disability, an area that has resulted in heated and protracted debates in philosophical circles in the last six or so decades focussing on such issues as normalization of bodies, embodiment, ontological, epistemological and moral issues of disability, disability and justice and so on. This has become a very vibrant area of discourse in recent times.

The recent increase in the discourse of delimited areas of, and specific subject matters in, African philosophy such as African ethics, African epistemology and African political philosophy has exposed the global community of scholars and researchers to fascinating ideas, theories, debate themes and issues in philosophy as they evolve in African contexts. However, there are many such important specific areas of African philosophy still underexplored. One such underexplored areas in African philosophy is the African philosophy of difference in general and the philosophy of disability in particular. This monograph, *African Philosophy and the Otherness of Albinism: White Skin, Black Race*, aims to explore, from a philosophical perspective, one of the most problematic, paradoxical and disturbing disability issues in African contexts and societies: albinism.

Recent and recurring experiences of persons with albinism in many African communities, such as the continuous stigmatisation and discrimination as well as the physical harming of such persons, show that the harmful beliefs that fostered and promoted the ill-treatment and killings of persons with albinism in traditional African societies are still very much present in modern African societies. Why are such harmful beliefs about persons with albinism persistent in modern Africa? What effective means can be explored in combating such beliefs? Existing literature on albinism in Africa has focussed primarily on exploring legal, health (such as medicine

x *Preface*

and genetics), cultural, human rights, and education issues of albinism in Africa. These perspectives in existing literature generally describe and expose the beliefs that are harmful to persons with albinism in African cultures and recommend ways of improving the lives of persons with albinism However, there is very little in existing literature on a philosophical perspective on albinism in Africa. It is this gap in scholarship that this monograph intends to fill. To be sure, a philosophical perspective would consist of a critical analysis of the ontological assumptions about being or reality, the epistemic framework, the ethical principles and implications, and the logical issues inherent in the harmful beliefs about albinism in African communities. Exploring the philosophical perspectives is essential in understanding the ideological commitments in African cultures that make such harmful beliefs about persons with albinism thrive and persist today in African places. It is also useful in identifying latent but fundamental aspects of tradition to focus on in seeking ways to improve the well-being of persons with albinism.

This book is therefore a critical reflection on, and interrogation of, the thick concept of albinism as understood within African contexts. Among other issues, it attempts to unravel the ontological roots of the harmful representations of albinism and of persons with albinism as, for instance, queer and harmful beings with superhuman abilities and powers. It also analyses the epistemological issues evolving from the African representation of albinism, such as issues regarding the processes of knowing and the role ignorance and an elitist virtue epistemology play in othering persons with albinism in African cultures; it also examines the issue of why false beliefs persist in the face of counterfactual evidences. Beyond these, it pays attention to the moral issues ensuing from the understanding of albinism in Africa, such as the justification of the maltreatment of persons with albinism to be found in African communalistic ethics, the duty and burden to care for persons with albinism and the challenges of an elitist virtue ethics for albinism in Africa. The peculiar existential challenges faced by persons with albinism in general and females with albinism in particular are also examined. They include a socially infused fear and dread, and the contemplation of suicide. The book concludes by exploring important aspects to focus on in finding solutions to the precarious situations faced by persons with albinism in African societies, such as the role of reconstructivism as a philosophy of education and the prospects and moral implications of genetic engineering and gene therapy for persons with albinism.

My interest in the philosophical discourse of albinism in African cultures has developed for two main reasons: first, a life-long lived experience of albinism as a form of difference. The physical and social challenges that resulted from my being white in a densely black populated community in Nigeria were essential in building and sustaining my interest in understanding albinism as a form of disability and its peculiarities in African contexts. The second is my training in Philosophy as a discipline. After completing my PhD in Philosophy in 2014, I became very interested in filling the gap

Preface xi

I had noticed in the literature on albinism in Africa: the lack of a philosophical perspective on the issue, which I felt was key to unravelling the intricacies of albinism, and the unpleasant experiences of persons with albinism in African societies due to the harmful representations of albinism in such societies. I do not, however, assume to have exhausted the issues that could evolve from an attempt to examine albinism in Africa from philosophical lenses in this monograph. But I do hope that the issues discussed herein will stir up further discussions in a very vibrant and important area of discourse of the philosophy of difference and disability in African spaces.

Acknowledgements

The ideas developed in this book emerged from approximately three years of research on the lived experiences of persons with albinism in Africa. But I could hardly find the time and space to synchronise these ideas scattered in many drafts into a book until I was selected as a Writing Fellow at the Johannesburg Institute of Advanced Studies (JIAS), University of Johannesburg, South Africa in 2017. The Writing Fellowship gave me the long awaited opportunity and space to develop these ideas into this book. Let me therefore begin by thanking Prof. Peter Vale, the Director of JIAS, and his reliable team for accommodating me and providing a very conducive environment to develop the first comprehensive manuscript. The administrative staff of the Institute, Johnny Selemani, Emelia Kamena and Prof. Ronit Frenkel were just awesome and I am grateful to them. The house manager, Ronald, and his team Seaka, Maria, and Johanna made life easy and comfortable. I am also very grateful to the other brilliant and friendly Writing Fellows who inspired me and challenged me in many ways through their constructive and critical comments during informal but productive conversations and during my seminars and lectures. I am particularly delighted to have met Prof. Pamela Maseko and Prof. Melissa Myambo whose comments and insights were always helpful.

The Writing Fellowship would not have been possible if the Vice Chancellor of my institution, Ambrose Alli University, Prof. I. A. Onimawo, the Dean of my Faculty, the Faculty of Arts, Prof. J. A. Onimhawo. and the Head of my Department, the Department of Philosophy, Assoc. Prof. Matthew A. Izibili, had not given approval for me to be away from duties in the University during the period I was a Writing Fellow at JIAS. I am therefore indebted to the University administration for granting me the opportunity to do this.

My charming wife and best friend, Sandra, and my beautiful children Evelyn, Ellen and Elliott were most amazing. Words cannot express my gratitude to them for all the days and nights they bore and allowed me to be away from home due to this project. It was difficult, but they understood how important this was for me. I am forever indebted to them for always supporting me, and I can barely put in words how much I love and owe them.

Acknowledgements　xiii

I can only say the same of my late father, Marcus, who passed on while I was researching on this project in 2016, my mum, Alice, my brothers Collins, Felix and Kester, and my sisters, Rita, Ivie and Itohan, who have always supported me and cared for me. I am forever indebted to them.

I also express my sincere gratitude to a mentor and a great scholar, Prof. Polycarp Ikuenobe, who created time out of his very busy schedule to read through the manuscript, make very useful comments and write the foreword to this book. I also thank Prof. Isaac E. Ukpokolo, Dr. Bjorn Freter, Dr. Yvette Franklin, and Dr. Dinah Laubisch for always being there and for always caring. Two persons that have been very active in the fight for the right, interests and well-being of persons with albinism in Africa, the United Nations Independent Expert on the Enjoyment of Human Rights by Persons with Albinism, Ms. Ikponwosa Ero, and Dr. Charllote Baker were very kind to go through the manuscript and write a blurb each for the book, and for this I am very grateful.

To the many who violently othered and persecuted me since childhood due to my visible difference and to the few who lovingly saw beyond, or loved, the difference, you may never understand how invaluable you were in making me who I am, and for this I am grateful.

Foreword

It is an honour to write a foreword to this book, partly because of my numerous connections to Dr. Elvis Imafidon. I have known of and about him from his published works only within the last two years. To my surprise, I found out recently that we have some personal and academic connections. He obtained his PhD from University of Ibadan, my *alma mater*; he attended (for his undergraduate degree) and he is currently teaching in the Department of Philosophy at Ambrose Alli University, Ekpoma, Nigeria (formerly Bendel State University), where my career started thirty-five years ago. As a young scholar, I was among the founding lecturers of this Department and University. I am glad to know that this Department is in the good hands of such a young, talented and hard-working scholar. Thus, it is with great pride that I write about the work of Dr. Imafidon on a significant issue.

This is a seminal book on albinism, the philosophical examination of its nature, the social or moral attitudes toward it, the foundations for such attitudes, and how albinism is understood in African traditions, in terms of perceiving albinism as a form of disability, 'difference', or 'abnormality' in African traditions. Dr. Imafidon brings a novel and an original philosophical perspective to the issue of albinism in African cultures — an issue that has not been previously addressed, at least, philosophically. To the best of my knowledge, this is the first book to address philosophically the issue albinism. This book addresses this issue in a comprehensive way, bringing to bear on the analysis, various philosophical perspectives: conceptual, biological, ontological, epistemological, metaphysical, ethical, existential and phenomenological. I find the ideas and arguments in the book and, the book as a whole, to be properly conceived, well-articulated, and conceptually and methodologically sound.

The book begins with a conceptual analysis of the idea or notion of albinism, and then, the metaphysical ontological and biological basis for categorizing, characterizing, identifying someone as a person with albinism. It explores how we form and justify beliefs about albinism, the truth or justificatory status of the beliefs we have about albinism or people with albinism, and whether such beliefs involve or are based on ignorance. It also explores

Foreword xv

how the false beliefs about albinism or people with albinism are perpetuated by cultures and cultural practices. It examines the normative moral status of these false beliefs and the negative attitudes they engender. It goes on to explore the ethical basis for the treatment of people with albinism, and whether such treatment can be morally justified.

This book also examines the existential and phenomenological approach or issues in albinism. In an effort to place the issue of albinism in an existentialist and phenomenological African cultural context, Dr. Imafidon discusses how, in general, cultural practices and norms, social context and community shape our existence, identity, lives and how we live our lives. He suggests that, by our actions and achievements, we can bring about changes in social or moral attitudes and practices in cultures and our communities. One element of Jean Paul Sartre's philosophy of existentialism is the idea that 'existence precedes essence', which suggests that we can, as rational autonomous beings, use our existence (the way we live) to shape or determine our (cultural-social or ontological) essence. This point is particularly underscored by what Dr. Imafidon is doing in this book, by seeking to use his life experience, work, scholarship and research to illuminate the circumstances of people with albinism in order to change people's attitudes, perspectives and how people with albinism are perceived.

This point is bolstered by and grounded in what is now commonly considered the African normative-processual view of personhood, which indicates that people define their or attain normative personhood based on their achievements and contributions to the community. However, the book also seeks to challenge, critically examine and change the social norms by which (in adhering to norms) people achieve and attain personhood. The book indicates that many people with albinism can rise, and have risen, above the negative cultural representations and attitudes, and they have made their existence and life meaningful, made significant contributions and have earned respect and honour. This is one way to change cultural attitudes and practices. The book discusses some efforts to overcome the negative 'othering' and representations of people with albinism. He indicates that these efforts have not been too effective or sufficient. I love the efforts to provide some prescriptions regarding how to create positive awareness and change attitudes. My specific pride involves the fact that it appears the author is using this book and his significant achievements in and contributions to philosophy to define his personhood and change negative attitudes.

This book's illuminating, multi-perspectival and multi-dimensional philosophical treatment of the issue of albinism in the context of disability studies is a timely, useful, significant and important contribution to the subject matter of African philosophy. I am of the view that this book is going to engender significant and numerous discussions about albinism, albinism as a disability, a basis for 'othering' people or identifying 'differences' or 'abnormality', and the general issues of disability in African cultures and

African philosophy. This is also a good contribution to applied normative ethics in relation to albinism and disability. I also suspect this book will have the heuristic value of contributing to further discussions and expansion of the range of issues and subject matter of African philosophy.

Polycarp Ikuenobe
Professor of Philosophy
Kent State University
April 2018

Introduction: Albinism, difference and the philosophical turn

Since the second half of the twentieth century, there has been a stronger and an increasing interest of philosophy in issues of disability. The flourishing of the philosophy of disability for more than four decades now, is to me, an inevitable consequence of two factors: (i.) In and just before the first half of the twentieth century, there was a substantive focus by philosophers on the question of difference, alterity or otherness. The works of philosophers such as Husserl, Derrida, Deleuze, Foucault, Levinas, Lacan and Beauvoir gained much prominence due to their focus on difference and alterity. Consequently, philosophers began to employ the theories of difference and otherness in the works of these philosophers to practical issues of difference such as race, gender and disability. Philosophy of disability therefore comes naturally under the umbrella of the philosophy of difference. Thus, the increasing interest in philosophizing about difference invariably meant an increase in philosophers' concern with the question of disability; (ii.) Disability studies has been around for a long time, but in the later part of the twentieth century, philosophers were becoming quite unsatisfied with the descriptive domains and models for the study of disability because such descriptive domains of discourse of disability failed to address essential philosophical concerns, such as the ontological characterisation of disability, the epistemic framework of disability and the moral normative questions of disability.[1]

African Philosophy and the Otherness of Albinism: White Skin, Black Race is a book ensuing from the same factors. As a philosopher in an African space, I have become fascinated in the last few years with the philosophy of difference and otherness, and I have become very much interested in applying time-tested theories in philosophy to experiences of otherness, such as concerning gender, ethnicity and disability, in my immediate environment. I have been particularly interested in the otherness of albinism as a disability in African societies. However, I am strongly worried that the dominant descriptive approach to albinism studies in Africa, as important as it is, may fail to explore essential normative questions relating to albinism, a task that philosophy can perform quite well. It is the need to enrich the domain of albinism studies in Africa by complementing the descriptive approach with

2   Introduction

a normative one that informs this work. But we may begin our philosophical task by exploring the nexus between albinism and difference and highlighting the importance of a normative philosophical discourse of albinism.

There is always uneasiness about being different from others within a community of selves. No matter the nature of the dissimilarity, the state of being different and unconventional radically and regularly confronts the differing subject. Being black in a densely white-community, being white in a densely black-community, being a Christian in a customarily Muslim society, being blind among thousands of persons who can see and striving to live a moral life in a highly morally bankrupt society are instances of otherness that constantly confronts the other or different. Difference and ideas about the different are thus mostly context dependent. When a black person in a densely white-community moves to a community crowded with blacks, the difference that confronts her naturally disappears. But there are few cases where difference transcends contexts and spaces. This is true for most cases of difference caused by disability. It is practically impossible for a person that is blind to overcome her difference by moving to a community of persons that are blind. However, even in such cases, the uneasiness and difficulty of dealing with the experience of being different may vary from one place to another due to varying conceptions and understandings of the nature of the difference.

Also, human experience shows that humans have an instinctive fear of something unconventional. Persons are usually uncomfortable with anything different from what they are accustomed to. They feel threatened with the presence of the other and would thus postulate theories to explain the other and take actions to confront the other, often in a manner of hostility. This has for long been experienced in all facets of human endeavours, such as religious, political, biological and cultural differences. We recall, for instance, the response of the Roman Catholic Church in the early stages of its history to differing teachings and beliefs about Christianity that were seen as contrary to that of the Church. The theory of heresy was immediately developed to forcefully deal with such differences in beliefs. In line with this theory, many were killed and tortured for holding a differing viewpoint. We recall quite recently the Nazi-Jewish violent othering. Thus, hostility toward the other or different is as old as human history.

Now, the question of the difference of bodily colour in corporealities and disability studies, for instance, is an old one revolving around questions of normalisation of bodies and resistance to bodily normalisation. Human societies have always produced corporeal norms, norms explicitly stating how the body should be, or ought to be like, which though may evolve from time to time, form the basis of normalisation for persons within such social contexts. One may quickly think of the ideal feminine figure in our age, which the female strives to normalise her body to fit into. Many body surgeons and pharmaceutical companies have made fortunes out of the norm of the ideal female body. Many female folks have spent lots of money dieting, doing surgeries, purchasing drugs and supplements not merely for health reasons but sometimes primarily for the 'right' normalised model figure. Those who do not strive for the normalisation of their bodies, through wilful or unwilful resistance to the norm, are tagged as different — fat, plumy, chubby, etc. — and presented and represented in various forms as the bodily other needing assistance for normalisation.

A similar bodily norm can be observed in African cultures that forms the basis for normalisation. in terms of colour, an African body ought to be dark or light skinned but certainly not white or pale. The resistance to this bodily norm not only by the presence of, but also by the inability to bring to normality, the white bodies in African places threatens the bodily norm in the community, and the community fights back by providing explanations for the corporeality of such white bodies in ways that others or differs them off from the community. Hence, to be white in a largely black-populated Africa is no joke. The difficulty and uneasiness of being white in an African community is more intense when a white-skinned person is born to African, black-skinned parents, a condition referred to as albinism. The history of human albinism in Africa is unfortunately a notorious one. The widening gap between the actual nature of the difference of persons with albinism in Africa and the generally hostile ideas held about such a difference is responsible for the notorious history of albinism in Africa, a history profusely punctuated with killing, maltreatment, dismembering, and stigmatisation of persons with albinism on the basis of wrong notions of difference.

The continuous entertainment of harmful ideas about albinism in African communities and the consequent ill-treatment of persons with albinism in modern African societies calls into question the African understanding of albinism as an other and a disability. It raises the question of why such harmful ideas about albinism still linger in modern day Africa and how such can be checkmated. Existing literature does well in describing such ideas held about albinism in African communities, exposing disturbing existential conditions that persons with albinism go thorough on a daily basis, and recommending ways for improving the wellbeing of persons with albinism in Africa. Thus, albinism in African has been explored in existing literature from such perspectives as medicine and genetics, culture, human rights, education and religion. However, what is lacking in existing literature and in these perspectives is an attempt to go beyond description and exposition, to a critical analysis of the normative principles and deeply entrenched ideas about reality in African traditions that stands under, or are foundational pillars for, ideas about albinism. A substantive and robust understanding of African ideas of being, knowledge and the good is key to understanding the African notion of albinism as well as any attempt to successfully negotiate such stance. Philosophy provides us with the necessary tools for actualising such a normative understanding of albinism in African traditions. But what does a philosophical approach to the study of albinism involve?

4   *Introduction*

Discourses and inquiries in philosophy often cut across and revolve around three interwoven areas of interest: the question of being or of what is; the question of knowledge; and the question of the good. But are these areas of interest peculiar to philosophy? Is science or religion, for instance, not concerned with questions of being, knowledge and the good? Science, for instance, studies specific beings and entities. It attempts to provide accurate and specific knowledge claims about the objects it studies, knowledge claims about their nature and regular patterns of behaviour. Science is not also completely indifferent about questions of value and the good because it, for instance, works within the framework of certain moral principles and guidelines that control its research and activities. Religion, on the other hand, lays claim to the existence of certain beings or entities. Christianity, for instance, holds the belief in such existents as God, angels, Jesus Christ, Satan and demons. Religion also tenaciously defends its knowledge claims about realities. Religion also expects its adherents to strictly follow some moral code. Hence religion and science, like philosophy, are concerned with questions of being, knowing and acting. So in what sense is a discourse or inquiry about such things distinctly philosophical? What essentially is the nature of a philosophical inquiry? And what makes the discourse of albinism in this work essentially philosophical.

Although philosophy is concerned with reality, knowledge and morality, subjects that are of interest to other fields, it does so in a distinct way. The Nigerian philosopher Olusegun Oladipo identifies three ways in which a philosophical discourse on these areas of interest is different from, say, a scientific inquiry.[2] First, a philosophical inquiry or discourse is general in nature. The questions that philosophy raises, for instance, about being, knowledge or the good, are about the general nature of such things. Philosophy is not concerned, as science is, with the nature of specific beings but rather with what belongs to beings in general, or, in other words, what gives any being at all (not this or that being) its beingness. While science studies this or that specific object or entity in the universe, philosophy concerns itself with analysing what stands under all beings, what all beings could have in common. Of course, we remember Thales' water, Anaximenes' air, Democritus' atoms and Plato's forms. The quest to understand the nature of being in general or what constitutes ultimate reality falls under the core branch of philosophy, metaphysics or ontology. Similarly, while science and other disciplines are concerned with acquiring and justifying knowledge about specific objects and events in the world, philosophy is concerned with the question of knowledge in general, that is, what it means to know anything at all, not this or that thing. Philosophy is thus concerned with understanding the conditions that must be satisfied for any proposition to be taken as knowledge.

Second, a philosophical discourse is a fundamental discourse. It is never a trivial one because it borders on issues that are of intrinsic interest to any rational human being. Inquiries about the general nature of reality, knowledge and the good are fundamental inquiries that any rational human being ought to be interested in. They are not issues to be taken for granted or treated with triviality, because such issues have immediate consequences on how we live and exist. Developing new models of cars, televisions and smart phones, inventing new lines of clothing, researching on the life of crocodiles and reptiles, research on the crossbreeding of flowers and a keen interest in the working of celestial bodies may be regarded as trivial since they do not have immediate consequences on how we live and exist. But understanding what makes any human action permissible or impermissible is not a trivial matter. It is a fundamental issue that confronts us every day of our lives.

Third, philosophical inquiries are abstract rather than concrete in nature. Science, for instance, deals with specific, concrete realities and attempts a physicalistic representation of those that are not so concrete. However, although the need to philosophise arises from the concrete experiences of daily life, philosophising itself is an activity of abstraction in so far as it attempts to arrive at general qualities or ideas from actual, specific and concrete existential experiences. The many -isms of philosophy bear witness to its highly cerebral activity of abstraction from concrete realties. Idealism, monism, materialism, Hegelianism, Kantianism, feminism, utilitarianism and the like are all attempts to abstract concrete realties of humans. Now that we have a clearer picture of what a philosophical discourse consists of, we are better equipped to anticipate what the contents of the philosophical discourse on albinism in Africa would be.

This monograph is an attempt to go beyond the social representations of albinism in African traditions, the description of specific and concrete ideas, knowledge claims and experiences of albinism in Africa to providing an analysis and critique of the general underlying assumption about the being of albinism in Africa, the epistemic framework on which knowledge claims about albinism are made, and the ethical issues evolving from the conception of albinism in Africa. It attempts to unravel and critically examine deeply entrenched ideological commitments about being, knowledge and the good in African traditions that make the harmful beliefs about persons with albinism persistent in modern times. It also seeks to expose latent but fundamental aspects of culture to focus on in search of viable solutions to the ill-treatment of persons with albinism.

But the quest for a philosophical inquiry into albinism in African traditions will not emerge properly if we do not first acquaint ourselves with the conceptions of albinism across African cultures, which we intend to subject to philosophical analysis. Hence, the first chapter of this book consists of an attempt to understand albinism in scientific terms and to streamline our discourse on albinism to persons with albinism as conceived in African cultures and traditions, bearing in mind that albinism is a genetic defect that occurs both in plants and other mammals. The chapter also examines contested conceptions of albinism in different communities from the different

6 *Introduction*

regions of Africa as both trivial and thick. It also discusses the physical and socio-cultural peculiarities of albinism in Africa.

Chapter two begins the philosophical inquiry with a focus on the ontology of albinism in African traditions. The chapter analyses the African notion of being which state that force is the ontological principle that stands under all existents. It discusses the various categories of beings in African traditions, paying particular attention to what makes a person a queer being in such an ontology and showing that persons with albinism do not meet the criteria for personhood, which makes them queer beings within the framework of thought. Persons with albinism are therefore conceived as an ontological other, and this conception of albinism within the realist ontology of African traditions results in a chronic ableism against persons with albinism.

Chapter three furthers the philosophical discourse by presenting an analysis of the epistemological issues surrounding albinism in African traditions. It begins with an examination of three formulations of the African theory of knowledge or African mode of knowing, which is essential in understanding the basis on which Africans acquire, justify and validate their knowledge claims about albinism. It also critically examines the deeply rooted epistemology of ignorance, consisting of the production and assimilation of harmful ideologies and false consciousness about albinism, which fosters the harm done to persons with albinism in African traditions.

The conception of albinism in Africa and the implication of that conception in the treatment of persons with albinism raises important moral questions. Is it morally justified within the African framework of thought to mistreat persons with albinism? What are the implications of a communalistic ethos for the treatment of persons with albinism? Who has the duty and obligation to care for persons with albinism, considering their peculiar difference and disability situation? What are the challenges of caring for persons with albinism or what is the nature of the burden of care for persons with albinism? How can the dignity of persons with albinism be protected? Finding answers to these questions forms the crux of chapter four. What becomes obvious in chapter four is that there is much that still needs to be done in caring for, and protecting the dignity of, persons with albinism.

As is common with all forms of difference and disability, PWAs are confronted with peculiar existential experiences as they live their daily lives. In line with the existentialist tradition in philosophy, chapter five examines some of the lived experiences of persons with albinism. Such peculiar lived experiences include fear and dread, stigmatisation, isolation, the contemplation of suicide and peculiar existential challenges faced by females with albinism such as the fear of rape, undesired singleness and unemployment.

The last chapter seeks to recommend ways of dealing with the issues of albinism in present-day Africa. It explores the role of reconstructive and awareness education and training in dealing with the deeply entrenched ideologies about albinism in African traditions and the role education plays in improving the quality of life of persons with albinism. It also examines the prospects and moral implication of genetic research in albinism for dealing with the challenges faced by persons with albinism on the African continent and beyond.

It is hoped that this book provides a better grasp of the nature of the issues involved with albinism, a grasp that goes beyond a mere description of the current state of affairs of albinism in Africa, but one that appreciates the essential normative principles and ideologies at play in understanding and resolving the issues faced by persons with albinism in Africa today.

Notes

1. David Christopher Ralston. *The Concept of Disability: A Philosophical Analysis.* Texas: Rice University Unpublished Doctor of Philosophy Thesis, 2011. ii.
2. Olusegun Oladipo. *Thinking about Philosophy: A General Guide.* Ibadan: Hope Publications, 2008. 12–15.

1 Albinism and African thick conceptualisations

There was a person who came in front of my eyes and called: 'Do you know you are money?'

— John Ngatia
(Kenya Albino Beauty Pageant Contestant, 2016)

The meaning of a concept is often debated or contested. There is hardly any concept that admits to a singular, uncontested, universal definition. But the contestation of the meaning of a concept could be trivial or essential. A trivially contested concept is a concept that has a factual meaning, and the debates about its meaning may not necessarily alter the facts about it. Such a concept has a reasonably precise description that can neither be denied nor disputed, or it is rather difficult to deny or dispute in the face of evidence by the different parties involved. Death, for instance, is a trivially contested concept. It is a fact that death means the end of life, the point when someone or something ceases to exist. This factual understanding of death is trivially contested among different schools of thought, religions and cultures of the world. Some argue that death is actually the process of gaining a higher or lower status of life in an otherworldly realm of existence, a necessary passage from here to there. Others argue that death is nothing but a deep sleep for a long period of time while awaiting resurrection. These conceptualisation of death are definitely trivial because they do not change the fact about death as the end of life. But as trivial as they are, they have a strong influence on those who have consciously or unconsciously assimilated them as normative representations of death.

An essentially contested concept, on the other hand, is a concept that, by its very nature, does not admit to a universal factual representation. It is thus debated by various schools of thought, groups, and cultures, and the nature of this debate is essential or fundamental because no singular group can lay claim to having *the* ideal understanding of the concept in question. There is a long list of such concepts: love, democracy, medicine, values, rationality, art, philanthropy, racism, rule of law, justice, hospitality, God, patriotism, beauty, knowledge and morality are just a few examples of essentially contested concepts. Each perspective of the concept enriches or challenges the

Albinism and African thick conceptualisations   9

available understanding of the concept. W.B. Gallie's classical analysis of essentially contested concepts in the 1950s comes to mind here. According to Gallie, such a concept is highly appraisive, not purely descriptive; it is inevitably controversial and thus involves endless dispute since its proper use are determined by their users; such disputes are nevertheless sustained by perfectly respectable arguments and evidence; though the disputing parties adhere to different views as to the proper use of the concept in question, nonetheless, each party recognises that his or her own use is contested by others, and each party has some appreciation of the different criteria in light of which other parties claim to be applying the concept; and each party continues to argue most seriously that his or her use of the concept is sound, even while, at times, realising that other participants in the dispute can make rational cases for their own view and that no conclusive argument can be advanced for any of the competing views.[1]

Albinism, the focal concept of this book, is not an essentially contested concept. Albinism is rather a trivially but highly contested concept among cultures, traditions and religions. It is a trivial contestation because although it is highly contested, its precise nature is highly factual and descriptive. The facts about it are strong and cannot be disputed. However, the different contested notions held about it by different groups may be trivial to the facts but remain important normative ideas about albinism because such notions and ideas affect people's attitude toward albinism in different contexts. We could therefore conclude that trivially contested concepts are also thick concepts because they have both a descriptive, factual dimension and a normative, social dimension to their definition and understanding. One can never solely focus on the former while ignoring the later in the discourse of albinism. In fact, this book emerges as a reaction primarily to the normative conceptions of albinism. Hence, although such normative conceptions might be trivial, they cannot be ignored in the discourse of albinism.

In this chapter, we begin by exploring the biological and scientific facts about albinism and the reasons why it is considered a form of disability. This is followed by an analysis of the trivial contestations but thick conceptualisations of albinism in different African cultures. The chapter then concludes by deducing from such thick conceptualisations some peculiarities of albinism in African cultures as distinct, say, from Western cultures.

The biological understanding of albinism in persons

Albinism refers to the condition where a living thing, plant or animal, completely or partially lacks the needed element(s) for *normal* pigmentation or colouring.[2] An entity that has albinism therefore has a pale, milk, red or white presentation of colour different from the normal colouring of members in its group. Hence, an entity with albinism is thus visibly different from others of its kind. In plants, for instance, the complete or partial lack

10   *Albinism and African thick conceptualisations*

of chlorophyll and chloroplast membranes results in albinism in plants. Such plants may then display pale colouring different from that of its class or group. Our interest in this work, however, is on albinism specifically in humans or persons.

Albinism in persons refers to a condition where a person partially or completely lacks pigmentation or colouring due to certain biological conditions such as the absence of melanin (the substance that gives a person his or her colour) and other genetic mutations. A person with albinism (PWA) visibly lacks pigment in all or some parts of his or her body including skin, hair and the iris and pupil of the eyes. Such persons generally have pale, milk- or pink-coloured skin, white, milk-coloured or blonde hair; and light-coloured (blue, pink or light brown) eyes. Human albinism can therefore occur in too different forms. It could be complete albinism, which is referred to in medical terms as oculocutaneous albinism (OCA), or partial albinism, which is known as ocular albinism (OA). The Vision of Children Foundation website gives an apt description of the differences between these two forms of human albinism:

> Human albinism can be divided broadly into two types, oculocutaneous albinism (OCA) and ocular albinism (OA), where "oculo" means eye and cutaneous means skin. These terms were devised in the late 1940s, when medical science was less sophisticated than it is now. The terminology sounds simple, but in reality, is probably incorrect, since all forms of albinism have relative deficiencies of pigment in the hair, skin and eyes. Historically, ocular albinism is an inherited disorder in which the eyes are deficient in the amount of melanin, which gives the eye its colour or pigment, while the skin and hair appear normal or near normal in coloration.[3]

It therefore means that oculocutaneous albinism affects not only the eyes but the skin and hair, even though the hair is obviously not accounted for in the deficient terminology. Hence, within our scope of discourse, we may simply refer to this form of human albinism as complete albinism that affects virtually all visible parts of the body. According to the Genetic Home Reference of the National Library of Medicine, in complete albinism:

> affected individuals typically have very fair skin and white or light-coloured hair. They have an increased risk of skin damage and skin cancers, including melanoma, with sun exposure. Oculocutaneous albinism also reduces pigmentation of the coloured part of the eye (the iris) and the light-sensitive tissue at the back of the eye (the retina). People with this condition usually have vision problems such as reduced sharpness; rapid, involuntary eye movements (nystagmus); and increased sensitivity to light.[4]

There are four different types of complete albinism. OCA1, OCA2, OCA3 and OCA4. OCA1 is characterized by white hair, very pale skin and light-coloured irises, and it is the most complete and medically challenging form of albinism. OCA2 is generally less severe than OCA1; the skin is usually a creamy white colour and hair may be light yellow, blond or light brown. OCA3 includes a form of albinism called rufous oculocutaneous albinism, which usually affects dark-skinned people. Affected individuals have reddish-brown skin, ginger or red hair and hazel or brown irises. OCA3 is often associated with milder vision abnormalities than the other forms of complete albinism. OCA4 has signs and symptoms similar to those seen with OCA2. Because their features overlap, the four types of complete albinism are most accurately distinguished by their genetic cause.[5] It is estimated that one out of every seventeen to twenty thousand persons has albinism globally, although this is not evenly distributed around the globe. In some societies such as Tanzania, it is estimated that one in every one-thousand, four-hundred persons has albinism, a figure that is fourteen times more prevalent than cases in other parts of the world.[6]

Ocular albinism, on the other hand, affects basically the eyes. But the terminology is also deficient because there are cases of albinism where the eyes and skin are not affected, but the hair is. In such cases, for instance, in Africa, the person has normal dark skin and eye colouring, but the hair is brown or red. Hence, we may simply refer to all such cases that affect parts of the visible body as partial albinism. Partial albinism is generally caused by reduced pigmentation rather than a complete lack of it and may lead to a number of challenges. In the partial albinism of the eye, for instance, even though the skin and hair are normal, the person may experience any of the following:

> reduced visual acuity (typically from approximately 20/30 to approximately 20/400); nystagmus (an uncontrollable, pendular, rapid movement of the eyes back and forth); strabismus (a muscle imbalance of the eyes in which the eyes are "crossed" rather than straight and parallel); and sensitivity to bright light. The reduced visual acuity may result in difficulty at school, such as trouble reading what is on a blackboard, except when the reading material is held very close, and difficulty with sports, particularly with small projectile objects. The reduced visual acuity may ultimately limit an affected individual's ability to obtain a driver's license, because most states require at least 20/70 vision (best corrected with glasses or contact lenses) to obtain at least a daylight-restricted driver's license.[7]

Thus, whether with complete or partial albinism, persons with albinism face a number of physical and social challenges because of their biological condition. The severity of the challenges faced may depend largely on the severity of the albinism.

12   *Albinism and African thick conceptualisations*

As far back as 1744, the French mathematician Pierre Louis Maupertuis was very much interested in what he termed the 'White Negro' (albinism among blacks), which led him to a number of wide speculations. In the words of Andrew Curran:

> The albino was absorbed into a scientific narrative in 1744 when Maupertuis used the concept to put forward a theory of shared origins or *monogenesis*. Positing that the *negre blanc* — quite literally a "white Negro" — was a racial throwback, a reversion to a primitive whiteness, Maupertuis inspired a new generation of thinkers, most notably the great French naturalist Buffon, to assert categorically that blacks had degenerated from a prototype white variety.[8]

A contrary speculation to Buffon's position was developed more than two centuries later by the Afrocentric scholar, Frances Cress Welshing in her 1990 collection of essays, *The Isis Paper: The Key to the Colours*.[9] As Mia Bay puts it:

> Welshing's book reinterprets world history according to her personal theory of colour confrontation. Among other things, she argues that white people originated as the "albino mutant offspring" of black-skinned African parents who cast out these defective children. Filled with implacable hostility towards their inhospitable parents, and a deep-rooted sense of inadequacy over their pale skin, the mutants wandered North to escape the equatorial sun. They ultimately settled in Europe they devoted themselves to the establishment of a universal system of white supremacy and domination... Welshing's story of the origin of the races is uniquely her own, but the issues her work addresses are old ones. By presenting white people as the flawed offspring of Africa, whose civilization emerged only after that of their African parents, Welshing is able to emphasize that black people are the parents of the entire family of people.[10]

Of course, Welshing's book was widely embraced by Afrocentrics the way Buffon's work was widely accepted by Eurocentrics. They were both nothing more than speculations of the role of albinism in deciding the superiority of one race over the other.

Hence, a sustained interest in the biological or scientific study of human albinism has been on for more than two centuries, although there are indications of earlier studies and interest in mediaeval writings as well as in the works of early and late classical authors such as Pliny, Mela and Ptolemy.[11] A number of such interests ended up in wide speculations about the nature of albinism as we see above. However, one of the earliest, most comprehensive and revealing scientific studies of albinism was carried out by Karl Pearson, E. Nettleship, and G. H. Usher and was published in 1911 with the title

A Monograph on Albinism in Man. The book provides a comprehensive discussion of human albinism. It covers such topics as the earliest observation of persons with albinism in recorded history, types of geographical distribution of persons with albinism, including albinism in Europe, China and Africa; a discussion of partial albinism and unnatural albinism (loss of pigmentation for different reasons after birth such as vitiligo or lencoderma). With particular reference to the scientific study of albinism in Africa, the authors did quite a lot in presenting their observations,[12] noting, however, some cultural inhibitions to getting accurate figures and data such as the fact that infants with albinism were often killed, and those who managed to stay alive were not easily accepted.[13]

Since then, and due to advancements in science and technology, there have been more accurate and informative scientific studies of albinism in recent times. From such available studies, we can draw the following conclusions about albinism specifically in humans:

1 Albinism is a congenital (existing at or before birth) disorder caused by reduced or the complete absence of melanin: the pigment responsible for giving colour to our skin, eyes and hair. Albinism is sometimes known as hypopigmentation.
2 Persons with albinism can live long, healthy lives just as anyone else. The biggest danger comes from skin cancer, which develops more easily from unprotected sun exposure.
3 Persons with albinism often have one or a few eye conditions, including poor eyesight, involuntary eye movements (nystagmus) and sensitivity to light (photophobia).
4 The cause of albinism is cellular. Malfunctioning genes do not produce melanin and cannot be made to.
5 Though the disorder is found in about 1 in 20,000 people in the United States, its prevalence is higher for other parts of the world where it can be as high as 1 in every 1,400 people in some parts of Africa.
6 People with albinism synthesize vitamin D five times faster than dark-skinned people. Since vitamin D is produced when ultraviolet-B light enters the skin, the lack of pigmentation means the light can enter more easily.
7 Though albinism does not require treatment, the skin and eye conditions that accompany it often do need specialized treatment.
8 Many different types of albinism exist. Oculocutaneous albinism is the most common and most severe, with a person's hair, skin and eyes remaining a pale white colour throughout their lives.
9 Some children born with less severe forms of albinism are born with white hair and skin that slightly darkens as they grow older.
10 One in 17,000 people have some form of albinism gene. Though it affects the sexes equally, males are more likely to have ocular albinism: a lack of pigment in the eyes.

14   *Albinism and African thick conceptualisations*

11   People with albinism face persecution and bullying all over the world. Some of this comes from beliefs that they are cursed or that their body parts have magical powers when used by witch doctors.

12   Around 1 in 70 people carry one albinism gene. If both parents carry the albinism gene, there is a 25 percent chance the child will be born with the disorder.

13   To be born with albinism, a baby must have defective genes from both its parents. If the baby inherits one normal and one albinism gene, enough melanin will be produced by the normal gene.

14   One of the most severe types of albinism is known as Hermansky-Pudlak syndrome. People with this variation are prone to bleeding, bruising and lung disease.

15   Albinism is most common in various groups of sub-Saharan Africa.

16   Scientists can test if a parent has an albino gene by testing if a hair follicle produces melanin.

17   Some lesser-informed men in East Africa — especially Tanzania, which has the largest population of people with albinism in Africa — believe that the mother of an albino child was unfaithful with a white man or that the baby is the ghost of a former European colonist.

18   Currently, there is no treatment that can cause the body to produce melanin and lessen the symptoms of albinism.

19   Albinism is genetic and thus is not contagious. And it doesn't make anyone less of a person. It's as genetic as having brown hair or blond hair, and we don't think less of people with brown or blond hair, so we shouldn't think differently about a person with albinism.[14]

Albinism as a disability

On what basis can we describe albinism as a disability? To answer this question, we need to first of all understand what disability is. Disability is a highly and an essentially contested concept in disability studies. It is defined and understood from different perspectives such as the medical, cultural and social perspectives. Its fundamental nature is perennially debated. But there are also facts about it that can only be trivially debated. It may be useful to focus on such facts in an attempt to understand disability. First, disability (in persons) is an impairment present from birth or occurring during one's lifetime that makes someone *unable* to do, or limited in doing, things or performing activities *normally* expected from her or him and includes the person's experience of that impairment in a social context. An impairment consists of a physical, non-physical (mental or psychological) or both physical and non-physical problem or alteration in a person's anatomy or body. Thus, disability is always at variance with normalcy. This idea of disability cuts across various models and perspectives of disability. For instance, the medical model emphasis the biological (physical and mental) impairment of disabled persons such as inability to hear, see, talk, walk, recognise colours, remember information and so on. The social model, on the other hand, emphasises the social experiences of persons with disability, their experience of being different, such as pity, bullying, maltreatment, experience of care and so on. While such models provide essential information about disability, it is more appropriate to have a balanced and comprehensive view that attempts to emphasize the various aspects of disability. The *World Report on Disability* therefore talks of a bio-psycho-social model that views disability as 'impairments, activity limitations and participation restrictions, referring to the negative aspects between an individual (with a health condition) and that individual's contextual factors (environmental and personal factors).'[15] Although this definition is encompassing, it fails to recognise that the interaction is not always negative but can and should also be positive.

Second, disability is a ubiquitous human condition. It forms an integral part of our everyday experience, and almost every human being at some point in life experiences some subtle or pronounced form of disability. The *World Report on Disability* succinctly expresses this point about disability:

> Disability is part of the human condition. Almost everyone will be temporarily or permanently impaired at some point in life, and those who survive to old age will experience increasing difficulties in functioning. Most extended families have a disabled member, and many non-disabled people take responsibility for supporting and caring for their relatives and friends with disabilities... Every epoch has faced the moral and political issue of how best to include and support people with disabilities. This issue will become more acute as the demographics of societies change and more people live to an old age.[16]

Hence, we are all confronted with disability, either we directly experience impairment, we care for someone who is impaired, or by our attitude or disposition, worsen or better the situation of those who are impaired.

Third, disability is usually construed within social and cultural contexts as a problem,[17] a negative difference-maker, something sub-optimal.[18] Such an understanding of disability as a problem does not, according to Titchkosky:

> ... arise simply because our bodies give us troubles; disability as a problem is presented to people through interaction, with the social and physical environment, and through the social production of knowledge. The over-determined sense in which our culture gives us disability as a problem is shared by the discipline of sociology in that social scientific research, textbooks, and course offerings in, for example, deviance, represent disability as a "problem" of the body gone wrong. This problem obtrudes into the social world and is studied by sociologists as such, thus representing disability as a social problem.[19]

16 *Albinism and African thick conceptualisations*

Although the medical notion of disability remains the most reliable authority on getting facts about disability, the social construction of disability cannot be taken for granted or relegated to the background. In fact, it must be taken very seriously because social representations, right or not, have real effects on real people. Dyer explains that the representation of people within a culture or society may not often succeed in comprehensively mirroring reality as it is, but yet there is something very real about a culture or society's representation of its people such as disabled persons because it influences the way such persons are treated and delineates what such persons can be within a given society. In fact, cultural forms of representation, Dyer argues, restrict and shape what can be said by and/or about any aspect of reality in a given place in a given society at a given time; they set the wider terms of limitations and possibilities for the representation of human experiences.[20] Titchkosky adds that the 'fundamental social character of representation lies in its ability to present a version of reality and not necessarily in its ability to "get it right." Representations have real consequences for real people, but these consequences go beyond the people being represented, since there are consequences for those who make these representations as well.'[21] Much of the focus of this work concerns a philosophical analysis of how the cultural representation of albinism in African communities have real consequences for persons with albinism and others in the communities.

With these three features of disability in mind, we can now adequately discuss albinism as a disability. Albinism is a disability for a number of reasons. First, it is a visible alteration or disorder in a person's anatomy that results in activity limitations or difficulties in performing certain tasks. For instance, one common body problem and consequently activity limitation for persons with albinism is one form or the other of visual impairment, which includes poor eyesight, involuntary eye movements (nystagmus) and sensitivity to light (photophobia). This leads to difficulty or reduction in their ability to perform certain activities such as reading, driving and other vision-sensitive duties. Students with albinism often have difficulties seeing what is written on the board, and the use of glasses may not necessarily improve the condition. Again, persons with albinism, particularly those with complete albinism (oculocutaneous albinism), cannot and should not be exposed to even a moderate amount of sunlight. Working in or constantly being under direct sunlight for the same amount of time a person with normal pigmentation should be exposed to sunlight can quickly result in skin cancer, which is life threatening. This is because there is a lack of the normal body pigmentation required to be able to be under sunlight. This surely results in limitations and difficulties in performing certain activities. A PWA conscious of his health and wellbeing will therefore not do any job or engage in any recreational activity that requires being exposed to the sun such as cultivating a piece of farmland, tanning, selling in an open market, outdoor sports and so on.

Also, in social and cultural contexts, albinism is represented as a disability in mostly negative ways that have real consequences for persons with albinism in such contexts and those with whom they interact. Such cultural and social representations influence the ways in which persons with albinism are mistreated and the sort of participation restrictions imposed on them. 'Participation restrictions are problems with involvement in any area of life — for example, facing discrimination in employment and transportation.'[22] PWAs face such participation restrictions with regards to employment, schooling and participation in the social and political aspects of their societies. In the section that follows, we pay closer attention to social representations of albinism in different African societies and how such representations foster the discrimination against and mistreatment of persons with albinism in Africa.

Albinism as a thick and contested concept in African thought

As mentioned earlier, albinism is not merely a trivially contested concept but also a thick concept. The term 'thick concept' was first introduced to the realm of moral discourse, particularly in the context of fact-value distinction to buttress the highly debated claim that certain ethical/moral concepts have both descriptive features as well as evaluative dimensions.[23] However, thick concepts can also be applied to describe any concept that has both descriptive and evaluative dimensions[24] such as aesthetic, linguistic and scientific concepts. It is therefore fitting, I believe, to describe albinism as a thick concept. This is because, as discussed above, it has descriptive biological features that are not in dispute. However, as I explore in this section with particular reference to African cultures, it also has normative features ensuing from the various representations of what albinism is in different social contexts. Hence, to get a good grasp of the evaluative dimension of albinism as a thick concept, we will pay close attention to social representations of albinism in African cultures.

As Dyer explains in the Introduction to *The Matter of Images: Essays on Representation*, any attempt to understand how members of social groups and categories are treated in any culture or society, must have (re) presentations of such social groups within such cultures or societies as its focal point. Discrimination, harassment, hate, reverencing and support for certain groups in a social system become open once we understand the representation of such groups within the social system.[25] In his words:

> How a group is represented, presented over again in cultural forms, how an image of a member of a group is taken as representative of that group, how that group is represented in terms of spoke for and on behalf of (whether they represent, speak for themselves or not), these all have to do with how members of groups see themselves and others like

18   *Albinism and African thick conceptualisations*

themselves, how they see their place in society, their right to the rights a society claims to ensure its citizens. Equally re-presentation, representativeness, representing have to do also with how others see members of a group and their place and rights, others who have the power to affect that place and those rights. How we are seen determine in part how we are treated; how we treat others is based on how we see them; such seeing comes from representation.[26]

Dyer's apt description of social/cultural representation is, for me, very insightful and instructive in understanding albinism in African traditions. The social representation of albinism in African cultural forms determine essentially how persons with albinism have come to view themselves within such cultures, the rights they have, their place in society, and how they are treated. We cannot understand the lived experiences of persons with albinism without understanding their social representation, and this remains the focal point of this work.

Dyer further identifies four basic features of representations within cultures and societies that are vital for our understanding of the cultural representation of albinism in African cultures:

First of all... representations are presentations, always and necessarily entail the use of codes and conventions of the available cultural forms of presentation. Such forms restrict and shape what can be said by and/ or about any aspect of reality in a given place in a given society at a given time...

Secondly, cultural forms do not have single determinate meanings – people make sense of them in different ways according to the cultural (including sub-cultural) codes available to them...

Thirdly, what is re-presented in representation is not directly reality itself but other representations... [partly because] reality is always more extensive and complicated than any system of representation can possibly comprehend, and we always sense that this is so – representation never "gets" reality which is why human history has produced so many different and changing ways of trying to get it...

The last point is... that it constitutes the very social grouping that it also represent... [it is in] the business of construction. Ethnic representation for instance is based not on inevitable categories pre-existing human consciousness but on the organisation of perception.[27]

In what follows, we will be fascinated with the way these features of representation play out in the representations of albinism in various African cultures and traditions and how such representations affect the way persons with albinism are viewed and treated. Interestingly, as we noted in the beginning of this chapter, such representations are trivially contested among different African communities because the contents of such representations

Albinism and African thick conceptualisations   19

differ from one place to another, sometimes contradicting themselves, and they do not negate the facts about albinism, even when they deliberately are meant to distort them. However, such representations are of immense interest to anyone wanting to understand albinism in Africa because they may not be true representations of reality and facts, but they are real insofar as they fundamentally affect the way people live and behave as and toward persons with albinism.

Broadly construed, albinism is socially and culturally represented as an unwelcomed abnormality or difference, much the same way other forms of disability are negatively designated in African traditions. Within and between cultures in African societies, there are varying descriptions of albinism in persons. However, such varying ideas about albinism all point to the same social and cultural representations of albinism as not only abnormal but repugnant; persons with albinism are considered abhorrent and disgusting within such cultural frameworks. Their experiences are shaped by averted glances and other types of avoidance that cut off practices of sociability. Pregnant women, for example, are often told to avoid looking at persons with albinism, lest they pass this quality to their child.[28] Specific negative descriptions and representations of persons with albinism are thus formulated to institutionalise the abnormal and repugnant nature of albinism.

Among the Yoruba people of Nigeria in West Africa, there are various explanations for albinism in humans. A popular notion of albinism is that persons with it are agents of divinities (*eniorisa* as they are often called) sent to families who have erred against some divinity or ancestral spirit as some form of punishment or curse. They are therefore often called *afin*, meaning horrible beings. For this reason, persons with albinism are often sent to serve in shrines, and some individuals draw the conclusion that since they are agents of the divinities, their body parts and blood must have superhuman powers that can be used for ritual purposes such as money-making rituals and charms for long life and different forms of protection.[29] In the words of Olugbenga Olagunju:

> The body parts of persons living with albinism make potent charms that can make people rich and successful... drinking the blood of a person with albinism gives extra magical powers, wherever one goes he will be honoured so they recite the incantation as follows:
>
> *Owokoko la fi n wogi*, we honour the tree because of the spot it possess
> *Owoorisa la fin woafin,* we honour the Albinos with the honour of the deity
> *E fi owotemiwo mi loni.* People should honour me today
>
> ... the blood and the hair of the Albino are potent for money making rituals... the ritualist uses the breast and private parts of the female Albinos for charm that enables people to live long and wealthy.[30]

20 *Albinism and African thick conceptualisations*

He further itemizes some other prevalent social representations of albinism among the Yoruba people. According to him, albinism is also believed to result from a woman getting pregnant after having sexual intercourse during her menstruation (this, of course, is scientifically impossible). It is also believed that albinism is contagious and can be contacted by getting close to a person with albinism.[31]

The Ibos of Eastern Nigeria share similar views with the Yoruba people. The repugnant way in which PWAs are viewed among the Ibos is obvious from the utterances of E.W. Ardener when he writes about attitude to skin pigmentation among the Ibos:

> Albinos, the extreme of paleness, however, are not admired, as their skins lack the essential smoothness and uniformity of texture and their many physical infirmities in any event render them *repulsive to normal Ibo*... The fact that the albino, who is at the extreme of the paleness spectrum, is *socially useless* may also play its part, as may the fact that Europeans are often thought to be weak, although this may itself be a product of the general belief... [A very light complexion man] fearing that his children might be albino... married a black wife. Emphases are mine.[32]

In fact, virtually all communities in sub-Saharan Africa have similar notions about albinism. As Muthee Thuku aptly puts it:

> In most communities across the world, albinism is hardly (or not) understood. Myths and misconceptions surround the condition. However, this is amplified in the sub-Saharan Africa largely because the light skin tone of PWAs [persons with albinism] stands out sharply in communities whose members are predominantly dark skinned. In some parts of sub-Saharan Africa, the condition was traditionally thought of as "a curse" or as some form of "punishment" from the gods or the ancestors for something wrong done by the parents. In some communities, it was thought that there was something wrong with the mother. For centuries, children born with albinism have been routinely killed immediately after birth by parents and mid-wives. Myths about albinism continue to persist in many parts of Africa.[33]

That these ideas about albinism persist today in the cultural representations of persons with albinism is obvious from the utterances people make, the manner in which people treat such persons, the manner in which persons with albinism view themselves, and, even more worrisome, the representation of such persons in movies, novels and the social media. For instance, the Nigerian film industry (popularly referred to as Nollywood) has been notorious in promoting violence against persons with albinism. Singled out are the film titled *End of the Wicked*, which portrays the main character

Albinism and African thick conceptualisations 21

(acted by a person with albinism) as a witch. Such films regularly promote superstitious beliefs such as that of witchcraft and highlight the spread of the idea that body parts of PWAs may have mystical powers. Many children, youth and adults with albinism in Nigeria have been found dead or have gone missing due to the belief that certain body parts can be used in rituals, to gain power, money, and success, and for the cure of impotency.[34]

Many Eastern African countries have also been known for their notorious cultural representations of persons with albinism and the inhuman consequent effects of such representations. Tanzania, Kenya, Burundi and Zimbabwe have, for many years, made international headlines due to their conceptions and treatment of persons with albinism. The conceptions of albinism within such societies are not sharply different from those already examined in Nigeria, but the effects have been much more tremendous. Tanzania has been the most notorious of the Eastern African countries in its representation and maltreatment of persons with albinism. In Tanzania and most parts of East Africa, traditional beliefs relating to the conception of a child with albinism as a punishment for misdemeanour and the notion of the intermediary position of the person with albinism between the physical world and the spirit world, run alongside the stereotypes of albinism, which include a fear that albinism is contagious and the belief that people with the condition are mentally handicapped. However, in recent years, a new set of beliefs has emerged that have been generated partly in response to current issues in sub-Saharan Africa but not deviating from traditional perspectives. The belief that sex with a person with albinism is a cure for AIDS is one of the most disturbing. The sale of body parts of persons with albinism as means of getting wealthy, in millions of dollars, and getting protection from harm are also quite new effects of old beliefs. The web of beliefs associated with albinism has a profound influence on the lives of people with the condition, from the moment of their birth until their death, interfering with access to education, employment and marriage.[35]

Between 2009 and 2010, there were a series of murders of persons with albinism in Tanzania by miners seeking wealth and protection. Bryceson, Jonsson and Sherrington explains that, 'a series of murders of albinos in Tanzania's north west mining frontier... are connected to gold and diamond miners' efforts to secure lucky charms for finding minerals and protection against danger while mining.'[36] This search for body parts of persons with albinism is largely associated with the notion in Tanzania that persons with albinism are ghosts having powers to be harnessed for personal gains. The effects of such a conception is so striking in the singular case shared by Malone Andrew in the *Daily Mail* newspaper of September 25th, 2009:

> Like a hunted animal run to ground, the little girl was cornered. Branded a "ghost" on account of her striking white skin, Mariam Emmanuel had been chased through her village, in a remote corner of Tanzania, by a bloodthirsty mob. Exhausted and terrified, the five-year-old slumped

22 *Albinism and African thick conceptualisations*

in the dust at the end of an alley. She whimpered and cowered while the adults surrounded her and sharpened their knives and machetes. Then they set to work, butchering her and dividing her remains between themselves. She was killed like an animal, by grown men who showed no compassion for another human being. Mariam's crime? She was an albino.

Mariam's case is one of numerous ones that have been experienced in Tanzania and other African countries in recent times.

Some of the social representations are at once irrational but very real within the social fabric and having real consequences for real people. Isaac Mwaura, a spokesperson for the Albinism Society of Kenya, expresses his surprise for such trivial contestations and unrealistic views about albinism in Kenya when he says:

It is funny that even in cosmopolitan Nairobi where orientation to human diversity is assumed, there have been weird accounts of people losing their appetite at the mere sight of a person with albinism, associating the condition with disease. Many are people who are convinced that persons with albinism are sterile or barren, that they are immortal, that they are mentally handicapped, or that they can cure HIV/AIDS! Others think that acquiring some body parts of those with albinism brings good luck and instant riches.[37]

These views we have examined above cut across most parts of Africa. They are inherent in the people's everyday perceptions of albinism. The situation is not different in South Africa,[38] Zimbabwe,[39] Namibia,[40] and many other African communities.[41] But, as seen above, these representations of persons with albinism have dire and quite peculiar consequences for persons with albinism all over the continent. This ranges from fear, murder, commodification of persons with albinism, psychological trauma, suicide and social exclusion. The founder of The Albino Foundation (TAF), Nigeria, summarises his personal experiences of the implication of such social representations. In his words, '... from relationships to the workplace, I have come face to face with these problems. I don't know where to start. I have been sent out of a party because I am albino; a woman has rejected me because I am an albino. I have been sacked from the work place because I am an albino.'[42] The existential challenges faced by persons with albinism will be substantially discussed in chapter five of this work. But one can safely conclude that the cultural representations, notions and beliefs about albinism in African traditional and modern societies do not only deviate far from reality but are harmful to the emotional, physical and social well-being of persons with albinism.

There has been an argument in some quarters that a number of these social representations are new and recent, and their ill effects are also recent and in line with modern economic and social yearnings of perpetuators.

Albinism and African thick conceptualisations 23

For instance, it is argued that it is in recent times that parts of persons with albinism are sort for moneymaking rituals, which in turn intensify the killings of persons with albinism. Charlotte Baker aptly captures this view when she says:

> ... in recent years, a new set of beliefs has emerged, that have been generated in response to current issues in sub-Saharan Africa. The belief that sex with people with albinism is a cure for AIDS is one of the most disturbing... the sale of body parts from people with albinism, like the phenomenon of children accused of witchcraft are "new" or "invented traditions" in the words... Whatever their origin, the web of beliefs associated with albinism has a profound influence on the lives of people with the condition, from the moment of their birth until their death, interfering with access to education, employment and marriage.[43]

Although it is quite true that a new set of representations of albinism has emerged and, by implication, new consequences, I argue in the following chapter that these new forms of representation are facets of old, deeply entrenched ideas about the other, the queer being in general, and albinism in particular in African traditions. These new forms of representation and more yet to come, we shall see, would inevitably emerge from the conception of albinism as queerness in African ontology.

The different representations of albinism that has become shared norms in different African traditions clearly show that albinism is a thick concept, which although can be clearly described in biological scientific terms is deeply shaded with normative ideas that have real consequences for persons with albinism. This work primarily ensues from a critique of the normative dimension of albinism as a thick concept in African traditions.

Peculiarities of albinism in Africa

> The very visible difference of a person with albinism [in Africa] has a profound effect on the personal identity of that individual... Nowhere can an albino be his real self — socially, at work, at school, at home — nowhere; it is a living nightmare.[44]

Persons with albinism in Africa face peculiar situations and circumstances presented by the very fact that they are in Africa. The ideas that persons with albinism are viewed as abnormal and as possessing some connection with the supernatural are not peculiarly African, although we could say it takes peculiar twists in African communities. As Alexander Krappe says:

> All "abnormal" phenomena are... likely to become the objects of superstitious fears or hopes; they are regarded as manifestations of some supernatural power or agency, which as such is usually held in

24 *Albinism and African thick conceptualisations*

awe, occasionally prayed to, and propitiated in the expectation that it may eventually be turned to the greater benefit and advantage of the worshippers.[45]

Here, however, I identify and discuss two experiences I consider prominently peculiar to the person with albinism in Africa. The first is the physical environmental factor and the second is the visible physical difference. The physical environment in which the person with albinism in Africa lives is mostly anti-albinism due to a very hot sunny climate. The sun is the most hazardous physical environmental substance to persons with albinism, and Africa, particularly West Africa, gets more than enough of a dose of it. The sun is the major cause of the skin damages that persons with albinism experience, and there is now an increasing rate of skin cancer suffered by persons with albinism caused by exposure to sun.[46] As Moloisane, Liebenberg, Lotter and De Villiers put it:

Dermatologists have recognized that the more melanin one has in the skin the less sun damage such as wrinkling, incidence of actinic keratoses, basal and squamous cell carcinomas, and melanoma occurs. People with albinism have no natural UV protection, therefore, their skin is more sensitive to sunlight and they develop sunburn. Under the tropical African sun, the melanindeficient skin of albinos develops wrinkles, lentigines, actinic keratoses (small reddish or tan thickenings with an irregular rough or scaly surface which develop on the face and the backs of hands, especially on bald scalps) and epitheliomata from which they may die in early adult life or in middle age.[47]

This peculiar situation becomes more challenging for certain reasons. First, a majority of persons with albinism in Africa are not educated or enlightened enough to know the cause of their damaged skin. Some believe the old tales in the community and live by them while doing nothing to protect their skin from the scotching sun. Some common reasons given for the damaged skin in many African societies include salt intake and some paranormal explanations. To cope with the problem of their skin, many persons with albinism stop eating salt altogether and bathe with certain medicated soaps, some of which are hash and contribute to the damaging of the skin. Second, those who know the primary source of skin damage are not able to manage the problem well, even when they are willing to do so. Sunscreens are expensive because they are mostly imported from the West and are often not affordable to a large part of the population of persons with albinism. Only very few are knowledgeable of local means to care for the situation such as the use of honey and aloe Vera plant gel. Again, although some scientists have attempted to produce effective, locally made sunscreen,[48] such attempts have mostly ended on paper with no support from government and other stakeholders to progress from theory to practice. Third, the sunny environmental challenge to the health of persons with albinism is compounded by the fact that in many communities in Africa, the nature of many types of work is such that they must be done under the sun. They include such work as farming, trading, hulking and many forms of apprenticeship. There is therefore urgent need to sensitise the population of persons with albinism on the cause and management of skin damage that is common with the disability.

The second peculiarity of albinism in Africa is the visible difference of a person with albinism. A person with albinism stands out in a typical African community in the same way a black person would stand out in a typical, densely white-populated European community. This standing out is odd and puts one in an awkward position, often attracting unnecessary attention. There is no hiding for a person with albinism in a typical African community; she or he is open to all for either love or hate or a combination of both. To be sure, some people in African communities have genuine love for persons with albinism. They befriend them and love them from the heart. This is often common with enlightened persons who are much more interested in the personality of a person than in the skin colour. But there are more against a person with albinism than for her because of her visible difference. This hinders employment, marriage, socialisation and freedom while promoting and fuelling ridicule, insults, hatred, commodification, killing, maiming and social exclusion.

The issues we have discussed so far in this chapter describe and expose us to the experiences of persons with albinism in Africa. They provide the raw materials for a critical and philosophical interrogation. The next chapter begins the journey of a philosophical analysis of these issues. The goal, of course, remains understanding the dilemmas, finding their roots and preferring solutions that address the problems from the roots.

Notes

1. See W. B. Gallie (1955-'56): 'Essentially Contested Concepts'. *Proceedings of the Aristotelian Society*, 56 167–198.
2. The question of the normalisation of pigmentation and bodies, or what colour makes a pigment or body normal is a protracted and perennial terrain of discourse in different disciplines including philosophy, leading, for instance, to issues of colour racism. We can assume here that albinism can be safely understood as a visible lack of pigmentation regardless of what colour a *normal* pigmentation is assumed to have by the different schools of thought involved in the debate.
3. Ocular Albinism. In *Vision of Children Foundation* website. http://www.visionofchildren.org/what-is-ocular-albinism/. par. 1.
4. James N. Parker and Philip M. Parker (Ed.) (2007). *Oculocutaneous Albinism: A Bibliography and Dictionary for Physicians, Patients and Genome Researchers*. San Diego: ICON Health Publications, 3–4.

26   *Albinism and African thick conceptualisations*

5. James N. Parker and Philip M. Parker. *Oculocutaneous Albinism* 4.
6. See 'Frequency of Albinism'. In *Under the Same Sun* website. http://www.underthesamesun.com/sites/default/files/Frequency%20of%20Albinism.pdf. par 1–2.
7. Ocular Albinism. In *Vision of Children Foundation* website. par. 5.
8. Andrew Curran (2009). 'Rethinking Race History: The Role of the Albino in French Enlightenment Life Science'. *History and Theory*, 48.3: 151.
9. Frances Cress Welshing (1991). *The Isis Paper: The Key to the Colours*. Chicago: Third Word Press.
10. Mia Bay. The Historical Origin of Afrocentrism (2000). *American Studies*, 45.4: 501.
11. Karl Pearson, E. Nettleship and G. H. Usher (1911). *A Monograph on Albinism in Man*. London: Dulau and Co Ltd. 11.
12. Karl Pearson, E. Nettleship and G. H. Usher. *A Monograph on Albinism in Man*. 112–157.
13. Karl Pearson, E. Nettleship and G. H. Usher. *A Monograph on Albinism in Man*. 117.
14. Adopted from Alex Salamanca. *25 Facts about People with Albinism that we Need to be Aware of.* In www.list25.com. par. 1–25.
15. World Health Organisation (2011). *World Report on Disability*. Malta: World Health Organisation. 4.
16. World Health Organisation. *World Report on Disability*. 3.
17. See Paul Abberly (1987). 'The Concept of Oppression and the Development of a Social Theory of Disability. *Disability, Handicap and Society'*, 2.1: 5–19; Tanya Titchkosky (2000). 'Disability Studies: Old and New'. *The Canadian Journal of Disability*, 25.2: 198.
18. Elizabeth Barnes (2009). 'Disability, Minority and Difference'. *Journal of Applied Philosophy*, 26.4: 337–340.
19. Tanya Titchkosky. 'Disability Studies: Old and New'. 198.
20. See Tanya Titchkosky. 'Disability Studies: Old and New'. 198; See also Richard Dyer (1993). *The Matter of Images: Essays on Representations*. London: Routledge. 4.
21. Tanya Titchkosky. 'Disability Studies: Old and New'. 198.
22. World Health Organisation. *World Report on Disability*. 5.
23. Roman Bonzon (2009). 'Thick Aesthetic Concepts'. *The Journal of Aesthetic and Art Criticism*, 67.2: 191. The first use of the term 'thick concept' can be found in Bernard Williams (1985). *Ethics and the Limits of Philosophy*. Cambridge: Harvard University Press.
24. For a detailed analysis of the descriptive and normative features of thick concepts, see Matti Eklund (2011), 'What are Think Concepts?' *Canadian Journal of Philosophy*, 41.1: 25–49.
25. Richard Dyer. *The Matter of Images*. 1.
26. Richard Dyer. *The Matter of Images*. 1.
27. Richard Dyer. *The Matter of Images*. 2–3.
28. Julie Livingston (2008). 'Disgust, Bodily Aesthetics and the Ethic of being Human in Botswana'. *Africa: The Journal of the International African Institute,* 78.2: 299.
29. Olugbenga Samuel Olagunju (2012). 'Toward a Biblical Response to Myth and Discrimination against the Human Rights of Albinos in Yorubaland'. *Journal of Studies in Social Science*, 1.1: 49.
30. Olugbenga Samuel Olagunju. 'Toward a Biblical Response to Myth and Discrimination against the Human Rights of Albinos in Yorubaland'. 50.
31. Olugbenga Samuel Olagunju, 'Toward a Biblical Response to Myth and Discrimination against the Human Rights of Albinos in Yorubaland'. 50.

Albinism and African thick conceptualisations 27

32. E. W. Ardener (1954). 'Some Ibo Attitude to Skin Pigmentation'. *Man*, 54: 71–72; emphases are mine.
33. Muthee Thuka. *Myth, Discrimination and the Call for Special Rights for Persons with Albinism in Sub-Saharan Africa*. https://albinismawareness.or.tz. 2.
34. Adediran Daniel Ikuomola (2015). 'Socio-Cultural Conception of Albinism and Sexuality: Challenges among Persons with Albinism (PWA) in South West, Nigeria. *International Journal of Arts and Humanities*, 4.2: 191.
35. Charlotte Baker. *Representing the tribe of ghosts: Stereotypes of albinism emerging from reports of recent attacks in Tanzania and Burundi*. www. inter-disciplinary.net>bakerwpaper. Accessed on September 9, 2015. 2.
36. Deborah Fahy Bryceson, Jesper Bosse Jonsson and Richard Sherrington (2010). 'Miners' Magic Artisanal Mining: The Albino Fetish and Murder in Tanzania'. *The Journal of Modern African Studies*, 48.3: 353–354.
37. Quoted in The Equal Rights Trust in partnership with the Kenya Human Rights Commission. *In the Spirit of Harambee*. London: The Equal Right Trust, 2012. 146.
38. M. Mswela and M. Nothling-Slabbert (2013). 'Colour Discrimination Against Persons with Albinism in South Africa'. *South African Journal of Biorethics and Law*, 6.1: 25–27; see also Adediran Daniel Ikuomola (2015). '"We Thought we would be Safe Here": Tanzanian Albinos in Kenya and South Africa'. *African Research Review: An International Multidisciplinary Journal*, 9.4: 37–54.
39. See Charlotte Baker, Patricia Lund, Richard Nyathi and Julie Taylor (2010). The Myth Surrounding People with Albinism in South Africa and Zimbabwe, *Journal of African Cultural Studies*, 22.2 169–181.
40. See Ruusa N. Ntinda (2009). 'Customary Practices and Children with Albinism in Namibia: A Constitutional Challenge'. In liver C. Ruppel (Ed., *Children's Rights in Namibia*. Windhoek, Namibia: Macmillan Education. 243–254.
41. See Thomas Probert (Ed.) (2014), *Unlawful Killings in Africa: a Study prepared for the UN Special Rapporteur on Extrajudicial, Summary or Arbitrary Executions*. Cambridge: Centre of Governance and Human Rights, University of Cambridge: 149–186; See also *Persons with Albinism,* Report of the Office of the United Nations High Commissioner for Human Rights to the Twenty-Fourth Session of the Human Rights Council of the United Nations' General Assembly, 2013: 1–18. Accessed on March 13, 2017 from: www.ohchr. org>A_HRC_24_57_ENG.
42. Quoted by Muthee Thuka (2011). 'Myth, Discrimination and the Call for Special Rights for Persons with Albinism in Sub-Saharan Africa'. 3. Accessed on March 23, 2017 from: http://www.underthesamesun.com/sites/default/files/MYTHS.Final_pdf.
43. Charlotte Baker. 'Representing the tribe of ghosts: Stereotypes of Albinism Emerging from Reports of Recent Attacks in Tanzania and Burundi'. Accessed on September 9, 2015 from: http://inter-disciplinary.net/bakerwpaper.
44. Charlotte Baker, Patricia Lund, Richard Nyathi and Julie Taylor. 'The Myth Surrounding People with Albinism in South Africa and Zimbabwe'. 173.
45. Alexander Krappe (2012). 'Albinos and Albinism in Iranian Tradition'. *Folklore*, 55.4: 170.
46. I. A. Chidothe and L. Masamba Neoadjuvant (2014). 'Chemotherapy in Albinos with Locally Advanced Skin Cancer at a Blantyre Hospital – Case Series'. *Malawi Medical Journal*, 26.3: 97–99.
47. M. L. Moloisane, W. Liebenberg, A. P. Lotter and M. De Villiers (2004). 'Formulation of a Topical Sun Protection Cream for People with Albinism'. *East and Central African Journal for Pharmaceutical Sciences*, 7.3: 60.
48. M. L. Moloisane, W. Liebenberg, A. P. Lotter and M. De Villiers. 'Formulation of a Topical Sun Protection Cream for People with Albinism'. 60–64.

2 The ontology of albinism in African traditions

Ontology is the theory of being — from the Greek words *ont* (being) and *logos* (theory, discourse or study). Since the seventeenth century, ontology is often used synonymously with metaphysics because of its concern with the general theory of being, or the essential features of what it means for any entity to be real or to exist. The use of the term *ontology* interchangeably with metaphysics helps to streamline the primary concern of metaphysics with the nature of being, of reality, which dates as far back as Parmenides, from other traditional concerns in metaphysics such as rational theology, rational cosmology and rational psychology.[1] In the history of philosophy, there have been attempts to present general theories of being that would account for the nature and structure of all forms of being in reality. But in recent times, particularly in the twentieth century, the idea of ontological relativity has been brought to the foreground. Ontological relativity implies that context, place and language are essential in formulating a theory of being. In other words, what we need to exist and the basic features of such existence is relative to the theory and language that we bring to the situation.[2] This view of ontology is defended, for instance, by Willard Van Orman Quine in his theory of ontological commitment. In his popular essay 'On What There Is', Quine says:

> A theory is committed to those and only those entities to which the bound variables of the theory must be capable of referring in order that the affirmations made in the theory be true.... So long as I adhere to my ontology, as opposed to McX's, I cannot allow my bound variables to refer to entities which belong to McX's ontology and not to mine. I can, however, consistently describe our disagreement by characterizing the statements which McX affirms. Provided merely that my ontology countenances linguistic forms, or at least concrete inscriptions and utterances, I can talk about McX's sentences.[3]

Quine's views stem, I believe, from the obvious incommensurability of numerous ontological theories and the manner in which specific ontologies have strong effects on those committed to it. Ontological commitments may vary between Christian and Buddhist ontologies or the ontology of science, but commitments to the theory of being in each of these contexts fundamentally affect what being is, and how being is characterised and related to within the specific ontology. It is in this sense that we can talk about ontological commitments in African traditions, a commitment to a theory of being that ensues from African places and African linguistic form. Within the framework of ontological relativity, I attempt in this chapter to develop what could be considered an African theory of being, that is, what it means for any being to exist or what the general features of being is in an African thought system. This is a very important step to take in understanding how the being of a person with albinism (PWA) is understood within an African form of life.

But it is important that we clarify the sense in which we employ the word *Africa*. This is because the word *Africa* does not refer to a specific place or a specific linguistic form. Rather, it is a space with many cultural contexts and linguistic forms. It thus seems better to speak of African ontologies, or ontologies in Africa, rather than speaking of an African ontology. Well it is possible to speak both about African ontologies and African ontology. When we speak about African ontologies, we refer to the theory of being ensuing from a particular African form of life, a cultural and linguistic schema. So we could, in this sense, speak of Yoruba ontology, Akan ontology, Zulu ontology and so on. However, when we talk about an African ontology, we do not mean that all African cultures have the same ontology, but rather that the theories of being in many African cultures have semblances and similarities even though they are embedded in different linguistic forms. It is also interesting to note that these different linguistic forms have quite similar structures across cultures. The similarities in the conception of being as well as knowledge and the good is very noticeable among sub-Saharan African cultures. This is why we can speak of an African philosophy, African epistemology, African ethics and the like.

Nonetheless, it is still important that while discussing African ontology, we should make references to how such semblances play out in specific cultures in Africa. Hence, I begin this chapter by presenting a theory of being that is deducible from the many sub-Saharan African cultures. This is followed by a detailed discussion of the categories of being that are included within such an African ontology. These expositions are necessary if we wish to understand how albinism is considered an other within African ontology. This chapter will also pay attention to the linguistic representations of albinism as an other within African traditions, bearing in mind that language is the house of being.

An African theory of being

The theory of being that has become popular in scholarly literature about African ontology is the vital force theory.[4] Like many other ontological theories, the force thesis is meant to engage a people's conception of being with

30   Ontology of albinism in African traditions

the aim of elucidating the general structures or outline of being as well as the substratum — that is, what remains present and enduring within the structure of being. To recast, the vital force theory presents a metaphysics of enduring presence as found in an African thought system.[5]

The vital force theory holds that in African traditions, there exists a world of two realms of existence — the visible and invisible, real and intrinsically linked to form a whole.[6] The beings existing in these two realms of a single existence are lively and active in varying degrees because they are vitalized, animated or energized by an ontological principle or essence called *vital force* that is given to them by the Supreme Being. Vital force is given different linguistic connotations in different cultures and traditions in sub-Sahara Africa, although having similar meanings. It is called *orion* (force), *etin* (strength) or *ahu* (energy or power) among the Esan people of Southern Nigeria.[7] It is referred to as *ike* among the Ibo people of Eastern Nigeria, *ntu* among the Bantu speaking people of Africa, *okra* among the Akan speaking people of Ghana, *mana* or *megbe* among the Mbuti people of Congo, and contestably *emi* among the Yoruba speaking people of Nigeria.

In theorizing about being in African traditions, some scholars have used the words *force* and *spirit* interchangeably.[8] Two main reasons can be identified for this: Spirit, just like force, is invisible; Spirit in an African community has a higher degree or vitality of force than physical entities and are believed to be able, in a number of ways to cause and (or) influence the vitality or life force in physical, visible entities. Idoniboye, therefore, sees spirits as the one entity that remains constant in an African belief system.[9] Ukhun also says the same about Esan ontology, that it lays strong emphasis on spirits rather than on material or physical entities:

> Spirits are sacrosanct and form the quintessential or the bedrock of existence of the traditional Esan tradition. In traditional Esan, the material has significance only in reference to the spiritual and not vice-versa... Every aspect of life of an Esan person is captured within a spiritual milieu and not necessarily in material terms. Although in Esan tradition a person may aspire to material acquisition or sees himself or herself as a physical entity, he or she is fully aware that there is a potent spiritual force behind his or her existence.[10]

However, the use of force interchangeably with spirit is faulty because force does not refer to an entity,[11] while spirit refers to this or that kind of entity in many African cultures. So, to avoid confusing a non-entity for an entity, it is safer to use the concept of 'force', or 'vital force', in speaking about the African ontological principle.

Perhaps a good starting point in understanding the concept of force in African ontology is by paying attention to Placide Tempels' *Bantu Philosophy*. Tempels' project in this work is primarily centred on an analysis

Ontology of albinism in African traditions 31

of 'vital force' as the 'inmost nature of being'[12] in Bantu tradition, the source of which is Supreme Being. The key to Bantu thought, he says, is the idea of vital force. He says therefore that:

> The key principle of Bantu philosophy is that of vital force. The activating and final aim of all Bantu effort is only the intensification of vital force. To protect it or to increase vital force, that is the motive or profound meaning in all their practices. It is the ideal which animates the life of the *muntu,* the only thing for which he is ready to suffer and to sacrifice himself.[13]

Tempels' goal in *Bantu Philosophy* is therefore to show that the nature of the universe to the African is nothing if not the universe of forces; these forces can weaken or strengthen the life of a person, and in the face of the fact that one's life force can be dangerously diminished or beneficially enhanced and strengthened, the best course of action for one is to take care to avoid the diminution of one's life force (which draws an obvious connection between the *is* and the *ought*, which we shall return to in due course). This last point is emphasised in chapters three ('Bantu Wisdom or Criteriology'), four ('The Theory of "Muntu" or Bantu Psychology') and five ('Bantu Ethics'), respectively. In them, every aspect of Bantu thought, action and practice is causally interpreted with regard to the diminution or strengthening of life force, as is evidenced in the treatment of witchcraft, sorcery, the medicine man, ancestorship, the king and the chief. The point made is that some of these actors diminish life force while some enhance it.[14] As a consequence, persons are cast in the role of manipulators; they manipulate the situation toward maintaining and strengthening their life forces.

Therefore, in articulating an African ontology, an essential point to be noted is that there is an '... energy of cosmic origin that permeates and lives within all that is — human beings, animals, plants, minerals and objects, as well as events. This common energy shared by all confers a common essence to everything in the world, and thus ensures the fundamental unity of all that exists ... This energy constitute the active, dynamic principle that animates creation, and which can be identified as life itself.'[15] In the words of Polycarp Ikuenobe:

> In the traditional African view, reality or nature is a continuum and a harmonious composite of various elements and forces. Human beings are a harmonious part of this composite reality, which is fundamentally, a set of mobile life forces. Natural objects and reality are interlocking forces. Reality always seeks to maintain an equilibrium among the network of elements and life forces.... Because reality or nature is a continuum, there is no conceptual or interactive gap between the human self, community, the dead, spiritual or metaphysical entities and

32 Ontology of albinism in African traditions

the phenomenal world; they are interrelated, they interact, and in some sense, one is an extension of the other.[16]

This principle of ontological unity has at least two immediate and fundamental implications: the principle of connectedness of all based on the common essence of vital force, and the principle of harmony based on the organic solidarity and complementarities of all forms.[17] The Supreme Being remains the source of this common essence, and for this reason, everything that shares of the divine essence is sacred.

Force is therefore described, and I believe correctly, by Stephen Okafor as 'phenomenon-aura'.[18] A 'phenomenon' is anything appeared or observed, especially if having scientific interests. An 'aura' is a subtle invisible essence or fluid said to emanate from human and animal bodies and even from things. Phenomenon-aura, therefore, is the emission of energy or force from an existent.[19] Viewing the conception of force in an African ontology, we realize that beings or entities are not only animated with force, they also emit an essence or force peculiar to each one of them in their causal relations, operations and interactions in the universe.[20]

Phenomenon-aura accounts for the following points concerning the concept of being in many African cultures: In a world of varying existents, or entities emitting varying degrees of force into the universe, they (the emitted energies) causally account for the experiences of joy, pain, death, illness, health, calamites, orderliness and so on. An existent possesses either a neutral aura, an active harmful aura or an active beneficial aura. Again, an existent, by its very position in a given place, atmosphere of event or mixture, may thereby be subject to a crossing and interaction of essences, which, in turn, create a new effect or aura. Some actors in an African community such as the medicine man, the witch or wizard, the witch doctor and the herbalist are manipulators of 'the realm of invisible auras', bringing either order or chaos to the community.[21]

Those who manipulate beings and their auras or forces have adequate knowledge of them and how to manipulate them to produce effect for good or for ill. The Supreme Being is seen as the source of both the phenomena and the auras. Evidently, therefore, the African believes in the influence of forces that are invisible casual agents and are part and parcel of their earthly affairs. They identify force as the ultimate working principle. In the Supreme Being resides force or energy, and he dispenses it at will.

The role of a particular entity or the extent to which it can be manipulated or become a manipulator in an African ontology in the causal interaction with other beings is determined by the degree of vital force possessed by the entity. Hence, within an African ontology, beings are categorised based on the perceived degree of vitality possessed by such beings. The next section pays attention to the hierarchical categorisation of being in an African ontology, showing where a person with albinism would fit into such a structure.

Categories of being in African ontology

African ontology consists of a hierarchy of interacting entities, an interaction made possible by the presence of force in each being. The hierarchy is also ranked and arranged based on the degree of vital force possessed by an entity and the extent to which a being has impact on other beings based on the exercise of force. In many African traditions, the Supreme Being is at the apex of the hierarchy, closely followed by the divinities, primordial and deified. Next to the divinities are the ancestors, and these are closely followed by what we could call 'manipular entities'. The human being is next to the manipular forces, and after them are the lesser beings such as animals and plants. Apart from these conventional sets of accepted entities, there is also the category of queer beings. In the next number of paragraphs, we shall examine these categories of beings and the nature of interaction that exist among them.

The Supreme Being is considered a real entity, standing as ontologically ultimate to any other entity in the category of being. The ontological supremacy of this entity is clearly seen in the names used in many African cultures to represent the Supreme Being, names that are mainly used to depict the idea that the Supreme Being is the source, creator and sustainer of the universe, of life, of being. The Supreme Being is viewed as all-powerful perfect and just. They recognize his majesty and mightiness. African traditions have many rituals, divinities, and manipular forces; peculiar rivers, trees, stones, spaces; dreams of and feelings toward the dead and so on. They have their sheer numinous powers, but the Supreme Being created the world that exhibits them.[22] It is because of the supreme nature of this being that it is not considered proper to approach this being directly but through intermediaries. This is a mark of respect and reverence for him. It is like the king-subject relationship[23] in some African traditional societies, where the king is not approached directly but through an intermediary. In the relationship between the African people and the Supreme Being, intermediaries therefore play a vital role. Olusegun Oladipo therefore says that:

> ... the Supreme Being in African cultures can be regarded as a typical religious object. He is, in most cases, regarded as the maker of the world and its sustainer and ruler; the origin and giver of life who is above all divinities and man; a supreme judge and a controller of human destiny. These attributes show that the Supreme Being in African culture is regarded as the ultimate reality. And He is a religious object. After all, they constantly mention Him in prayers andin times of difficulties, even though no direct worship of Him is entertained in most cases. Generally, then, the Supreme Being... can be regarded as the ultimate point of reference in whatever may be called African traditional religion.[24]

Next in the hierarchy of beings are the divinities. The belief in the existence of divinities is a major feature of the traditional thought of the African

34   *Ontology of albinism in African traditions*

people. In African ontology, this category of beings is basically subdivided into two: (i.) the primordial divinities and, (ii.) the deified divinities. The primordial divinities are called 'sons of the Supreme Being'. They are spiritual forces brought into being with regard to the divine ordering of the universe. They are ministers of the Supreme Being with derived powers. The Supreme Being assigns each of them a portfolio. They act as intermediaries between the Supreme Being and the human being. They are largely nature- or object–inhabiting spirits by having temporary dwelling places in features of nature such as rivers, lakes, lagoons, streams, trees, forests, mountains, groves, hills and so on. From there they emit their powers, energies or forces for the benefit of the people.[25]

Deified divinities, on the other hand, are heroes and founding fathers who have contributed immensely to the founding of a community and after physical death are believed to be in a position to influence positively the lives of the physically living by relating their problems to the Supreme Being. A person who sacrificed himself to save his community, a person who started a settlement, or a person who performed great feats for his community was, at his death, deified and venerated and became the primary divinity for the respective community. Shrines and statues are erected for them and festivals are held to commemorate their lives and feats. The function of these divinities, both primordial and deified, is to place the individual in an interplay of forces, where if persons venerate and appease them, the living are believed to be protected from misfortunes and evil spiritual forces in general. The traditional African person is therefore required to show loyalty to these divinities to avoid being doomed, for they are believed to have the power to either make or mar her or him, to either increase or diminish her or his vital force depending on the kind of relationship he or she has with them. The ancestors, in Lee M. Brown's words:

> … are individuals who were once [physically] alive, but are nonetheless still capable of agency. Having agency is to be understood as having a capacity to initiate, on one's own accord, actions that have intended consequences for oneself or for others. It is believed that the awareness of the intention of ancestral spirits provides grounds for understanding physical occurrences.[26]

In African traditions, ancestors are members of the African community who have *properly* departed the physical realm of existence to the non-physical. They are those who have completed their course here in the land of the physically living and have gone to the spiritual abode of the physically dead. However, an essential point to note is that not all who die become an ancestor in African traditions. For one to become an ancestor, she or he must be a person and not a queer being — a point we shall return to subsequently — must have lived a community-accepted or culturally accepted lifestyle, must have lived to a ripe old age, must have children to

Ontology of albinism in African traditions 35

honour his or her death, and must have died a good death (as distinct from bad death, where the person's death results from suicide or unexplainable circumstances). For example, the Akan people see a person who is morally bankrupt, a person who dies mysteriously and tragically, as being disqualified from being an ancestor. An ancestor is one who has lived to a ripe old age in an exemplary manner or did much to enhance the prestige and standing of the family, tribe and clan.[27] Kwasi Wiredu shares the same view that 'living a full and meaningful life is a condition for becoming an ancestor.'[28] In many sub-Saharan African cultures, too, only men who have fulfilled the above requirements qualify to become an ancestor. Women who may qualify do not become ancestors. This, of course, raises certain issues concerning the gender bias and sexist treatment of women, which is not within our immediate concern in this work.

For a person to become an ancestor, it is also important that she or he is properly buried — that is, the necessary burial rites must be done for the fulfilled person to enter the ancestral cult. The burial of the dead in African communities involves many rites of passage to the ancestral cult, the constituents of which may vary in some form from one community to another. These rites of passage are therefore garnished with religious underpinnings.[29] During the rites of passage or burial rites, the first son or the most eldest brother is installed as the new family head, the representative of the ancestor in the world of the physically living, having the duties of mediating between the kin and the ancestor.

The ancestors are thus intrinsically intertwined with the living; their consent is sought regarding family decisions. Anyone who erred in the family and has been left behind, must appease them for forgiveness to avert punishment and to live a better life. Nothing is done without their involvement in the family. A person's prestige increases with her age, values, generosity, courage in warfare and haunting wisdom, and respect for elders and ancestors. To such a person, it is believed tha ancestors grant the reward of success in life in all its ramifications.[30] The daily flux of existence in traditional African communities affirms and reaffirms the ancestral presence and an impossibility of its absence. This is attested to by the shrines found at many turns and the utterances in the offering of libation that punctuates the daily flow of life.[31] Thus, the Akan maxim 'When a person dies, he is not (really) dead'[32] is a true depiction of the nature of African traditions. This being the picture, the dead do not just fall into oblivion because they continue to be involved in the affairs of the living; the living are, in fact, named after them.[33] This is aptly captured by Benezet Bujo in the following lines:

> The relationship between those living on earth and the ancestors is very close, since the living owe their existence to the ancestors from whom they receive everything necessary for life. On the other hand, the living dead can "enjoy" their being ancestors only through the living clan

36 Ontology of albinism in African traditions

community. In this way, a kind of "interaction" – hierarchically organised from top to bottom and vice versa – is created.... The goal of this interaction is the increase of vitality within the clan[34]

Thus, ancestors are themselves still continuing persons, still very much a part of the living community.[35]

In African traditions, there exist some supernatural forces that are neither divinities nor ancestors but either manipulate or are manipulated in such a way that they become beneficial or harmful to the physically living. They are manipulated in sorcery, witchcraft and magic of certain ends.[36] They include roaming spirits (particularly of the improperly dead) and supernatural forces like witches and wizards. Hence, we can categorise such entities as manipular beings. For instance, persons who have harnessed the manipular force of witchcraft are often seen as evil persons who use their elevated energy to cause tension in the family and society. Yemi Elebuibon expresses this belief in the Yoruba culture. According to him, Yoruba has two types of evil supernatural powers; the first is the power or force wielded by *Ajogun* (belligerent enemies of the person) and the second is that of *Eleye* or *Aye* (witches). Generally speaking they use their supernatural powers to work against man's interest by trying to delay or totally prevent the realization of one's destiny or by diminishing one's life force.[37]

Barry Hallen and J.O. Sodipo gives a general sketch of the manner in which witches (or wizards) are perceived in African traditions:

> Witches meet in secret assembles at night; when travelling to these assembles, they take on the form of an animal and leave their physical bodies behind. Witches prey upon non-witches who are neither deserving of, nor responsible for, the misfortunes they suffer. Often the witch is thought to 'consume' the body or force of its victim in some physical and/or non-physical fashion. The physical symptoms of this in the victim are diseases or any wasting, lingering illness. Witches are sometimes thought to derive certain of their powers from a 'witchcraft substance', either internal to the body of the witch or kept by her in some external, secret place.[38]

G. Sogolo adds also that the act of witches are always evil and destructive; they cause the death of people, make men impotent and women barren, cause failure in all forms of human endeavours, etc.[39]

Not all manipular forces are evil. Some aid in the maintenance of justice in the community. It is believed, for instance, that if someone commits murder, rape, adultery, causes misfortune for another using some non-physical means, or engages in any such social vices, not only will the person incur the wrath of ancestors, divinities and the Supreme Being, but also that of manipular forces. This is because, in a case of the murder of a young person, for instance, the African believes that the spirit of the victim will avenge

Ontology of albinism in African traditions 37

her untimely death. And when the culprit becomes ill without any scientific diagnosis or cure, people believe that she has been caught by the spirit.

The activities of manipular forces surely reveal an interplay and operation of forces that are neither divinities, ancestors, nor the Supreme Being, but affect the life of the living through witchcraft, magic, sorcery, healing, rituals and the like. in this category of beings, the human person is fully involved This is because, in some cases (like in the case of witchcraft), she is the being who increases her vital force or energizes herself beyond her normal life force degree by the invocation of manipular forces through initiation or rituals in order to either harm (as in the case of a witch)or aid (as in the case of a witch doctor) the life of her fellows. She is also at the receiving end of the manipulations of manipular forces. This is why there is the belief that the force that the Supreme Being gives to the free and responsible beings he has created is neutral; they either become good or evil depending on how they freely use their force or energy to the benefit of humans and society. The very fact of the existence of spiritual beings, especially those that can mar the person's life, helps to strengthen the relationship between persons, the ancestors, the divinities and the Supreme Being.

Next in the hierarchy of beings is the human person. There is much to say about the African concept of a person. In fact, much has been said on the topic in existing literature. We shall, however, limit the analysis here mainly to the ontological view of the being of man in order not to deviate from the scope of discourse. The person in African traditions is a composite whole of a number of substances: material, immaterial and even quasi-material substances. He has a body, spirit, mind and destiny. All of these put together does not yet become a person until a spark of God's energy or force vitalizes or energizes the composite and gives him life. The physical body is concrete and tangible. The spirit, on the other hand, is the spirit of the individual. It is what roams about, reincarnates, joins the ancestral cult, or becomes a deified divinity after the demise of the body. Though often taken as an immaterial substance, it is also alleged to be a quasi-material substance, which strong medicine men can see. In African ontology, lower beings than men, such as animals, plants minerals and, interestingly, queer beings do not possess spirit, only force. The mind is yet another immaterial substance of the person regarded by African ontology as the seat of thought, strength and memory.

In African traditions, it is strongly defended that a person has a destiny. The destiny of a person is what the Supreme Being endorses a person to become when he arrives here on earth. It is referred to as *Ori* in Yoruba ontology, *chi* in Ibo ontology and *nkrubea* in Akan ontology.[40] Evil forces can militate against a person from actualizing her chosen destiny. The person can ignore her'self-actualization process'[41] or destiny due to ill behaviour and unwillingness to yield to the voice within (the destiny guardian). The philosophical problem concerning freedom and responsibility does not arise here. This is because the idea of destiny confirms one's freedom and

38   *Ontology of albinism in African traditions*

responsibility. This is because when a person chooses her destiny before the Supreme Being, she is free to follow it up by heeding to the voice of the destiny guardian, or rejecting it, but in either case, facing the consequences. These components of the human being show why a person's life goes beyond the material physical world and why death simply leads to another form of existence, a rite of passage that allows one to gain another existential status, that of an ancestor, for instance.

Just below the human being in the hierarchy are things, basically animals, plants and minerals. These things either have a low degree of vitality (like in animals) or are inactive forces (like in plants or minerals) until acted upon either by a person or by other spiritual beings. A leaf, for example, lies inactive in the bush until someone gets it, acts on it, and it emits its aura of healing.

What is interestingly striking about these things is that their energy or force is hardly fixed or stable. This is because spiritual forces, good or evil, can easily inhabit them due to their inactive nature — they can hardly resist such inhabitation — and control or direct their behaviour or disposition; it is the animating of sustaining, creative force of the universe.[42] This is a common belief in African communities. Trees, birds (specifically owls), animals (e.g., cats) or bodies of water are inhabited by forces. Witches are normally known to inhabit owls; deities (deified and primordial) are known to inhabit natural entities such as rivers, earth, metal, etc. This makes these things act with a very high degree of force, though it is really not theirs. Things, therefore, can at a time be inactive and at another time become active even more than those beings above them in the hierarchy. The only reason why they cannot overtake the person in the hierarchy is because their demise marks their end; they have no spirit in them.

The last in the category of beings in African traditions, one that is of much interest to us in the discourse we are right now engaged in is what I would term 'queer beings'. An entity or event is described as queer if it is at variance with what is usual or normal, that is, if it differs in some odd or strange way from what is ordinary. Something queer is something suspicious, unconventional and strange. A queer being in African ontology is a being that may visibly appear as a human being but, due to lack of, or possession of, certain ontic qualities, is seen as not fitting within the categories of human beings due to its unusual nature. Hence, queer beings may look human, but they are not regarded as humans nor treated as such in African traditions. The list of the kinds of entities that may fall within this category of being vary from one sub-Saharan African culture to the other. Generally, however, persons with one form of disability or persons born with any form of deformity (e.g., persons with albinism) would fall under this group. In some cases, twins, triplets and quadruplets, little persons, persons with angular kyphosis, and the like would be treated as queer beings.

The treatment of queer beings varies, too, across cultures. Due to their unusual nature, some are seen as some kind of favourable divine presence

Ontology of albinism in African traditions 39

that deserves care and reverencing, while others are seen as an unfavourable divine presence, some sort of curse or punishment from supernatural entities that deserves to be done away with or, at least, abhorred. Take for example the birth of twins. In some cultures such as the Yoruba culture, twins or triplets are reverenced and taken to be a good sign of favour from the ancestors, divinities and the Supreme Being. They are therefore expected to be treated as princes and princesses. However, a number of communities around Abuja Nigeria, such as Yaba, Gulida, Gomani, Tepase, Dawaki, Warambi, Kiyi and Shetuko villages are still to date engaged in the killing of twins because they are considered as queer beings that bring bad luck. We recall, of course, the work of the Scottish missionary Mitchell Slessor to abolish the killing of twins in sub-Saharan Africa, particularly Nigeria. Hence, in most cases, queer beings are killed immediately after birth, thrown into the evil forest or, in cases where they escape being killed mostly due to modern social structures, they face maltreatment, stigmatisation and social exclusion for much of their lives. The social institutions on ground are therefore properly structured to establish, perpetuate and maintain the queerness of such entities.

In virtually every African culture or tradition, however, persons with albinism are not just queer beings, but queer beings with abhorrent representations. In what follows, we shall attempt a detailed and critical analysis of the idea of persons with albinism as queer beings.

Persons with albinism as queer beings

In African ontology, persons with albinism may in all respects visibly appear to be human, except, of course, for the lack of pigmentation. But they are, in fact, excluded from the human category of beings. Rather, persons with albinism are viewed as queer, unusual beings. To be sure, when the word *queerness* is used, it immediately presents the idea of oddness, difference and unusualness. But beyond these definitions, it intrinsically connotes counterfeit, worthless, questionable and suspicious. Hence, when we talk about queer money, for instance, we do not only mean that the money is unusual or different but that it is questionable, suspicious and redundant counterfeit. Understanding persons with albinism as queer beings in these ways is much felt in African societies. Their unusual nature stems not only from their visible physical difference but also from the ideas about the nature of their being presented and represented down the ages in the worldviews of African traditional societies. We had discussed such sociocultural representations of albinism in African traditions in the previous chapter. At this junction, however, it is important that we pay attention to the ontological differences between human beings and persons with albinism as queer beings that accounts for their exclusion from the human category of being.

One important distinction between human beings considered as normal and those considered as queer, with particular reference to persons with

40 *Ontology of albinism in African traditions*

albinism, is the presence and absence of the spirit element of the human being that lives on in the spiritual realm of existence after physical death. It is evident from African traditions that while human beings possess not just vital force, but also spirit, which makes them capable of becoming an ancestor, a manipular spirit, or a deified divinity, persons with albinism, as queer beings, may have vital force but do not have spirit. It is therefore not possible, for instance, to talk of a person with albinism as becoming an ancestor after death. A person with albinism is therefore less of a being than a human being. Such a person is also not viewed in the same way a human being is viewed as possessing certain essential ontological qualities such as coming into being with a destiny chosen before the Supreme Being. Rather, the coming into being of a person with albinism is viewed as an outcome of a curse placed on the child bearer, the husband of the child bearer or the family at large due to some wrong doing, from a higher force (such as an ancestor or divinity) due to some wrong doing. Hence, a family that gives birth to a person with albinism is seen as unfavoured by some higher forces and faces ridicule within the community. For this reason, persons with albinism are conceived as a human other, *something* different from the approved and accepted notion of a human being. A person with albinism as an other is thus not expected to participate or take the lead in human social and religious activities within the community. It is not mandatory for him to receive proper burial rites even though he succeeds in raising a family, having children and living a community accepted form of life. Basically, a person with albinism is not expected to be treated as a human being.

Another interrelated point to be underscored about albinism in African traditions can best be understood if we, first of all, say a few things about the fundamental need for preservation of the community of beings in African traditions. Communal harmony and equilibrium is essential and fundamental because beings or forces interact and find meaning in the community. The community itself is an aggregate of interacting cosmic forces, as well as structures established to foster and sustain the established and most needed interaction. Accepted beings within the ontological structure and the community are therefore intrinsically interwoven and cannot be conceived as existing separately at any point. Cosmic forces find meaning in their space of dwelling. Consider, for example, the being of the ancestor. It is impossible to conceive an ancestor as separate from the kin. This is because it is within his kin that he is not only venerated, but also where a shrine is erected for him; it is because of him that the whole kin come together, at least once a year, to pay homage and respect to him. He is called on issues of morality, conflict, social problems, health matters, joys and virtually all events confronting the family. This is where his existence finds meaning and where his force becomes useful. In the same vein, the kin also do not conceive of theirselves at any point as being independent of their ancestors. On social, religious, moral, spiritual, health, political

Ontology of albinism in African traditions 41

matters or otherwise, they seek the decision or consent of their ancestors, they appease to him when any family member does wrong in order to calm his temper and reaffirm their loyalty to him. They thank him for the birth of a child, for good harvest, for protection from enemies and so on. the kin and the ancestors therefore enjoy a relationship that is reciprocal. Benezet Bujo says, for example, regarding the relationship between a person and his or her ancestors on health matters:

> The community of the diseased is also not forgotten since a disease might be caused by the disturbed relationship of the patient with the world of those who have passed away....Health, therefore, implies safe integration into the bi-dimensional community as the place where life grows.... [For] If interpersonal relationships are not well maintained, sickness can affect the members.[43]

Hence, interpersonal relationship is necessary for survival of any being in the ontological structure. This is one reason why communal harmony is essential. It is what Stephen O. Okafor captures as *commensality*. Commensality, in practice, means 'the act of eating together or sharing in a common meal'. However, from what has been said above, it becomes necessary to note its primary and secondary senses. In its primary sense, it is the philosophical or ideological criterion for all forms of social or political relationships; a mechanism that militates against social excommunication and tension-ridden rivalries. This surely has enormous benefits for the development of any community or society. It makes for peace and social harmony. In its secondary sense, it is the possibility and practice of sharing in all forms of common and conventional meals on family, communal or national levels; or between individuals; between the living and the living-dead; between the community and their divinities or Supreme Being.[44] Therefore all cosmic forces interact and relate in the established structures of the community to promote peace, order and tranquillity and to checkmate ill-behaviour or anything that seems to threaten the much needed unity of beings. The famous lines of John Mbiti readily comes to mind here.

> Only in terms of other people does the individual become conscious of his own being, his own duties, his privileges and responsibilities towards himself and towards other people. When he suffers, he does not suffer alone but with the corporate group; when he rejoices, he rejoices not alone but with his kinsmen, his neighbours and relatives whether dead or alive. Whatever happens to the individual happens to the whole group and whatever happens to the whole group happens to the individual. The individual can only say: "I am, because we are; and since we are, therefore I am." This is the cardinal point in the understanding of the African view of man.[45]

42   *Ontology of albinism in African traditions*

Another important aspect of the relationship and interaction of forces in the Esan community is vividly seen in the idea of causality or causal agency. As Polycarp Ikuenobe says:

> The proper or harmonious interaction among forces and lack thereof, provide the basis for explaining causal phenomena with respect to various events or occurrences. Harmony in interaction among forces brings about good events and lack of harmony in interaction among forces brings about bad events such as death and disease. Human actions in relation to community and nature are central to the ability to create harmony.[46]

Every event, happening or phenomenon experienced in the community is caused by a causal agency — physical or non-physical. All beings in African societies are causal agencies, and events in the community are explained with reference to them. Beings and their interaction are therefore the basis for the explanation, predication, and control of events in the community. One point must be stressed here. Spiritual forces are not the only causes of events in the African community. Indeed, all beings are involved — physical and non-physical. G. Sogolo says, for example, about the Azande that:

> They provide descriptions of objects and explanations of events in theoretical categories not tied to magical or religious beliefs. The Azande have principles and beliefs about how to hunt for animals... the kind of soil that would produce harvest... knowledge of nutritional techniques, the food that nourishes and that which does not; that which is poisonous and that which is not; it would therefore be a mistake to suggest that in these areas of their daily activities the Azande always resort to magical or religious explanations.[47]

Therefore, causality in the Esan community reflects the interaction between the physical and non-physical in human existence. The African operates with the idea that every event has a cause but not every event has a scientifically explainable or verifiable cause in a positivistic sense. Chinua Achebe also depicts this about Igbo metaphysics in his classic *Things fall Apart*. This is typified in Okoli's death. The only thing we know about Okoli is that he joined the new religion, that he 'brought the church into serious conflict with the clan... by killing the sacred python, the emanation of the god of water... The royal python was the most revered animal in Mbanta and all the surrounding clans. It was addressed as "Our Father" and was allowed to go wherever it chose'.[48] When the people learned that Okoli had killed the python on account of the new religion, they were infuriated; yet, they believed the gods would fend for themselves: 'It is not our custom to fight for our gods... Let us not presume to do so now. If a man kills the sacred

Ontology of albinism in African traditions 43

python in the secrecy of his hut, the matter lies between him and the god'.[49] And surely enough, Okoli fell ill and died, showing that '... the gods were still able to fight their own battles'.[50]

In sum, the two main reasons why communal harmony is very essential in the community are: (i.) to guarantee survival and (ii.) to provide causal explanations. Now, if communal harmony and equilibrium is this important, then the community has the crucial responsibility of preventing or doing away with anything considered a threat to the preservation of the community. For instance, moral bankruptcy of a person, or not living by community-approved standards is considered a threat to the structure of beings. This is because a morally bankrupt person doing things that are frowned at by the ancestors or divinities would cause frictions and unhealthy relationships between her kin and her ancestors. This brings about disequilibrium in the relationship among beings and becomes a threat to communal harmony. For this reason, morally bankrupt persons in African traditions may be considered persons in the ontological sense as having all the necessary constituents of the beings of persons but would not be considered as persons in the social sense and would be stripped of all social status and positions until she repented of the wrongdoing.

Similarly, many queer beings are seen as threats to the established harmony of being and to the vital force of the human being. For instance, many African traditions codify within their worldviews the need to avoid and abhor persons with albinism. If persons with albinism are beings produced from the anger and punitive measures of supernatural entities, then associating with them may lead to suffering from the same vengeful anger that brought them into being. Hence, children are told to stay away from such persons; pregnant women are threatened not to look at persons with albinism, lest they give birth to something like them; persons with albinism are largely excluded from social gatherings or activities. This is because having relations with persons with albinism will result in incurring the wrath of some supernatural entity, which will bring about frictions in the community of beings. In fact, among the Yoruba people, they are believed to be the properties of the supernatural entities that begot them. Hence, it is conventional within the Yoruba culture to make such persons serve in the shrine of a divinity rather than stay home with the family. In this way, persons with albinism are completely isolated away from the main human societies and become servants to some chief priest in some isolated shrine.

Again, there are two immediate consequences of the idea that persons with albinism come into being through the punitive acts of some supernatural forces. First, as it was common in many sub-Saharan African cultures, the new born infant with albinism is killed or thrown away in the forest as a form of sacrifice to appease the angry supernatural entity. Hence, it was customary to kill infants born with albinism at birth. Although occurrence of this has reduced due to the experience of modernity, it has not completely been eradicated. There are still indications of the killing of infants with

44   *Ontology of albinism in African traditions*

albinism in many communities in Africa to date. Second, persons with albinism who, for some reason, survive death as infants are thought to possess some peculiar kind of force that can be manipulated or harnessed for certain ends. Medicine men spread the idea that body parts of persons with albinism can be manipulated with the aid of manipular forces to, for instance, provide protection, good health and wealth for humans. In this scenario, persons with albinism are nothing more than things or objects whose force can be extracted or harnessed for certain ends. Those who are involved in the dismembering and killing of persons with albinism do not feel the guilt that a human being has been killed, because such persons are not, in the first place, considered as a human being. There is no spirit element departing the dead body of the person with albinism to a spiritual realm of existence as, for instance, a manipular force seeking revenge for her death or an ancestor joining the ancestral cult. Hence, in the last few decades, there has been a notorious history of killings of persons with albinism in modern times for such reasons as luck charms, wealth and health, with East Africa (particularly Tanzania) making notorious headlines.

Hence, the othering of persons with albinism as queer beings in African ontology and the manner in which the queerness of their beings has been presented and represented through the history of African cultures have had dire consequences for such persons and continue to do so. Persons with albinism do not only face ontological exclusion but social exclusion. Their othering is deeply entrenched in the ontological and social institutions of the African community. The social exclusion experienced by persons with albinism today can therefore not be tackled without first paying attention to the alterity encoded into the African theory of being in sub-Saharan African traditions.

Questioning the ontological asumptions about albinism

A number of issues arise from the ontological othering of persons with albinism in African traditions. There is, for instance, an apparent contradiction in the general theory of being in African cultures and the specific ideas about albinism thereof. Three things stand out from an African theory of being: (i.) all existents are connected because they share a common essence or ontological principle, vital force. This explains causal agency and relationship and the importance of communal harmony and equilibrium for the preservation of the community of beings; (ii.) the Supreme Being is the source of vital force, which makes all things sacred and potentially of great value; and (iii.) force is in itself neutral until it is acted with or acted upon, which implies that no entity is innately bad or good. If these conclusions about African ontology are true, then the ontological representations of persons with albinism deviate largely from the dominant line of thought about being and reality in African traditions for a number of reasons.

First, although persons with albinism are visibly different, and alleged to be queer and unusual in a densely black-populated African community, they ought not to be ontologically unusual since they share the same common essence, vital force, with other beings. The principle of being ought to enclose rather than isolate as queer the being of persons with albinism as human beings. If we had a hundred apples in a box, ninety-eight of which are green and two red, the two red apples do not cease being apples simply because they are *different*. They are simply what they are, apples with different colours. The attempt to claim and maintain that the two red apples are no longer apples but an unusual kind of fruit is to deliberately isolate the red apples merely to ensure that only green apples remain in the box and the status quo is maintained. The ontological representation of persons with albinism, therefore, seems to me an attempt to actively produce false consciousness about such persons by capitalising on their visible difference with the view of completely isolating them from the social box of black Africans in the respective communities. Institutionalising the isolation of persons with albinism from human persons through deeply entrenched ideas about being makes it possible for community members to evade their responsibilities and obligations toward such persons, an issue we shall be returning to in the fourth chapter.

Second, the person with albinism (cum some other allegedly queer beings in certain African places) seems to be the one who is innately born with a harmful vital force rather than a neutral essence as it is the case with other beings. A human being in the African theory of being can only become harmful or evil through sustained actions and conduct that go against socially recommended norms of behaviour. She is not born with an evil vital force. Even when she becomes morally bankrupt, she is only isolated from being a person in a social-normative sense, not in an ontological sense. But a person with albinism is alleged to be born harmful and evil because she is the consequence of the punitive actions of a supernatural entity. Even sitting close to or passing by a person with albinism is considered detrimental to the well-being of accepted human beings. In some African communities, it is important that a person touches any metal substance (such as a metal button on the cloth one is putting on) when she gazes, by chance, on a person with albinism on the road, in the market or in some other place, to avoid being hurt by the evil essence of the person with albinism. Social and ontological exclusion cannot be more deeply entrenched. But the manner in which it is entrenched obviously goes against the very nature of the essence of African ontology.

There is an enormous gulf between modern, empirical and scientific facts about the coming-to-be of albinism and the ontological characterisation and normative representations of albinism in African traditions. This fact-norm distinction of the thick concept of albinism in African places is also observable in other queer beings such as the gap between scientific facts about twins, triplets and little persons, and the representations of such persons

46　*Ontology of albinism in African traditions*

in traditional cultures. There is nothing in the deeply entrenched ideas about persons with albinism that points to the facts about such persons that we now have in modern times, facts that make it easier for such persons to cope with their condition. In the next chapter we shall return to the issue of the gap between the truth and false consciousness about albinism and the role actively produced ignorance plays in maintaining such a gap. However, it is worrisome that even though many in modern Africa are now aware of the biological facts about albinism, the awareness has achieved only very little in reducing the discrimination and isolation of such persons in African community. Why is this so? It is because African conception of being is presented, represented, and assimilated into individual consciousness as a realist form of ontology, a theory of being that takes the status of a given, an objective, infallible, independent structure of reality. When the African talks about ancestors and divinities and queer beings, she is not referring to some idea conjured up in an attempt to make sense of human experiences (which is what they actually are). Rather, she is convinced that she is speaking about something real and tangible even though not always physical. So when a person with albinism is represented as a ghost or a divine agent or the product of a curse, such representations are not mere ideas in the mind but real representation of real existents. This realist stance on African theory of being makes it difficult for many Africans to do away with such representations of persons with albinism and embrace the factual and observable explanations for their being.

These issues show clearly that the ideas about albinism in African ontology are not only questionable but are highly speculative. However, they continue to have real consequences for persons with albinism. There is, therefore, an urgent need to uproot such speculative but deeply entrenched ideas about the otherness of persons with albinism. But the theoretical roots are deep and successfully fertilised with ideas about the supernatural. Hence, a lot needs to be done in demystifying albinism through massive education and enlightenment projects, intense and massively funded medical research and health education/care programs and the strengthening of already ongoing intervention. But before paying attention to these areas in chapter six, more needs to be done in unearthing the roots of the dilemma faced by persons with albinism in Africa. This last section of this chapter and the next four chapters do just so.

The linguistic turn: albinism and linguistic ableism

> Language is the house of Being and it is by dwelling [in this house] that man ek-sist.[51]

Martin Heidegger's words show that language plays a crucial role in our understanding of being. Heidegger, in *Being and Time,* describes language as a modality of the uncovering of entities as entities. Language is, at every point, embedded in and presupposes existence. It is that out of which individual speakers speak and upon which they depend; this dependence is described by him as a 'showing' (*Zeige*) that reaches into all regions of presence and lets what is in each case present appear and mis-appear (*rerscheinen*) out of them. Heidegger's point is that it is 'the word' that first brings a thing into its being. Being is discovered and illuminated through language. Language is the supreme event of human existence because it enables persons to bring what exist into the open and preserve it in potential form for later generations. Linguistic terms arise from an encounter with beings. Language is also the most significant event of human experience as well as the most dangerous of possessions insofar as it can be called a possession at all. It can therefore be misused in a manner that veils rather than illuminate being. Hence, the thinker who would illuminate Being must dig down through the accumulations of meanings and vague connotations of a word to reach the original truth that it embodies. This is one task Heidegger is good at carrying out: penetrating into the utmost recesses of his native German and classical Greek in order to discover what Being is. What is real to a person or group of people and the nature of such reality is captured in words. Language illuminates Being as it unfolds. The contents of language ought, therefore, to be temporal; and finite needing updates and revisions as reality unfolds and man's experiences change.[52]

In African traditions, the perception about albinism and the consequent ableism and discrimination against persons with albinism is vividly captured in the generic words or names used to represent persons with albinism. Among the Yoruba people, for instance, persons with albinism are called *afin*, which means 'horrible'. It is common among people in South Africa to refer to a person with albinism as *isishawa*, which means 'cursed'. In Zimbabwe, persons with albinism are referred to as *sope*, a word used to indicate that such persons are possessed with evil spirits. In Tanzania, persons with albinism are referred to as *zeruzeru*, meaning 'ghost people'. These are just a few of the many derogatory and ableist terms used against persons with albinism in many African societies. Such words are taken as an apt description of reality. They become part of the people's consciousness, both young and old. Hence, when a group of young children are walking back home from school and catch sight of a person with albinism in some village in Tanzania, they are not in doubt of what entity in reality they are perceiving or encountering; they are encountering the reality within their particular world of a *zeruzeru*; so they take to their heels while screaming 'zeruzeru, zeruzeru...'.

The ableist linguistic representations of albinism in African societies remain one of the worst nightmares of a person with albinism. She is confronted on a daily basis not only with gazes and actions of disapproval, but with words, whispered, chanted or screamed, that remind her of being within the place in which she finds herself. Close family members mock and tease her with ableist words, bold children chant derogatory terms, clapping

48 *Ontology of albinism in African traditions*

their hands and hooting at her on the streets, fearful ones whisper the words as they run for safety. Fingers point and mouth open to identify her with those words in the school, at the market place, in the church, in the bus and other social places. It is a daily and unending nightmare.

There are two immediate implications of the ableist language used against persons with albinism. First, language is used in African traditions as an effective means of presenting and representing ideas of being and existence. Hence, the idea that persons with albinism are queer beings that should be avoided are captured in language using simple words and phrases that are passed on from generation to generation. It becomes an effective means through which members of society learn about their worldviews without needing to be given a lecture on the ontology of the people. Language is such an effective means because it is assimilated from infancy as a perfect representation of what is real and does not often have mechanisms for self-scrutiny and revisions. The linguistic scheme of a people in sub-Saharan African is simply handed down from generation to generation. As the young grow, they absorb it and use it to relate with being. The old see it as a duty to preserve it from extinction and pass it to the next generation. To be sure, new terms are formed to account for new realities, but old terms are simply left the way they are in a manner that indicates that the being they house, the reality they represent, is fixed and unchanging.

Second, if the ableism and discrimination against persons with albinism is to be checkmated, the linguistic schemes that shore it up in African societies cannot simply be preserved from generation to generation without revision. New understanding of old experiences that were not captured in the language needs to be reflected now in the language for future generations. It is fundamental that new facts about albinism that were not present in the old order be encoded into the language of the people. It is an important way of gradually doing away with the false ideas about albinism that were deeply encoded into the language of the people. It is also important that efforts are made by all stakeholders to institutionalise such ableist terms and the use of them as not normal descriptions of reality but as derogatory and offensive terms that should be abhorred. Dealing with the discrimination and derogation of persons with albinism inherent in African languages is an important step to take in improving the quality of life of persons with albinism.

From the foregoing, it is clear that albinism is an ontological other in African traditions. Persons with albinism are seen as queer beings different from human beings due to their visible differences and certain characterisations of their being, characterisations that deny them a neutral vital energy that all beings have and the sacredness and dignity due to them. The ideas about albinism are further encoded into linguistic words, which intensifies the ableism suffered by persons with albinism. It is more worrisome that many persons in African communities, including persons with albinism, assimilate and live by these ideas and knowledge claims, taking them to be true and factual about albinism. Not all who become aware of the scientific

Ontology of albinism in African traditions 49

explanation for albinism are willing to let go of the claims made about such persons within their framework of thought. It is therefore important to pay closer attention to how such knowledge about albinism is produced, acquired, assimilated and justified within African communities. This will be our focus in the next chapter.

Notes

1. Nicholas Bunnin and Jiyuan Yu (2004). *The Blackwell Dictionary of Western Philosophy*. Malden MA: Blackwell Publishing. 491.
2. Nicholas Bunnin and Jiyuan Yu, *The Blackwell Dictionary of Western Philosophy*. 491.
3. Willard Van Orman Quine (1953). 'On What there Is'. *The Review of Metaphysics*, 2 (1): 33–35.
4. The force thesis has been popularized by Placide Tempels (1959) in his classic *Bantu Philosophy*. Paris: Presence Africaine; and by Alexis Kagame (1976) in his *La Philosophie Bantu Comparee*. Paris. For a summary of this view see D. N. Kaphagawani (2004) 'African Conceptions of a Person: A Critical Survey'; Kwasi Wiredu (Ed.) *A Companion to African Philosophy*. Malden, MA: Blackwell Publishing. 335–337.
5. Cf. C. B. Guignon (Ed.) (1996). Introduction to *The Cambridge Companion to Heidegger*. Cambridge: Cambridge University Press. 4.
6. Cf. Christopher E. Ukhun (2006). 'Metaphysical Authoritarianism and the Moral Agent in Esan Traditional Thought'. *Uma: Journal of Philosophy and Religious Studies* 1.1: 145–46.
7. Christopher G. Okojie (2005). *Esan Dictionary*. Lagos: Perfect Printers Ltd. 23, 242, 120.
8. For instance, Jim I. Unah (2004) interchangeably uses 'force' and 'spirit' in his paper, 'The Nature of African Metaphysics'. In Jim I. Unah (Ed.) *Metaphysics, Phenomenology and African Philosophy*. Lagos: FADEC Publishers. 337–55.
9. D. E. Idoniboye (1973). 'The Idea of African Philosophy: The Concept of Spirits in African Metaphysics'. *Second Order* 11.1: 83.
10. Christopher E. Ukhun (1978). 'Metaphysical Authoritarianism and the Moral Agent in Esan Traditional Thought'. 146–47.
11. There are, however, indications that some African traditions personify the principle of vital force. For instance, it is referred to as the 'high god' among the Bambara people of Mali. But as J. H. Driberg argues, the high god does not exist as an entity in Africa. See J. H. Driberg (1936). 'The Secular Aspect of Ancestor Worship in Africa'. *Supplement to the Journal of the Royal African Society*, XXXV.
12. Placide Tempels, *Bantu Philosophy*. 175.
13. Placide Tempels, *Bantu Philosophy*. 114.
14. Stephen O. Okafor (1982). 'Bantu Philosophy: Placide Tempels Revisited'. *Journal of Religion in Africa* 13.2: 84–85.
15. John M. Plumey (1975). 'The Cosmology of Ancient Egypt'. In C. Blacker, and M. Loewe (Eds.), *Ancient Cosmologies*. London: George Allen & Unwin. 24.
16. Polycarp Ikuenobe (2006). *Philosophical Perspective on Communalism and Morality in African Traditions*. London: Lexington Books. 63–64.
17. M. A. Mazama (2002). 'Afrocentricity and African Spirituality'. *Journal of Black Studies* 33.2: 219–20. See also F. N. Ndubuisi (2004). 'A Conception of Man in African Communalism'. In Jim I. Unah (Ed.) *Metaphysics, Phenomenology and African Philosophy*. Lagos: FADEC Publishers. 424.

50   *Ontology of albinism in African traditions*

18. Stephen O. Okafor. 'Bantu Philosophy: Placide Tempels Revisited'. 94.
19. Stephen O. Okafor. 'Bantu Philosophy: Placide Tempels Revisited'. 95.
20. Elvis Imafidon (2011). 'Rethinking the Individual's Place in an African (Esan) Ontology'. *Cultura: International Journal of Philosophy of Culture and Axiology* 8.1: 96.
21. See Christopher E. Ukhun and Nathaniel A. Inegbedion (2007). 'Ontological Validation of Land Tenureship in Esan Tradition'. *Studies in Tribes and Tribals* 5.1: 19.
22. Stephen O. Okafor. 'Bantu Philosophy: Placide Tempels Revisited'. 97.
23. Cf. J. S. Ukpong (1983). 'The Problem of God and Sacrifice in African Traditional Religion'. *Journal of Religion in Africa* 14.3: 198–201.
24. Olusegun Oladipo. (2004). 'Religion in African Culture: Some Conceptual Issues'. Wiredu, K. (Ed.) *A Companion to African Philosophy*. Malden, MA: Blackwell Publishing. 357.
25. See Peter Ali. (2006) *EsanTraditional Values and the Roman Catholic Church. A Comparative Discourse*. Lagos: Decraft Communications. 45–47.
26. Lee M. Brown (2004). 'Understanding and Ontology in African Traditional Thought'. Lee M. Brown, (Ed). *African Philosophy: New and Traditional Perspectives*. Oxford: Oxford University Press. 158.
27. John Pobee (1976). 'Aspects of African Traditional Religion'. *Sociological Analysis*, 37.1: 7–8.
28. Kwasi Wiredu (1992). 'Death and After Life in African Culture'. In K. Wiredu and K. Gyekye Eds. *Person and Community: Ghanaian Philosophical Studies*. Washington D.C: The Council for Research in Values and Philosophy. 143.
29. Peter O. Iwelomen (2008). 'Burial Rites and Inheritance Laws in Esanland'. In P. O. Iwelomen, (Ed.) *Who is Who in Esan Land*. Ekpoma: Esan Magazine Publication. 270–271.
30. A. W. Wolfe (1959). Man's Relation to Man in Africa. *American Anthropologist* 61.4: 608.
31. J. C. McCall (1996). 'Rethinking Ancestors in Africa'. *African Journal of the International African Institute* 65.2: 258.
32. Kwame Gyekye (1996). *African Cultural Values: An Introduction*. Accra: Sankafa Publishing Company. 13.
33. John Pobee. Aspects of African Traditional Religion. 8.
34. Benezet Bujo (1998). *The Ethical Dimension of Community: The African Model and the Dialogue between North and South*. Nairobi: Paulines Publications. 16.
35. Ifeanyi A. Menkiti (2004). 'On the Normative Conception of a Person'. In K. Wiredu, (Ed.) *A Companion to African Philosophy*. Malden, MA: Blackwell Publishing. 327.
36. Godfrey O. Ozumba (2004). 'African Traditional Metaphysics'. *Quadlibet Online Journal of Christian Theology and Philosophy*. 6.3: Accessed on January 15, 2005 from http://www.Quadlibet.net.
37. Yemi Elebuibon (2008). *Invisible Powers of the Metaphysical World: A Peep into the World of Witches*. Ibadan: Creative Books. 17.
38. Barry Hallen and J. O. Sodipo (1997). *Knowledge, Belief and Witchcraft: Analytic Experiments in African Philosophy*. Stanford: Stanford University Press. 93–94.
39. Godwin Sogolo (1993). *Foundations of African Philosophy: A Definitive Analysis of Conceptual; Issues in African Thought*. Ibadan: Ibadan University Press. 99.
40. For a detailed explanation of *Ori* in Yoruba thought, see Segun Gbadegensin (2004). 'An Outline of a Theory of Destiny'. In Lee M. Brown (Ed.) *African Philosophy: New and Traditional Perspectives*. Oxford: Oxford University Press. 51–68.

Ontology of albinism in African traditions 51

41. Leke Adeofe (2004) gives a fine analysis of Destiny as individual's "self-actualization process" in his paper: Personal Identity in African Metaphysics. Lee M. Brown, (Ed.) *African Philosophy: New and Traditional Perspectives.* Oxford: Oxford University Press. 69–83.
42. A. B. Ekanola (2006). Metaphysical Issues in African Philosophy. Oladipo O. (Ed.) *Core Issues in African Philosophy.* Ibadan: Hope Publications. 78.
43. Benezet Bujo. *The Ethical Dimension of Community: The African Model and the Dialogue between North and South.* 182–183.
44. Stephen O. Okafor. 'Bantu Philosophy: Placide Tempels Revisited'. 93.
45. John S. Mbiti (1969). 'African Religion and Philosophy'. London: Heinemann Publisher. 108–109.
46. Polycarp Ikuenobe. 'Philosophical Perspective on Communalism and Morality in African Traditions'. 63.
47. Godwin Sogolo. *Foundations of African Philosophy: A Definitive Analysis of Conceptual; Issues in African Thought.* 72–73.
48. Chinua Achebe (1969). *Things Fall Apart.* New York: Ballantine Press. 147.
49. Chinua Achebe, Things Fall Apart. 148.
50. Chinua Achebe, Things Fall Apart. 150.
51. Martin Heidegger, quoted by Frederick A. Olafson (1996). 'The Unity of Heidegger's Thought'. In Charles B. Guignon Ed., *The Cambridge Companion to Heidegger.* Cambridge: Cambridge University Press. 118.
52. See G. G. Gray (1952). 'Heidegger's Being'. *The Journal of Philosophy* 49.12: 415–422.

3 The epistemology of albinism in African traditions

The ideas about the coming-to-be and the nature of the being of persons with albinism clearly indicates that African indigenous communities possess a body of knowledge and truth claims about such persons as queer beings that have been institutionalized into society and preserved by social structures that influence the way communities deal with persons with albinism, as well as how such persons view themselves within such particular worlds. This immediately raises some epistemological questions about such knowledge claims, how they are acquired, justified and preserved in human society. What is the basis of human knowledge in African traditional communities, or what does it mean for an African to claim to know in an African context and, in this case, to know certain things about albinism and be sure that her knowledge of such a being is true? How does an African explain the reliability of her knowledge claims about albinism? How does she explain the nexus, for instance, between the amputated limb of a person with albinism and protection from bad luck or creation of wealth? How does an African person acquire what he knows about albinism, or what are the processes of knowing in African communities? What role does utility and inculcation play in the preservation of beliefs and knowledge claims about albinism in modern times even in the face of biological facts about the human condition? What role does ignorance and the active production of falsehood play in the knowledge process in African communities? What is the connection between constituted authority and the reliability of knowledge? These are important epistemological questions that arise from the ideas about albinism in African communities, epistemology being the theory, study or discourse of knowledge.

In what follows, I begin with an attempt to construct an African theory of knowledge by theorizing three interrelated levels on which an African can claim to know anything: (i.) knowledge understood as first-hand information; (ii.) knowing consistency with established beliefs; and (iii.) knowledge as implying 'we know that'. I show in each case that the ideas about albinism as a queer human condition are ideas that community members can claim to have reliable knowledge about as different from having a mere personal opinion or 'voice' in the matter. This is followed, I believe necessarily, with

Epistemology of albinism   53

an examination of the African processes of knowing or modes of knowledge acquisition. It is obvious that what the African knows about albinism and any other matter is gradually inculcated and assimilated from birth to death through social epistemic structures of learning and training that can, in many ways, authoritatively impose the community's ways on the individual and his will.

I then proceed to examine certain factors responsible for the strong persistence of the belief in the supernatural agency of persons with albinism in whole or in part, leading to the commodification of such persons even in the age of science and modernity, which, far from being a perfect mode of thought and having its own many flaws and limitations, provides us with factual, verifiable information about albinism as a human condition. Here I pay close attention to two key factors: the power of inculcation and the power of utility. I further dwell on utility in terms of how African community members provide explanations for the knowledge claims they hold, not in some conventional sense of outlining the belief, truth and justification of the claim, but by simply showing the utility or function of the claim. And this is very evident in how people defend their claims about albinism. Lastly, in this chapter, I pay close attention to what I consider a crucial aspect to decipher any attempt to understand the epistemic framework from which ideas about such unusual human conditions such as albinism stem from. It is the role of ignorance and actively produced falsehood in the knowledge production process. I conclude by highlighting the essential ingredients of a robust polycentric, global epistemological programme as essential for overcoming the shortcomings of an African approach to knowledge.

African theory of knowledge I: Knowledge as first-hand information

In the first level of the theorisation of knowledge in African traditions, to know is to have first-hand information or a personal experience of an object or an event. In other words, an African knows what she has personally sensed or experienced and there is no question or doubts about it. The person who claims to know in this level of epistemic competence has witnessed or experienced what she knows first-hand through the senses. Consider this scenario A: In a Yoruba community, Dayo tells her friends that Alabi's wife has given birth to a strange baby with white pale skin, an *afin*, at the midwife's house. The friends ask her: 'How do you know this?' She responds: 'I saw it myself. I was there, and I am just returning from the midwife's house.' Consider the second scenario B: Dayo tells her friends that Alabi's wife has given birth to a strange baby with white pale skin, an *afin*, at the midwife's house. The friends ask her: 'How do you know this?' She responds: 'Well, Jomoke told me just now, near the market on my way here.' In scenario A, the knowledge claim is not in question because Dayo had a first-hand experience of the information she was providing. The matter ends there and

54 *Epistemology of albinism*

does not raise any scepticism or disputes. This is essentially because the hearers, Dayo's friends, are convinced that since Dayo saw what she claims to know, they can also verify the claim themselves by going to the midwife's house to see the strange baby. However, in scenario B, Dayo's friends would be sceptical because Dayo's knowledge claim is not first-hand information. Their respond to Dayo's statement that she heard it from Jomoke will likely be to ask Dayo if she saw the baby herself. If Dayo replies in the negative, her friends would likely advise her to witness her claim first-hand before she shares her knowledge with others.

This level of theorizing in African traditions is aptly developed by Barry Hallen in his essay 'Yoruba Moral Epistemology'. According to him, within the Yoruba thought system:

> Persons are said to *mo* (to "know") or to have *imo* ("knowledge") only of something they have witnessed in a first-hand or personal manner. The example most frequently cited by discussants, virtually as a paradigm, is visual perception of a scene or an event as it is taking place. *Imo* is said to apply to sensory perception generally, even if what may be experienced directly by touch is more limited than is the case with perception. *Imo* implies a good deal more than mere sensation, of course. Perception implies cognition as well, meaning that the persons concerned must comprehend that and what they are experiencing. The terms *"ooto"/"otito"* are associated with *"imo"* in certain respects that parallel the manner in which "true" and "truth" are paired with "know"/"knowledge" in the English language. In the English language "truth" is principally a property of propositional knowledge, of statements human beings make about things, while in Yoruba *ooto* may be a property of both propositions and certain forms of experience.[1]

Hallen therefore draws a distinction between first-hand and second-hand information. Second-hand information, as distinct from the direct experience of first-hand information, is the propositional knowledge highly valued in Western epistemology. And this is information that 'cannot be tested or proven in a decisive manner by most people and therefore has to be accepted as true because it "agrees" with common sense or because it "corresponds" to or "coheres" with the very limited amount of information that people are able to test and confirm in a first-hand or direct manner.'[2]

The distinction that Hallen makes between first-hand and second-hand information is akin to the distinction John Hospers makes between facts as actual states-of-affairs and facts as true propositions.[3] Facts as actual states-of-affairs is not propositional per say but refers to the configuration of things around us, how the objects and events in the world happen to be and our experiences of them. Facts as true proposition, on the other hand, are statements that are true by virtue of the fact that they can be verified directly or indirectly, and it is in this sense that we talk about scientific facts

Epistemology of albinism 55

and knowledge. Knowledge in African traditions, according to Hallen in this first level of theorisation, would consist of the first reports or information about actual state-of-affairs as experienced by the reporter or informant.

A number of issues arise from living the theory of knowledge in African traditions to this level alone. For one thing, this manner of claiming to know is not peculiar to Africans alone. It is, in fact, a common sense way of claiming to know by humans in general — I can lay claim to knowing what I saw or directly witnessed without needing to subject it to any rigorous form of verification. I know that I saw a cat outside my house just now, and I know I am watching CNN while sitting on the couch. I also know that the community head is going to his farm, because I saw him on the farm road walking toward his farm with his farming tools. These are not knowledge claims that are often subjected to some rigorous form of verification. Nonetheless, there are latent issues arising from knowledge as first-hand information.

There is the issue of the moral standing of the informant. This is precisely the point Hallen brings out in his essay. If I experience an event first-hand, and I relate it to two or three other persons, for what I relate to them to be taken as knowledge for them the same way I do, they must have complete trust in my honesty, credibility and reliability as an informant at that moment. If there has been several cases in the past where I related a first-hand experience and it later turned out to be false or largely incorrect in description, then my honesty and reliability would be called into question whenever I give first-hand information about an event or an object. This will only result in episteme solipsism, where I know but others do not know what I know. Similarly, if my first-hand information has always proved to be apt and correct, then it is likely that even when I make a mistake or provide inappropriate description of my knowledge claims, others will still take my information as accurate knowledge. Consider, for example, this scenario: If Dayo's information about the birth of an infant with albinism at the midwife's house turns out to be true in the same way virtually all her previous first-hand information to her friends were true, her friends become morally obliged to accept any other first-hand claims she brings forward. If after some days, Dayo reports to her friends that she *heard* the baby crying in a strange way, like an owl, in the parents' house, her friends would accept her information as knowledge because she has earned the epistemic virtue to make such a claim, and her claim is in many ways in line with already existing beliefs about such babies. But Dayo is certain within her that the cry of the baby did not really sound like that of an owl.

Dayo's new first-hand information brings us to another issue with this level of conceptualising knowledge in African traditions. This is the problem with accurate and objective descriptions of events. The competency of objectively describing events and objects is never foolproof. There are always flaws, biases and idiosyncrasies inherent in the description of objects and events. If the mother of an infant with albinism and the witch doctor of the community are told to give first-hand information of the baby they see

56 *Epistemology of albinism*

right in front of them, they are most likely to vary in their descriptions due to personal feelings and biases. Knowledge as first-hand information does not therefore give us a comprehensive account of an African view of human knowledge. Besides, it mainly accounts for the visible and tangible objects and events, and it is difficult to on the basis of it accounts for the many invisible agencies and experiences that Africans claim to be knowledgeable about and on which basis a majority of their objects, beliefs and events are explained.

African theory of knowledge II: Knowledge as consistency with established beliefs

In this level of epistemic competence, persons in an African community can claim to know if the knowledge claim is consistent or coherent with an established body of beliefs. Such established beliefs in African traditions include the belief in the agency of invisible entities such as ancestors, divinities and manipular forces; the belief in the interaction of beings that could result in either the strengthening or weakening of one's vital force; the belief in specific kinds of rituals and taboos; the belief in the high epistemic competence of a community elder as a custodian of the traditions of the people; the belief in queer beings and their nature; in manipular forces; in the Supreme Being and so on. Knowledge claims made by specific persons within specific spheres of existence must fit within such consistent sets of beliefs in order for others not to become sceptical of such claims. Consider this scenario: Among the Esan people of Southern Nigeria, it is an established belief that when a married woman has extramarital affair, she incurs the punishments of ancestors of her husband's kin. The punishment is such that a child she had with the husband becomes ill without any medical remedy for the ailment.

At the point when the medical attention has been sought for a child consistently without any diagnosis and, by implication, any known remedy, the husband and his kin can make specific knowledge claims about the situation. They would claim to know that the woman in question has committed adultery even when there may be no factual evidence to back up the claim. This is because the claim is consistent with established beliefs regarding the signs of a cheating wife. On the basis of knowing this, the woman is summoned to a meeting where she is asked to speak the truth, which is expected to corroborate what the husband and his kin already *know*. In virtually every case I am aware of, the woman does confess to having cheated on the husband, because she is warned that delaying the confession may result in the death of her child. When she confesses, and the necessary appeasement rituals are done — rituals that include the slaughtering of a goat provided by the woman and the sharing of the meat among the husband's kin, and the parading of the woman around the community as some form of deterring measures — the child recovers from the strange illness.[4]

Epistemology of albinism 57

Therefore, to make specific knowledge claims about albinism or persons with albinism is to make a claim that is consistent with the established beliefs about albinism within the African framework of thought. If *x* claims to know that the infant with albinism given birth to by the wife would bring bad luck to him and his family and, thus, decides to hand the baby over to the chief priest to be thrown away in the evil forest or to serve at the chief priest shrine, or he decides to let the child grow in his home but refuses to care for the child's needs such as schooling, his claim to know would be a justified claim because it is consistent with the established beliefs in his community about persons with albinism as queer beings. If *y* claims to know that *z* must have given birth to a baby with albinism because she or the husband has done something evil that they are being punished for, *y*'s knowledge claim would be accepted as consistent with established beliefs about albinism. Similarly, if *a* claims to know that she performed badly in her interview because she had gazed at a person with albinism while on her way for the interview, she would also be making a claim consistent with established beliefs about albinism, which makes her claims not merely an opinion but a knowledge claim.

However, if *x* makes a claim within a typical sub-Saharan African community to know that his new-born baby, although having albinism, is just another human being with a biological defect and deserving of care and attention, he would be making a claim that is not consistent with established beliefs, and his claim could, at any point, be called into question. As funny as this may sound, it is still very true of the experience of albinism in modern African societies. Many persons still feel it is a waste of hard-earned funds to spend money in sending a child with albinism to school. As a person with albinism, I have experienced first-hand strong challenges to my parents' claim to know facts about albinism that are inconsistent with established beliefs in the community. When I did something wrong in junior college — specifically, not being able to take down notes written on the board due to poor vision — my class teacher was always quick to tell me that it would have been better if I was thrown into the evil forest when I was born rather than allowing my parents to waste money on me. Hence, persons are expected to fit within the framework of knowledge in making knowledge claims to avoid making claims that become sceptical and questionable.

Knowledge as consistency with established beliefs does not require knowing why an object or event is taken the way it is. It simply requires knowing that it is taken the way it is within a larger framework of thought. To know is, therefore, to be knowledgeable in the ways of the people, not necessarily having some explanation for why the ways of the people are such and such. A member of the Esan community, for instance, knows that if the woman confesses, the goat is slaughtered and the woman is paraded around the community, the ill child will become well. The three events, she knows, are essential components of the process of appeasing the husband's ancestors to avert the punishment that befalls a woman who commits adultery. There

58   *Epistemology of albinism*

are not accidental components of the process. The Esan may not be able to explain why the goat needs to be slaughtered or why the woman in question needs to be paraded around the community.[5] However, he knows that if the essential components of the confession and atonement process are carried out, the woman will receive pardon for her wrongdoing and the child will get well. He may not be able to explain the causal connections between visible and invisible agencies, but he is certain of the connections, and we shall return to why such connections are deeply established and sustained in his belief system, even without some cogent explanation for them. In the same vein, x does not know why there is a connection between his new born baby with albinism and bad luck, but he knows that there is a connection, because the connection is an established belief. A does not know why there is a connection between her interview that went bad and her gazing at a person with albinism, but she is certain of her knowledge that there is a connection, because it is an established belief.

In light of emerging facts about albinism in modern times as a human condition caused by the lack of melanin, these established and consistent beliefs in African traditions about the nature of albinism are called into question. And herein lies the major challenge to knowledge as consistent with the established body of beliefs: the question of the gap between rationality and consistency, where the former must include elements of truth and the later may completely lack them. This has been aptly discussed by Kwame Anthony Appiah in his essay 'African Studies and the Concept of Knowledge.' Ideally speaking, as Appiah explains, rationality ought to be linked with the quest for truth:

> Rationality is best conceived of as an ideal, both in the sense that it is something worth aiming for and in the sense that it is something we are incapable of realizing. It is an ideal that bears an important internal relation to that other great cognitive ideal, Truth. And, I suggest, we might say that rationality in belief consists in being disposed so to react to evidence and reflection that you change your beliefs in ways that make it more likely that they are true. If this is right, then we can see at once why inconsistency in belief is a sign of irrationality: for having a pair of inconsistent beliefs *guarantees* that you have at least one false belief, as inconsistent beliefs are precisely beliefs that cannot all be true.[6]

Hence, ideally speaking, it would be expected that a rational person would let go of some set of beliefs about albinism, no matter how established and consistent they are, in the light of a new sets of beliefs that are completely inconsistent with the former but are not only internally consistent but are factually true and can be verified. It would be a sign of irrationality to want to hold two inconsistent sets of beliefs side by side; it is, in fact, impossible to do so because one is not consistent with the other. Thus, the rational move would be to let go of the less truthful set of consistent beliefs for the more truthful representations of reality.

Therefore, having a consistent set of beliefs as the basis for knowing is not enough. The set of beliefs must also be largely true. In Appiah's words:

> ... consistency, as an ideal, is not enough. For someone could have a perfectly consistent set of beliefs about the world, almost every one of which was not only false but obviously false. It is *consistent* to hold, with Descartes in one of his sceptical moments, that all my experiences are caused by a wicked demon, and, to dress the fantasy in modern garb, there is no inconsistency in supporting the paranoid fantasy that the world is "really" a cube containing only my brain in a bath, a lot of wires, and a wicked scientist. But, though consistent, this belief is not rational: we are all, I hope, agreed that reacting to sensory evidence in *this* way does not increase the likelihood that your beliefs will be true.[7]

Thus, to claim to know specific things about persons with albinism on the basis of a consistent set of ideas that are obviously false is not a rational move to make and calls such knowledge into question because 'a person who starts with a consistent set of beliefs can arrive, by way of reasonable principles of evidence, at the most fantastic untruths.'[8]

Acceptably, persons in traditional pre-colonial African societies with no alternative set of beliefs to their ideas about albinism cannot be blamed for the knowledge claims they hold about albinism. It is normal and reasonable for persons in every mode of thought to hold tenaciously to beliefs within that form of life in the absence of countervailing evidence. In fact, even in situations where there is countervailing evidence, it is difficult to let go of the less factual beliefs that have been held for a long period of time. We see this many times in the history of science as a form of thought, and Thomas Kuhn has helped us see how jealously scientists hold on to a model even when there are good evidences to let go. It is so difficult that it would need a scientific revolution in the Copernican sense to overcome the old less truthful set of beliefs.[9] The question then is: Why are the sets of established beliefs about albinism still very prevalent in modern African societies in the face of factual counteracting evidences? What sustains false beliefs? I shall return to these questions in a moment — in the section on the persistence of established false beliefs — because if we must succeed in overcoming harmful knowledge claims about albinism, we must, first of all, find a way to deal with the prevalent sets of beliefs about albinism that shore them up and find a way of bridging the gap between a consistent set of established beliefs and the cognitive ideal of truth. But first, let us pay attention to a third level of the theorization of knowledge, one that is very vital for understanding the African mode of knowing.

60 *Epistemology of albinism*

African theory of knowledge III: Knowledge as shared knowledge

The third level of the theorisation of knowledge in African traditions stems from the ontological essence of being in African traditions that has become popular in existing literature, the communalistic principle. Basically, the communalistic principle emphasises that the community has ontological priority over individual entities in every area of thought, which makes its survival fundamental. With particular reference to the relationship between the community and individuals, the ontological priority of the community over the person is clearly seen in the following facts: that an individual person is born into an existing human society and therefore into a human culture; that is, the human person does not voluntarily choose to enter into a human community; also, the human person is at once a cultural being, and the human person cannot live in isolation from other persons, hence she must form relationships with others; these social relationships are necessary, not contingent, and the person is constituted thusly, but only partly, by social relationships in which she necessarily finds herself.[10]

Based on these ontological facts about the being of the person as subsumed under the being of the community, it is implied that the community has the crucial moral responsibility of providing normative guidance and setting the standards for individual persons on every matter arising from social interactions such as standards of morality and epistemic competence. The moral right of the community to do this is not simply because it has ontological priority over individual entities in the community, but also because it is seen as the only way the community can survive and individual interests protected. Hence there is an emphasis on shared standards and shared norms as crucial for the survival of both the community and the person.

Flowing from this background, claiming to know something is claiming to know what others know. Knowledge is thus shared knowledge — What I know is what we know. As Bert Hamminga puts it, 'the African "knowing subject" is not an individual person.'[11] It is the community. When I claim to know x, I am not making a claim to have come to the knowledge of something through some solitary mental exercise; rather I claim to know x because we as a group know x, and others share in my knowledge of x. In Hamminga's words:

> Since togetherness is the highest value, we want to share our views. All of them. Hence we always agree with everybody. Standing up and saying: "I have a radically different opinion" would not, as it often does in the West, draw attention to what I have to say. Instead, I am likely to be led before my clan leaders before I even had the chance to continue my speech. Among us, you simply never have radically different opinions. That is because, and that is why we are *together*. Togetherness is our ultimate criterion of any action, the pursuit of knowledge being just one of them.[12]

Hence, knowledge claims about ancestors, the maleficent nature of witch-craft, the way to harvest and store crops, the types and functions of different divinities, the right ways to live and the nature of queer beings are all shared knowledge perpetuated by communal structures, and individual members are expected to fit into these structures. Fitting into these structures of shared ontic and shared epistemic ideas, no matter how difficult it may be, is fundamental for the survival of the community and individual members. This is why a radically different view from shared knowledge, for instance, is often not welcomed even when the radically different view is evidently factual. As Hamminga says:

> The clan or tribe is the knowing subject. All knowledge is power. All power comes from the forces preceding us: our ancestors. These are three maxims that have a status comparable to the law of conservation of energy in western science: if some of your thoughts do not tally with it, that means you have made some error. So even if the tribe changes its mind, as for instance tribes, facing AIDS, nowadays do on sexual relations, this is an accommodation to new circumstances, according to the traditional view agreed upon, yes *decreed* by the ancestors.[13]

In this level of knowing in African traditions, knowledge claims about albinism are, thus, shared. To claim to know something about the being of a person with albinism is to make a claim that is shared such that when x says, 'I know that a person with albinism is so and so', she is saying in effect that 'We know that a person with albinism is so and so. To make a radically different knowledge claim about albinism is to make a claim that is controversial and may be denied as knowledge even when such claims are evidently factual. One is not expected to think outside the knowledge box in African traditional communities, and this has in many ways eaten deep into modern African societies. If a young lady in an African society, for instance, sees albinism differently, perhaps in biological terms, and on the basis of her different understanding becomes comfortable in dating and getting married to a young man with albinism, her action would become a shocker to family members, friends, and persons in her community. Their shock stems from their thinking that the girl *does not know* what albinism is to the extent that she is willing to be married to a person with albinism, or that she *knows* and she is yet willing to ignore all what she knows and go ahead with her relationship with such a person. To be sure, *knowing* here has to do with the shared knowledge of albinism. Her own differing knowledge claims are completely ignored in the assessment process of her decision, even if she has clearly explained herself to family members and friends. The same scenario can be observed when the manager of a firm recommends the employment of a person with albinism. Fellow workers would find this odd and contrary to what is known about albinism. Hence, a knowledge claim about albinism ensuing from an individual subject that is radically different from what is

62   *Epistemology of albinism*

inter-subjectively known is mainly treated as an opinion, a voice standing out in the matter, but one that needs to be as subtle as possible and not become louder than the voice of the group, because that would threaten the much needed communal harmony. As Hamminga puts it, 'if in an African group there are inconsistent proposals, the *group as a togetherness* is in quite a[n]... uncomfortable state of mind. The state has to be resolved quickly. It decreases vitality, it inhibits action.'[14]

To be sure, an immediate matter that raises concerns when we talk about the collective approach to being, knowledge and the like in African traditions is the manner in which it overrides a person's will and discourages individual creativity, even of ideas. This has been responsible in African scholarship for the protracted and heated individual-community debate that has resulted in essentially two theories, radical communitarian theory and moderate communitarian theory.[15] To avoid deviating too far from the issues at hand in this chapter, I do not intend to get involved just right now with this debate. But one thing is clear, the community of selves superimposes its will and ideas on persons whose individual wills and ideas must fit within communal expectations. One obvious consequence of this is that in African scholarship today, we primarily have at our disposal African theories or worldviews and ideas evolving from an African space. We rarely have ideas about the nature of things proposed and developed by individual members of an African community as we may have in the West. When personal voices are subdued, and the community's voice reigns supreme, the community easily becomes authoritarian and anachronistic, and its ideas outlast their use. It is now obvious in the face of alternative and factual theories about albinism that ideas about the human condition in African communities are clearly untrue, authoritarian and anachronistic, even though they persevere, as we shall soon see, for certain reasons. But they cannot be sustained for too long if the right things are done.

Again, that an idea is shared by many does not guarantee that the idea is true or can pass as knowledge. Many times in human history, an idea can be held by many as a true and objective knowledge claim without any evidence in support of the claim. It is so much upheld as knowledge that it influences how people act and react to related matters. That the invisible agency of the Bermuda triangle is widely held to the extent that it has become known by many as the Devil's Triangle does not make the ideas about it true, factual knowledge claims. The widely held view among European tribes that African tribes and, indeed, non-European tribes are less human and pre-logical may have influenced European action and reaction for centuries until now, but it was far from being what we can today call a true knowledge claim. In the same vein, although the ideas about persons with albinism in African communities were shared ideas, they were not necessarily true, as it has become obvious today. Hence, if a group of persons are content with attributing the status of knowledge to a claim simply because many or all in the group have come to accept it, then they are

Epistemology of albinism 63

most likely going to have a bulk of claims that would turn out to be false claims in the face of counterfactual evidence.

But it remains a major component of knowledge that what is known must, among other things, be an inter-subjectively shared knowledge rather than something known only to the subjective self. This is not a peculiar requirement to knowing in African traditions. It is essential for any form of knowledge claim. Hence, one way to raise the status of the scientific and biological facts about albinism to that of knowledge in modern African societies is to find ways of making the knowledge claims more popular, acceptable and shared among many members of African communities. This depends largely on identifying the right channels through which this can be done. We shall return to this issue in the last chapter. At the moment, I would like to pay closer attention to a very important issue. Why do the ideas about albinism in African traditions still flourish and survive today even though they have been found lacking in facts? To answer this question, we need to say a few things first about the processes of acquiring knowledge about albinism in African traditions.

Processes of knowing

Mario Martinez rightly says that 'any theory that attempts to define the process of knowing requires an explanation of how information is accessed, stored and retrieved in order to understand how learning takes place.'[16] This is because understanding the process of knowing in any given space invariably sheds light on how what is known is stored and sustained through time. Here, I would like to present a communo-cognitive theory of the process of knowing about persons with albinism and, indeed, anything in African traditions. By a communo-cognitive theory, I simply mean that the process of knowing in African traditions and the related cognitive features such as learning and remembering is essentially a community-centred process, controlled by the community and its structures. This is precisely why knowledge is seen as shared knowledge since the process of accessing and acquiring such knowledge is determined by institutions established and controlled by the community.

Once a person is born into a community in African traditions, she immediately begins to develop her cognitive abilities by gaining access to the institutions available in the community through which she can learn, understand and remember the ways and standards of the people. There are two key institutions in any African community having the epistemic competence to impact knowledge into individual persons. They are the family and the elite class. Let us begin with the place of the family in the cognitive development of the person.

Many traditional African communities operate the extended-family system, in the sense that the community is organized in terms of kinship. But this can easily be misinterpreted in a way that it would seem the nuclear

64 *Epistemology of albinism*

family is not important. The nuclear family still plays a very important role in the upbringing of a child. Of course, a child is born into a community and she is raised by the community. But important phases of training and learning about life that a child receives come from her parents. The parents have the primary responsibility of bringing up the child in a way acceptable to the community buy helping her acquire shared community knowledge.[17] This is obvious for two reasons: first, when a person deviates from the way that is known to the community, the immediate family takes the blame. If, for example, a child fails to greet an elderly person, the elder is apt to ask the child, 'Did your mother and father not train you well?' This implies that the immediate family of the child is expected to ensure that the child is accustomed to the standards of the people. Second, the parents have the status of an elder to their children, which gives them the competence and obligation to inculcate in them the right ideas and values.

The role of the family in the cognitive development of the child in line with community values is clearly seen in the notion of a family name. The notion of a family name in African traditions describes whether a particular family has a good family name, that is, the said family is competent and in-tune with a community-accepted lifestyle, or a bad family name, that is, a family that has competence in the traditional ways of life but fails to live by it. A good family name is developed, tested and earned with time to the extent that it can be handed down from one generation to another. The only way this is possible, however, is if the parents, especially the family head (the father) instil in the children the shared knowledge and standards practiced by the family, both through deliberate training and through personal actions. A bad family name is also developed with time. It is natural that no person is perfect and would therefore not always do what is right or what is expected of him. This is not enough to earn a person or a family a bad name. But when a family member radically or persistently deviates from the accepted standards, it brings a bad name to her family.

Hence, it becomes normal for a family member to discriminate or stigmatise a person with albinism because she has been trained by both words and action in the family to do so. She learns from the way the father, mother and older family members and relatives relate with such persons from a distance. She has inculcated and continues to remember the normalcy of the social exclusion and isolation of such persons from normal human society. She is cognitively aware of the stigma and the shame that families with persons with albinism go through. She has also come to know that normal people are not supposed to form an intimate relationship, such as marriage, with persons with albinism. So, if a family member grows up and brings home a person with albinism for marriage, she threatens the family name and opens the way for outsiders to question the epistemic competence and effectiveness of the upbringing of the child. The parents and other family members would naturally refuse to support the union in order to avoid tarnishing the family name, because the said action of the individual member would bring shame

Epistemology of albinism 65

to the family since it is not part of the shared knowledge for a person to associate with such a queer being in such an intimate manner. The refusal to support the union between a family member and a person with albinism in modern times can be intense, violent and traumatic for the family member and, in most cases, it often succeeds in ending the courtship. But if the family member insists on going ahead with the union without the support of the family, she brings shame to the family and would likely be cut off by angry family members. With regards to the elite class, Albert Onobhayedo says that:

> Prior to the advent of Western education, elitism did not derive from literacy. Yet, it is possible to point to the traditional rulers... and their chiefs, the elders..., priests, heroes as well as professional craftsmen as the elite of traditional [African] communities. They were the opinion leaders and custodian of the customs and values of the people. They ensured that the younger ones were groomed to be conformists within the traditional settings. They also provided leadership in politics, industry, religion as well as individual and community health management. The ordinary subjects generally obeyed and emulated these supposedly knowledgeable and well-adjusted members of their community.[18]

The group of persons which Onobhayedo refers to as the traditional African elite — kings, chiefs, priests, elderly ones, professional craftsmen, etc. — can simply be referred to as the custodians of the community to whom the young ones and 'ordinary people' look up to. They are accorded tremendous authority, respect and power in traditional African communities, and they occupy a status where their epistemic competence, will and dictations are not questioned. Instead, they are taken as representing the epistemic competence and will of the community of beings, both visible and invisible. The respect and reverence accorded these ones in these communities is made particularly obvious in a general name or title given to any elder in traditional Esan community of Southern Nigeria, *Owanlen*. *Owanlẹn* translates as 'wise one'.

It is meant to indicate that the bearer of such a title is a repository of the customs and traditions of the people and, by implication, he is the custodian of the traditions of the people. He is therefore primarily responsible in protecting that tradition and preventing it from oblivion. The elite class thus have the crucial responsibility of maintaining and sustaining communal equilibrium by internalizing into members of the community the values and norms that will bind them together.

Anelite is seen as a fully developed moral and knowledgeable person who has important roles in forms of communal and social responsibilities, which include training the young ones both through words — through storytelling, adages and folklore — and action, prodding others, or praising others as the case may be, in order to help them achieve moral and epistemic

66   *Epistemology of albinism*

competence, which is crucial for attaining personhood and possibly elitism. This duty requires the elder to display his wealth of knowledge in his judgement by exhibiting rich and comprehensive sensitivity. An elder, by his very action, is teaching and morally educating the young ones by modelling his actions for them. This is why he is a mentor and a role model for the people to emulate. Thus, an important part of the process of training is the ability of the younger ones to imitate the actions of the elders.[19] This is why before an African traditional community confers a clearly stated elitist position on anyone, he must have fulfilled the roles expected of him by the community and be very conversant with the cultural practices, beliefs and values of the community for the obvious reason that others will look up to him. For if he is not well informed about these things, he will become someone who misleads the younger ones. This is thoroughly avoided. Learning of values by the younger ones from the elders reveals that:

> ... the community as an informal educational structure represents a hierarchy of moral authority and teaching responsibilities, where those in the top hierarchy teach and reinforce for those in the lower hierarchy how they ought to behave in order to achieve harmony. In this hierarchy children are at the lowest level and the elders, who are not only the custodian of the tradition, but are people of wisdom (epistemically and morally), are at the top. The highest moral status in the community is being an elder or chief, or, in some cases, king or queen.[20]

It is therefore not strange that the younger generation assimilate the ideas about albinism held by the elite class and approach albinism in the same way the elders or members of the elite class approach it. If they see albinism differently, it would imply that the elite class failed in their responsibility to train them to become epistemically competent in the ways of the people. Hence, the status quo is maintained to a process of learning where the views of those at the top of the hierarchy are infused into those in the lower ranks of the lower hierarchy. This is an effective means of cognitive development, because the elite class, or indeed the family, would never claim that these are their own ideas or knowledge claims. But it is always made clear in the learning process that the knowledge being transferred is a community-based knowledge that goes beyond any particular member of the elite class and that all beings in the community, both visible and invisible, have been involved in the knowledge production process.

Why do (false) beliefs persist?

Why do people hold on tenaciously to beliefs and knowledge claims even when there are obvious counterfactual evidences to such claims? More specifically, why do many persons in African communities still cling doggedly to certain notions about albinism even when they are evidently false? It is quite obvious from our discourse so far that the survival value of these sets of beliefs about albinism in modern African communities is not determined by their being true or reasonable.[21] As Appiah says, for instance, 'anyone who has read Evans-Pritchard's elegant discussion of Zande witchcraft beliefs will remember how easy it is to make sense of the idea that a whole set of false beliefs could nevertheless be part of what holds a community together. But the point does not need labouring; since Freud we can all understand why, for example, it might be more useful to believe that you love someone than to recognize that you do not.'[22]. So, if truth and reason doesn't essentially count in helping a belief survive even when there are reasons to let it go, what then does? There are two essential reasons, I believe, why this happens. First, a person growing up in an African community becomes habitually dependent on ready-made patterns of beliefs. Second, utility or functional explanation play a crucial role in the sustenance of beliefs.

In traditional African societies, a person is born into ready-made or already provided patterns of beliefs that she gradually becomes addicted to or depends on habitually as she grows up. Her addiction to such patterns of belief is really no fault of hers because she hardly has any evidence within such a closed society to counter the set of beliefs, and even when there are isolated and recalcitrant cases that seem not to fit quite well within the established pattern of belief, it is not enough to let the belief go, not after realising the heavy weight of tradition behind such beliefs.[23] This attitude displayed by the person in African traditional communities is, to be sure, not peculiar to her. The same attitude is obvious in the history of science. It takes more than the availability of alternative ideas and counterfactual evidence for a theory to be let go in the sciences. Appiah puts it succinctly:

> ... it may seem strange to suggest that accepting beliefs from one's culture and holding onto them in the absence of countervailing evidence can be reasonable, if it can lead to having beliefs that are... so wildly false. But to think otherwise is to mistake the relatively deplorable nature of our epistemic position in the universe. It is just fundamentally correct that there is no requirement other than consistency that we can place on our beliefs in advance, in order to increase their likelihood of being true; and that a person who starts with a consistent set of beliefs can arrive, by way of reasonable principles of evidence, at the most fantastic untruths. The wisdom of epistemological modesty is, surely, one of the lessons of the history of natural science...[24]

Hence, persons in African communities — including those communities in modern Africa that are still very indigenous and traditional and still rely heavily on traditional ideas about life — would cling to the ideas about albinism they have grown up with and become habitually used to, even though such beliefs are not true. They are unlikely to let go of these established patterns of beliefs simply because a differing viewpoint emerges from another form of life.

68   *Epistemology of albinism*

But the more worrisome situation has to do with how we can account for why many persons in African *modern* communities who we could say have a fair enough grasp of modern ways of life — trained in Western formal education, having some basic medical knowledge, having information about the cause of albinism, and so on — still would not let go of the traditional beliefs about albinism. The way they relate with persons with albinism, their utterances and comments about the condition and persons with albinism in informal settings show that they are still very much addicted to the established patterns of beliefs in their communities. The truth is many Africans do not see Western education and science as a mode of knowing and learning new ways or ideas that may be useful in evaluating shared beliefs in African traditions. Many simply see the formal education process as a necessary requirement for survival in modern societies, such as becoming aware of certain useful information and getting hold of a degree certificate in order to get a white collar job. It is therefore not surprising that there are still medical doctors, healthcare workers, lawyers, academic professors, political leaders and the like who still relate to persons with albinism on the basis of shared-knowledge within the community, which persistently determines their actions and behaviour. One reason why it is difficult for even such ones to let go of false beliefs is because they see these sets of false beliefs as stemming from the agency of invisible forces. Such agency is alleged to be so evident in everyday life that they simply would not let go of such false beliefs simply because Western science cannot access them and they are also sure that such agency is very useful in explaining events. In Appiah's words:

> The evidence that spirits exist is *obvious*: priests go into trance, people get better after the application of spiritual remedies, people die regularly from the action of inimical spirits. The reinterpretation of this evidence, in terms of medical-scientific theories or of psychology, requires that there be such alternative theories and that people have some reason to believe in them; but again and again, and especially in the area of mental and social life, the traditional view is likely to be confirmed.[25]

And this brings us to the second point on why false beliefs persist: The utility value of such beliefs in terms of explaining events, that is established patterns of beliefs, provide functional or teleological explanation of events. African traditional and modern societies exist in a big web of causal relations. Things do not happen by chance or coincidence. Every event has a purpose and meaning. No event is contingent but necessary. It is no coincidence that the owl cries in the night and the child dies in the morning, that the woman commits adultery and her child becomes incurably ill else she confesses, that a man does some evil and the wife gives birth to a child with albinism, that a person suffers some bad luck after coming in contact with a person with albinism. These series of causally related events help individual

Epistemology of albinism 69

persons to make sense of the world they live in. So, it is not likely for them to let go of the set of beliefs that gives meaning and purpose to their existence.

Furthermore, the appeal to agency essentially includes invisible agents and forces. The role of invisible forces in the unfolding of events in the universe is taken very seriously in an African space. Hence, when an incurable illness or albinism is seen as the result of some invisible being, it is not questioned. In fact, it is welcomed because it explains the events and ensures that no event is left unexplained. It doesn't just explain events; the expected consequences are often felt in every area of life. And if such causal explanation of events is reliable in making sense of the world the African lives in, why would she let it go even in modern times? Take, for instance, the glaring evidences that the body parts of persons with albinism sell for a whooping sum of $75,000, USD, or more in East Africa.[26] In the face of such realities, how do you explain to a seemingly modern African that the person who has spent such a huge amount of money to acquire the body of a person with albinism did it without a clear purpose in mind? How do you explain that both the seller and the buyer are not fully convinced of the efficacy of their beliefs that they are able to invest such time and money into it? Hence, families arrange to sell their member with albinism, relatives connive to kidnap and kill a person with albinism to make money or to gain some favours from invisible agents.[27]

The point to draw from all this is that it will take much more than the mere availability of counterfactual evidence to certain false beliefs in African traditional form of life to make people let go of such false beliefs. To achieve a model-shift in the perception of albinism in African societies, an ideological revolution must obviously take place, and it must be a deliberate one championed and sustained by all stakeholders for a long period of time. The new model must provide better functional explanation, not in some classroom in a university, but to the market woman in a village in East Africa as to why, for instance, a child is born with albinism and how the condition can be avoided in the first place. To be sure, these explanations are available and certainly reliable; they are not just being said in the right place and in the right way. The cognitive process is inadequate in getting the message home. In the last chapter of this work, we shall examine some ways to achieve this arduous task.

Ignorance and systemically produced falsehood

A recent trend in epistemology is the attempt to examine 'the complex phenomena of ignorance, which has as its aim as identifying different forms of ignorance, examining how they are produced and sustained, and what role they play in knowledge practices.'[28] It aims to 'promote the study of ignorance, by developing tools for understanding how and why various forms of knowing have "not come to be", or disappeared, or have been delayed or long neglected, for better or for worse, at various points in history.'[29]

70   *Epistemology of albinism*

This is the branch of epistemology known as the epistemology of ignorance. According to Linda Martin Alcoff:

> The idea of an epistemology of ignorance attempts to explain and account for the fact that such substantive practices of ignorance — wilful ignorance, for example, and socially acceptable but faulty justificatory practices — are structural. This is to say that there are identities and social locations and modes of belief formation, all produced by structural social conditions of a variety of sorts, that are in some cases epistemically disadvantaged or defective.[30]

My goal in this section falls in these lines of thought. I am concerned here about how ignorance played a crucial role in the production of knowledge about albinism in African traditions and how the ideas about albinism were institutionalised into such society through a systemically produced falsehood that stemmed from ignorance, deliberate or otherwise.

In the early stages of the development of African communities, building community was paramount and seen as the primary means of communal and individual survival. African elite classes, as the custodians of the customs and traditions of the people, were saddled with the crucial responsibility of establishing and sustaining the much needed harmony among beings in African communities. Hence, when they noticed anything abnormal or extraordinary, something different due to ignorance about the other and other from the status quo, out of fear of being a threat to the accepted nature of things, theories were formulated and falsehoods were deliberately and systematically produced about the abnormal, ideas that dichotomised the normal from the abnormal, ensuring the superiority of the former over the latter. Such theories were institutionalised, presented and re-presented in various forms from generation to generation until they attained the status of 'objective ontologies of truth' spiced with religiously garnished ideologies.

These constructed ideas and representations were mostly far from factual. They were falsehoods deduced from ignorance but nonetheless institutionalised and entrenched into the socio-cultural system because they were goal-directed: to protect the status quo and overcome the fear of the other. Hence, for instance, such social representations are not different from the racial contract drawn by European tribes against non-European races in the past. It is a contract drawn by the normal against the abnormal, the self against the other. It stems from wilful ignorance produced and sustained to attain certain goals. These actively and deliberately produced falsehoods are not factual, true, or justifiable, but they are systemic and structural, deeply entrenched into society and having real consequences for real people.

As we have seen, the consequences of such deeply entrenched social representations about albinism in African traditions coated with ignorance and falsehood are real and troubling. It is not news that persons with albinism continue to face unfair and unjust treatment. Due to the harmful ideas

Epistemology of albinism 71

about them in the consciousness of Africans, they continually face stigmatisation, social exclusion, maltreatment, dismembering and even murder. They are hunted for their body parts; they lack access to basic things in life such as education, marriage, employment, good health care and cordial familial relationships. Until such social representations are overturned and the ignorance and falsehood inherent in them made obvious to the market woman and the school student, persons with albinism are likely to continue to experience such injustice, partiality and unfairness.

The epistemological issues that we have been engaged in thus far clearly show that the knowledge about albinism in African traditional and modern societies is riddled with systemic ignorance and falsehoods that continue to serve as a veil that hinders the actual facts about albinism. And as we have seen, such untruths about albinism are part of a consistent and reliable set of beliefs that are not only deeply entrenched in African thought systems, cherished and shared by Africans but are seen as providing functional explanations for objects and events. Any attempt to overthrow these deeply rooted ideologies about albinism must be as penetrative, popular and useful in managing and dealing with albinism both by persons with albinism and other community members. I shall return to these concerns in due course.

Notes

1. Barry Hallen (2004). 'Yoruba Moral Epistemology'. In Kwasi Wiredu Ed., *A Companion to African Philosophy* (Malden MA: Blackwell Publishing). 298.
2. Barry Hallen, 'Yoruba Moral Epistemology', 298.
3. John Hospers (1973) *An Introduction to Philosophical Analysis* (London: Routledge and Kegan Paul Ltd.).
4. For details on the intricacies of adultery among the Esan people of southern Nigeria, see Justina O. Ehiakhamen, 'Beyond Culpability: Approaching Male Impotency through Legitimated Adultery in Esan Metaphysics'. In Elvis Imafidon and John A. I. Bewaji (Eds.), *Ontologized Ethics: New Essays in African Meta-ethics* (Lanham: Lexington Books). 121–131.
5. The distinction between essential and accidental components of a ritual in African traditions is clearly drawn by Kwame Anthony Appiah (2005). 'African Studies and the Concept of knowledge'. In Bert Hamminga Ed., *Knowledge Cultures: Comparative Western and African Epistemology* (Amsterdam: Rodopi). 26–27.
6. Kwame Anthony Appiah, 'African Studies and the Concept of Knowledge'. 34.
7. Kwame Anthony Appiah, 'African Studies and the Concept of Knowledge'. 34–35.
8. Kwame Anthony Appiah, 'African Studies and the Concept of Knowledge'. 35.
9. See Thomas Kuhn.
10. Kwame Gyekye (1992). 'Person and Community in African Thought'. In Kwasi Wiredu and Kwame Gyekye Eds., *Person and Community: Ghanaian Philosophical Studies* (Washington DC: The Council for Research in Values and Philosophy). 104.
11. Bert Hamminga (2005). 'Epistemology from the African Point of View'. In Bert Hamminga Ed., *Knowledge Cultures: Comparative Western and African Epistemology* (Amsterdam: Rodopi). 57.

72 *Epistemology of albinism*

12. Bert Hamminga, 'Epistemology from the African Point of View'. 58.
13. Bert Hamminga, 'Epistemology from the African Point of View'. 59.
14. Bert Hamminga, 'Epistemology from the African Point of View'. 60.
15. See, for instance. Olatunji O. Oyeshile (2006). 'The Individual-Community Relationship as an Issue in Social and Political Philosophy'. In Olusegun Oladipo Ed., *Core Issue in African Philosophy* (Ibadan: Hope Publications). 102–119.
16. Mario E. Martinez (2001). 'The Process of Knowing: A Biocognitive Epistemology'. *The Journal of Mind and Behaviour*, 22 (4): 407.
17. S. Baskerville (2009). 'Freedom of the Family: The Family Crisis and the Future of Western Civilization'. *Humanitas* XXII.1&2: 170.
18. Albert Onobhayedo (2007). 'Western Education and Social Change in Esan Land'. *IRORO: A Journal of Arts* 7.1 & 2: 270–271.
19. Polycarp Ikuenobe (2006). *Philosophical Perspective on Communalism and Morality in African Traditions.* (Lanham: Lexington Books). 136.
20. Polycarp Ikuenobe, *Philosophical Perspective on Communalism and Morality in African Traditions.* 137.
21. Kwame Anthony Appiah, 'African Studies and the Concept of Knowledge'. 35.
22. Kwame Anthony Appiah, 'African Studies and the Concept of Knowledge'. 35.
23. See Evans-Pritchard (1976). *Witchcraft, Oracles and Magic among the Azande* (Oxford: Clarendon Press).
24. Kwame Anthony Appiah, 'African Studies and the Concept of Knowledge'. 35.
25. Kwame Anthony Appiah, 'African Studies and the Concept of Knowledge'. 36.
26. See Flora Drury (2015). 'Hunted Down like Animals and Sold by their own Families for $75,000: Tanzania's Albinos hacked Apart by Witchdoctors who believe their body parts "bring luck" in Sick Trade Fueled by the Country's Elite'. In *The Daily Mail Online.* Accessed from: http://www.dailymail.co.uk/news/article-2922243/Hunted-like-animals-sold-families-75-000-Tanzania-s-albinos-hacked-apart-witchdoctors-believe-body-parts-bring-luck-sick-trade-fuelled-country-s-elite.html.
27. See Flora Drury, 'Hunted Down like Animals and Sold by their own Families for $75,000 …'
28. S. Sullivan and T. Nancy (Eds.), Introduction to *Race and Epistemologies of Ignorance.* 1.
29. R. N. Proctor and S. Londa (Eds.) (2008), Introduction to *Agnotology: The Making and Unmaking of Ignorance.* (Stanford: Stanford University Press). vii.
30. L. M. Alcoff (2007). 'Epistemologies of Ignorance: Three Types'. In S. Sullivan and T. Nancy (Eds.), *Race and Epistemologies of Ignorance.* (Albany: State University of New York Press). 40–41.

4   The ethics of albinism in African traditions

Every human society operates within the framework of certain accepted norms or standards of proper behaviour, some ethical principles that help persons within such societies determine whether their actions or the actions of others are permissible or not. Such norms or principles that guide human actions become customs and form regular patterns that persons within the society fit into because they are believed to have resulted from the rich cultural heritage of the people and have been useful in maintaining order and peace in the society. Hence, although such ethical norms are used in evaluating the actions of persons, they are themselves not often subjected to evaluation; their relevance, value and efficiency in determining the rightness or wrongness of an action is often not subjected to rigorous critique within the form of life in which they are held. But every now and then, when weighed against universal moral norms of human action, some ethical principles within certain forms of life become problematic and their value is evaluated and questioned. This, of course, has resulted in the perennial debate between moral universalism and moral relativism.

To be sure, there are certain norms of action that ought to apply, given similar conditions, to every person regardless of race, sex, culture religion and other relative characterisation. It is, for instance, wrong in principle to deny a young child or an elderly person food simply because she does not contribute to providing the food; it is right to be honest and truthful, to show hospitality and kindness. But if these are indeed universal principles, how are we to understand and make sense of, for instance, the practice of taking the elderly to the sea and setting her adrift on a floating iceberg in traditional Eskimo because they could no longer care for their survival? Within the Eskimo tradition, such an action was, of course, regarded as permissible and it was indeed a custom, although it may not have been in line with universal expectations of care, hospitality and kindness, particularly toward the elderly. The obvious tension between universal and context-based moral expectations is not an easy one because the Eskimos would provide strong reasons and justifications for their actions, ranging from religious beliefs of an afterlife to the need for group survival. But are the justifications provided within certain contexts for its departure from universal moral expectations sufficient enough?

74 *Ethics of albinism in African traditions*

The objectives of this chapter ensue from a similar tension between universal moral expectations and real customs and ethos of behaviour in particular contexts. Are there reasons, and if there are, are the reasons sufficient, for the widening gap between the universal moral expectations in the treatment of persons with albinism and the actual customs and ethos of behaviour toward such persons in African communities? How do accepted norms of action in African communities affect the well-being of persons with albinism? To answer these and related questions, I begin by exploring an African moral theory, that is, the fundamental moral principle of human action in African thought. I then proceed to examine a ground for the moral justification of the discrimination against persons with albinism in African communities. This is followed by an analysis of other essential issues concerning the ill-treatment of persons with albinism, such as the question of moral responsibility toward those considered an other in African context, the challenges of caring for a disabled person and the problems associated with inherent elite-virtue ethics in African traditions.

An African theory of the good

What is the theory of the good among sub-Saharan African traditions? What basic moral theory can be deduced from such thought systems that determine the permissibility or impermissibility of particular actions? In his paper 'Toward an African Moral Theory',[1] Thaddeus Metz provides an apt and comprehensive normative moral principle that accounts for what makes an action good or otherwise in African traditions by developing an African moral theory. This theory of the good is intrinsically linked with the goal of maintaining communal harmony or equilibrium among beings in the African community as a necessary and sufficient factor for survival. Consequently, the primary and most important goal of existence is to establish, maintain and sustain this communal harmony in the interest and welfare of both the community as a collective whole and individual persons within the community. Hence, the idea of the good in African traditions is essentially communitarian in nature, aiming to sustain community. As Polycarp Ikuenobe aptly puts it:

> This idea of harmony or the goal of maintaining harmony for the human good and well-being is the foundation for communalism, which implies the need to impose social responsibilities on people in order to rationally perpetuate the relevant traditions and maintain harmony. So, maintaining harmony with the aid of the community is an essential human interest. The idea of pursuing and maintaining human welfare and interests is at the moral centre of communalism and the moral conception of personhood in African traditions. ... As such, communalism prescribes that people should act in a way that would enhance their own interest within the framework of pursuing

Ethics of albinism in African traditions   75

the goal of human well-being and welfare in the context of natural harmony in their communities.[2]

G. Setiloane adds that if we have understood community in African traditions as inclusive of all lives, and that the success of life is found in the ability to maintain a healthy relationship with other beings, then the moral imperative and contract will, by implication, be to maintain harmony in the community and to ensure its continuance. The cycle of ritual life is to sustain the wholeness of the community of human beings, nature and the elements.[3]

Thaddeus Metz offers six possible ways that such an African moral theory, which emphasises communal harmony for human well-being can be formulated. He terms an African moral theory '*Ubuntu*' (U) because of the communal basis of African ethics. *Ubuntu,* as a word used mainly by the Zulu people of South Africa, roughly translates as humanness, and it features in the maxim that 'a person is a person through other persons', meaning that one's identity as a human being causally and even metaphysically depends on a community.[4] Bearing this in mind, Metz, proposes the following six formulations as the most likely formulations of an African moral theory:

U1: An action is right just insofar as it respects a person's dignity; an act is wrong to the extent that it degrades humanity.

U2: An action is right just insofar as it promotes the well-being of others; an act is wrong to the extent that it fails to enhance the welfare of one's fellows.

U3: An action is right just insofar as it promotes the well-being of others without violating their rights; an act is wrong to the extent that it either violates rights or fails to enhance the welfare of one's fellows without violating rights.

U4: An action is right just insofar as it positively relates to others and thereby realizes oneself; an act is wrong to the extent that it does not perfect one's valuable nature as a social being.

U5: An action is right just insofar as it is in solidarity with groups whose survival is threatened; an act is wrong to the extent that it fails to support a vulnerable community.

U6: An action is right just insofar as it produces harmony and reduces discord; an act is wrong to the extent that it fails to develop community.[5]

He elaborates on each of them, showing, for good reasons, why U6 presents a better formulation than others. To be sure, as he rightly argues, U4 remains the most conventional formulation that has become a dominant interpretation of African ethics available in many literatures.[6] This is because most scholars see the maxim 'to be a person through other persons' as a call for an agent to develop his or her personhood.[7] However, Metz identifies a number of issues with U4. Instead of others' welfare being the relevant good for a moral agent to promote, here it is the realization of one's distinctively human and valuable nature, specifically, one's special ability to engage in communal relationships. It lays too much emphasis on self-realization and

76 *Ethics of albinism in African traditions*

this has counter-intuitive implications. Suppose that you are the breadwinner of your kin; both your immediate and extended family members depend on you for sustenance and the provision of their material needs, which you do quite well. It then happens that your business or means of income crumble, and you are well aware that in a few weeks you will be unable to provide for the needs of others who depend on you. If then a friend convinces you that you could become very rich before the end of those few weeks if you could provide the limbs of a person with albinism to a certain witch doctor in your community for some money ritual, it would follow that, to maximize your self-realization, you would need to kill a person with albinism so as to acquire his limbs or, at the very least, go to the human parts black market to buy the limbs from another person who has done the killing already. Of course, in killing or buying human parts, you would not be realizing yourself, for the theory says that to realize yourself you must do so by positively supporting other persons in some way. However, since you can positively support other persons in the long-term only by acquiring more wealth, which in this case you have done through killing another person or buying the body parts of another person, the theory counter-intuitively seems to permit murder for one's own benefit. A straightforward way to resolve this problem would be to build constraints into the theory, so that an act is right if and only if it develops one's social nature without violating the rights of others. That manoeuvre avoids the counterexample.[8] However, this version of the self-realization theory still faces the problem that it can never permit, let alone require, giving up one's life for others, even for one's children since one's self-realization would thereby end. One can obviously question whether killing oneself when necessary to help others is invariably a way to maximize the realization of one's communal nature. Even if it is granted that sacrificing one's life for another person is such a high 'spike' in the expression of one's communal nature that one could not express more of it if one were instead to stay alive, U4 still suffers from an inherently egoistic factor. If one asks why one should help others, for example, this theory says that the basic justificatory reason to do so (though not the proper motive for doing so) is that it will help *me* by making me more of a better person. This will obviously be antithetical to the whole idea of communal harmony stressed as a necessity in African traditions.[9]

Hence, Metz offers U6 as a more promising theoretical formulation of African ethics. This is because, as opposed to well-being or self-realization, this account of *Ubuntu* (U) posits certain relationships as constitutive of the good that a moral agent ought to promote. 'What is right is what connects people together; what separates people is wrong.'[10] In accordance with U6, therefore, An African ought to act, as a matter of duty, only in ways that will establish, promote and sustain peaceful coexistence, harmony and equilibrium between him/her and other beings — visible and invisible — in the community. Thus, actions that ensure communal harmony are permissible, while actions that cause discord are impermissible. The justification

Ethics of albinism in African traditions 77

of this African moral theory is that communal and individual interests are only attainable if and only if the theory is strictly adhered to. This justification is the reason why some scholars have argued that the emphasis on communal harmony is not antithetical to the long term rational life plan of the individual, for, as Polycarp Ikuenobe says, such communal interest provides the basis for the individual to pursue his rational life plan in a social and safe context.[11]

The theory of morality offered by U6 is aptly captured by Desmond Tutu when he says that:

> Harmony, friendliness, community are great goods. Social harmony is for us the *summumbonum* — the greatest good. Anything that subverts or undermines this sought-after good is to be avoided like the plague. Anger, resentment, lust for revenge, even success through aggressive competitiveness, are corrosive of this good.[12]

P. J. Nel adds that:

> An act of violence is viewed as an act disturbing the equilibrium or balance of the community. An indecent act which destroys community life... will not be left unpunished in this world; retribution is not retained for the hereafter only. The moral imperative is co-habitual in the sense that it is part of the entire concept of being, part of a comprehensive community.[13]

This is what underlies the notion of moral humanism in African traditional societies where what is morally good or bad is appreciated in the context of its contribution to the well-being and dignity of humankind and the community in particular.[14] Kwasi Wiredu has been a strong advocate of the unique moral humanistic character of African traditions. In his words:

> It has often been said that our traditional outlook was intensely humanistic. It seems to me that, as far as the basis of the traditional ethic is concerned, this claim is abundantly justified. Traditional thinking about the foundations of morality is refreshingly non-super naturalistic. Not that one can find in traditional sources elaborated theories of humanism. But anyone who reflects on our traditional ways of speaking about morality is bound to be struck by the pre-occupation with human welfare.[15]

J. A. Aigbodioh adds that:

> African communalism implies a co-dependency ethos. This means that communal life in Africa served the purpose of inculcating in the minds of African persons the strong moral feeling of togetherness, mutual

78   *Ethics of albinism in African traditions*

interdependence of individuals in the society and the realistic sense of confidence that the co-operation and sympathetic understanding of, and from, brothers and sisters are always at the disposal of everyone. This ethos, which defines the African human nature, is generally considered to be a source and a mark of strength, potency, might and unity rather than of weakness.[16]

Kwame Gyekye sums up the communalistic/humanistic ethic of African traditions in these words:

In the light of the relentless concern among the African people for the welfare of each member of the communal society, it would be appropriate to expect the ethics espoused in African societies to be a social ethics... A moral system that emphasizes concern for the well-being of every member of the society and should be distinguished from a system that emphasizes the interest and welfare of the individual to the (almost) total disregard of the interests of the others... [Thus] A list of moral values equated with the good in African societies will include kindness, compassion, generosity, hospitality, faithfulness, truthfulness, concern for others, and the action that brings peace, justice, dignity, respect and happiness.[17]

The argument for the moral humanism of African moral theory has resulted in a heated debate among scholars on whether morality in African traditions had a religious or humanistic foundation. Having examined the humanistic perspective, it is important that we understand the religious perspective as well. The argument for the religious foundation of morality in African traditions can be stated thusly: If the Supreme Being is the origin and source of life, if he is the creator of all beings and energizes them with the force of life, then it follows logically that he is not only the source of man's conscience, but also the source of his sense of right and wrong.[18] Based on this argument, many scholars have defended the view that religion is the source of morality in African traditions. It is easy to locate John Mbiti in this camp. Mbiti states it clearly that, 'God gave the moral order to people so that they might live happily and in harmony with one another.'[19] This is because Mbiti believes strongly that African life is intensely religious in all spheres of living and ethics is only a special case of this religious orientation to life; all moral norms come from God. Bolaji Idowu has also been in the forefront of advocating this religious view of morality. As he says:

Our own view is that morality is basically the fruit of religion and that, to begin with, it was dependent upon it. Man's conception of deity has everything to do with what is taken to be the norm of morality... The sense of right and wrong by degree of God has always been part of human nature... Morality is the fruit of religion.[20]

Ethics of albinism in African traditions   79

We have already examined the claims of the other camp on the humanistic character of morality in African traditional societies. For some strong reasons presented by this camp (the humanist camp), it is difficult to deny the fact that although African traditional societies were very religious due to the presence of, and relationship with, supernatural entities, moral norms were primarily intended to maintain social equilibrium and communal harmony. Kwame Gyekye says, therefore, that:

> It would be more correct to say that African moral values derive from the experience of the people in living together or in trying to evolve a common and harmonious social life. That is, the moral values of the African people have a social and humanistic basis rather than a religious basis and are fashioned according to the people's own understanding of the nature of human society, human relations, human goals and the meaning of human life.[21]

But admitting this point of the humanistic camp does not necessarily negate that of the other camp (those who hold the religious view). This is because even if we agree that morality in African traditions is basically humanistic, we cannot at the same time disprove the fact that religion served as an effective means for *enforcing* such socially motivated moral norms. In this sense of the relationship between morality and religion, we can then understand better what Mbiti means when he says that one should view morality as an authoritative code of conduct directly sanctioned by the Supreme Being. The moral code is therefore not autonomous, but its autonomy is derived from the Supreme Being. Any breach of the moral code would accordingly be an offence against the Supreme Being and his instructions.[22]

Since the primary goal of existence in African communities is to maintain equilibrium and harmony among beings in the community as a necessary factor for survival, it therefore means that the community, in the words of Ifeanyi A. Menkiti, 'plays a vital role both as catalyst and as prescriber of norms'.[23] The community is thus saddled with a crucial responsibility of ensuring that there is order in the system and achieving this crucial responsibility involves the establishment of structures and institutions of community saddled with the duty of prescribing norms and rules of behaviour that are acceptable to the community to the extent that they, at least, promote communal harmony. Abiding by such norms or rules will mean living up to the expectations of the community, while violating such rules will mean going against the expectations of the community, and this will not go without its consequences.

Norms of behaviour are effectively enforced with the authority of the holy. It is this authority that ensures easy compliance to these norms and rules of conduct. This authority, which is to be found in the religious beliefs of the people, serve as ideologies (garnished with notions about the supernatural) used to enforce a moral standard that meets with the expectations of the

80 Ethics of albinism in African traditions

community. Ideology here represents any ready-made set of ideas adopted as the exclusive basis for the organization of society, a set of dogmas to be imposed with force if necessary, to achieve certain ends.[24] In this case, ideologies represent the set of religious dogmas or unquestioned notions about the supernatural meant to enforce the moral norms of the African community. Religion becomes the authority for ensuring compliance to moral codes of conduct.

The tie between religion and morality thus punctuates every aspect of the life of the African. But this is not in any way strange. Religion has often played a particularly important role in ethics down the ages of Western thought because it has been a useful instrument for enforcing moral codes. One should do this and not do that because God has said so. Much of the ancient and medieval ethics of the Western world hinged on religious precepts. The medieval philosophers in particular found God a very useful resort, the point in which all arguments ended. Thus, that the same pattern of strategic reasoning existed in African traditional societies simply goes a long way to buttress the fact that humans have always depended on religion as an unquestioned ideology for enforcing moral norms. As Elechi Amadi says in his *Ethics in Nigerian Culture*:

> The overall effect of all these is to enforce a moral standard acceptable to a particular society. A secular interpretation leads to the conclusion that moral precepts have always had their origin in the mind of man. Even when deities are said to have laid them down, they have had to do so through the mind of man. It would appear, then, that while man formulates the moral code, he enlists the influence of religion for its enforcement. In other words, *in ethics man proposes, god enforces*.[25]

Does African moral theory justify harming persons with albinism?

That persons with albinism in many African communities suffer many forms of harm is to state the obvious. These include stigmatisation and discrimination, killing, maiming, commodification of their body parts, social exclusion, denial of education and employment, and harmful representation such as labelling them as witches and wizards, the personification of a curse and the property of supernatural entities. Such actions against a person would normally be considered morally impermissible and wrong. To wilfully cause harm to another person is, under most circumstances, considered wrong. In circumstances where they might be assumed to be permissible by perpetuators, such as subjecting a convicted serial killer to death by electrification, hanging or firing squad, tactful senicide among the Eskimos due to difficulties of survival, and the extremely painful circumcision rites that still take place in many African communities as a part of manhood initiation rituals, they become very controversial, resulting in heated and protracted debates

Ethics of albinism in African traditions 81

on the permissibility or otherwise of the action, such as whether the reasons for performing such actions is enough to justify the action itself.

If the permissibility or impermissibility of actions in sub-Saharan Africa is intrinsically hinged on the African moral theory discussed above, would the harmful treatment of persons with albinism be permissible or impermissible within the framework of the moral theory? Again, do the perpetuators of such harm against such persons feel they are justified to do so? Do they feel they have done something right or wrong? We can best answer these questions by returning to the idea of moral humanism in African indigenous ethics. Suppose that a store of grains is needed to be kept safe as the only means for survival of a village and it is thus kept safe. But there remains one threat to this store of grains: rodents. Would it be wrong to set traps in the storehouse to catch such rodents and kill them? The chorus answer would be in the negative in so far as the killing of such rodents preserves the grains in the store and ensures the survival of the community.

As discussed in chapter two of this work, persons with albinism are described as queer and harmful beings in African traditional thought. They are seen as threat to the harmony and equilibrium among beings in the community. Since the harmony of beings in an African community is an essential good that must be pursued for the well-being and interests of both individual persons and the community at large, doing away with or causing harm to anything that produces discord or that threatens the much needed harmony is permissible. Take for instance, the case of a morally bankrupt person in an African community. In many African communities, such a person is ostracised for not living a community-accepted lifestyle because to continuously entertain and support such a person would be to encourage actions that would breed discord and disequilibrium. Suppose in an African traditional community where polygamy is still very much in practice, it is forbidden for a man to have sexual relations with any of his father's wives or concubines because it would not only bring shame to the family but also make the ancestors of the kin angry, thereby causing disequilibrium and discord between the family and their ancestors. It would be morally justified from the perspective of the African moral theory to ostracise for a period of time a man who breaks this rule because his actions threaten the communality of the community. It would take a series of rituals to bring the man back to the community after genuine repentance is shown. Similarly, the need to preserve community and abhor discord also stands under the justification provided for which persons who suffer from certain understood or incurable diseases were camped far away from the community. Such communities — and this, of course, is not peculiar to traditional African communities — feared that not doing so threatens the very existence of the individual persons within the community and the community at large.

Now, many African communities see certain beings and forces, including witches, wizards and queer beings such as persons with albinism as threat to personal and communal well-being. The ontic and ontological

82 *Ethics of albinism in African traditions*

representations of such entities characterises them as something evil, harmful and worth avoiding by any means possible. More importantly, a person with albinism is not considered a human being but a lesser sort of being. Coming in contact with a person with albinism, for instance, is seen as bringing bad luck. In fact, the very fact of giving birth to a person with albinism is identified as a bad omen for the family and as signifying divine punishment for some past actions by either or both of the parents. Hence, the understanding of the being of persons with albinism in African traditional communities favours the harming or cruel treatment of such beings as a source of wellbeing and good luck. Doing away with an infant with albinism by dumping her in the evil forest or dedicating her to serve at the shrine of a chief priest is seen as a way of getting rid of the curse that would have otherwise brought calamity to the family. Getting the body parts of a person with albinism, such as the fingers, hair, bones and limbs, for money rituals is seen as an effective means of enriching oneself and providing for others in the community. Forcefully having sexual relations with a young teenage girl with albinism is seen by some as a way of getting cured of HIV/AIDS. These instances clearly show that harming persons with albinism is much more beneficial for personal and communal interests than caring for them. However, an objection may be raised against these instances because they seek first for self-preservation and ones' self-realization and put the community as secondary (as seen in the U4 formulation above). This sort of understanding of African ethics has already been criticised above as not being a true reflection of the nature of the good in African traditions. Nonetheless, within the U6 formulation, the person with albinism doesn't still fare well because her presence in the community is seen as inhibiting and endangering the development of community rather than contributing to it.

Hence, African moral humanism justifies the cruel treatment of persons with albinism. When persons within an African community cause harm, maltreat, stigmatise and discriminate against persons with albinism, they do not often feel they are doing something wrong in the same way they would feel when they are hurting a fellow human for two reasons. First, their interaction with a person with albinism, cruel as it may be, is not considered the same as an interaction they would have with a fellow human being; second, the ill-treatment of persons with albinism protects the community from harm.

Another perspective from which we may view the ill-treatment of persons with albinism consists of a set of arguments from utility. An African could argue, for instance, of the need to kill infants with albinism or isolate them from the social life of the community in a manner that is less coated with religious ideas. Such arguments hold that such actions were taken primarily in traditional communities for the preservation of the community from empirical reasons and on the grounds of their usefulness. Persons with albinism have a fragile skin that could not withstand the heat of the African sun. This implies that they could not have been able to work in farms or

Ethics of albinism in African traditions   83

raise animals and carry out other outdoor activities without bringing too much burden of ill-health to the family and the community — ill-health that the community could not treat or cope with. Again, persons with albinism have poor vision. They could not have coped as hunters, for instance. They would have contributed nothing to the community's well-being, but merely become a burden to the family in particular and the community in general. Hence, it was best to get rid of them at an early stage by killing the infant with albinism or abandoning her in the forest to be killed by wild animals to save both the victim and the community much pain and headache. In much milder situations, they were kept alive but not allowed to participate in the usual activities in the community.

This understanding of the harm done against persons with albinism argues that the supernatural/religious ideas about albinism were simply formulated by the community to cover up the empirical facts about the being of albinism and to enforce compliance with the decisions about how they should be treated. It might be difficult to compel a mother to dump her new born baby with albinism in the evil forest because the child would find it difficult to survive. She might insist on caring for the child no matter what. But if the ideologies she has met on ground states that such a child is cursed and would bring misfortune to her, her husband and the entire kin, it would be easier to make her comply and get rid of the child. Here, it is once more obvious, as maintained in the previous section, that religion plays a key role in enforcing moral norms.

These arguments, from the utility of harm, akin to those Eskimos have given concerning senicide, raise even more fundamental moral questions. What duties or obligations do we have toward caring for a person with a disability? Do disabilities reduce the moral worth of a person? Is our relationship with others determined by convenience and does it disappear when we cannot benefit from the other? The following section pays more attention to these questions.

The duty to, and burden of, care

According to Eva Feder Kittay, the term _care_ can denote three interrelated things: a labour, an attitude or a virtue. As labour, it is the duty of maintaining others and ourselves when we are in a condition of need. It requires skills on the part of the caregiver and uptake on the part of the one cared for. It is most noticed in its absence, most appreciated when it can be least reciprocated. As an attitude, caring denotes a positive, affective bond and investment in another's well-being. The labour can be done without the appropriate attitude. Yet without the attitude of care, the open responsiveness to another that is so essential to understanding what another requires is not possible. That is, the labour unaccompanied by the attitude of care will not be good care. Care, as a virtue, is a disposition manifested in caring behaviour (the labour and attitude) in which a shift takes place from the interest in our life situation to the situation of the other, the one in

84   *Ethics of albinism in African traditions*

need of care. Relations of affection facilitate care, but the disposition can be directed at strangers as well as intimates.[26]

These components of care reveal that care involves a spectrum of activities taking place between the caregiver and the one being cared for. It may, for instance, involve taking responsibility for protecting and advancing the interests of the one being cared for. It may also consist of supporting and providing for the needs of the one being cared for such as food, clothing, money and so on as seen, for instance, in the case of a parent caring for a child. It may also include a positive emotional attachment to the one being cared for that is deeply rooted in love and respect and felt strongly by the one being cared for; it's an attachment that gives her a sense of security, that she is cherished and loved by someone. More importantly, if the three interrelated components must be involved in care-giving, such that not only care as labour stands out, for instance, care must involve choice and volition.[27] This is why the feminist critique of African women (and women of African origins in the diaspora) in assuming the primary role of caring for their families and doing most all the chores needed to care for family members, such as caring for the baby, cooking, shopping farming and the like, is questionable. Many of these women do not see themselves as being compelled to carry out these duties of care. For such ones, such care-giving is what defines them and gives their lives meaning; they find joy and fulfilment in doing it. They are disposed and emotionally attached to it. Of course, there is no doubt that there were and still are individual cases of abuse of such care-giving in African societies. But to advocate that African women in general do away with the disposition to care for others, particularly the family, is to impede the choice they have made to care.

Care is thus 'a relational value lived out in particular relationships set within specific cultural, social and economic contexts.'[28] Many times, the caregiver gives more and puts in more work than the one being cared for. It is often difficult to have equal reciprocity in care-giving. In this regard, focus on the equality of the reciprocity of care between two persons — where each assumes the role of giver or receiver at a given point in time — may obscure the very essence of care and present care-giving as oppressive and subjugating to the caregiver because such equality is rarely obtainable in relationships. When a mother cares for a child — disabled or non-disabled, when a daughter cares for an elderly, frail father and when a man cares for his dog, equal reciprocity of care for the former is hardly obtainable from the latter. Even in the case of a married couple committed to their union, the man and the wife would not always be able to reciprocate the same quality and quantity of care that one gives to the other.

As suggested by Barbara H. Andolsen, it may therefore be more feasible to make mutuality rather than reciprocity of care the focal point of care-giving. In her words:

> ... mutuality names a dimension that we long for in relationships... mutuality is a term that denotes a positive, usually a loving, reciprocity.

Ethics of albinism in African traditions 85

Mutuality indicates a pattern of shared giving and receiving of good things, including intangibles such as respect. Feminist ethicists have examined friendship as an important paradigm of mutuality. Erotic relationships, properly constituted, are another important paradigm... mutuality in the context of care... do[es] not require strict equality... Mutuality can name a shared commitment to remain open or "present" to one another with all the other's strengths and weaknesses, even when the two "partners" vulnerabilities are not (at least roughly) balanced. Mutuality must not only enhance and deepen what is most fully human in each party to a relationship, but also preserve and support what is human when it is threatened by physical or mental decline.[29]

Consider, for instance, the relationship of care existing between a mother and a ten-year-old son who has muscular dystrophy. It is certainly a difficult position for a mother to be in as a caregiver for a child. But her joy comes not from any expectancy that the son will someday reciprocate in quite equal value her care for him, but from the smiles, the 'Thank you, Mum' and 'I love you, Mum' that her son consistently tells her, showing love, respect and appreciation for her hard work and care. At times when she has given up, weighed down by the burden of care, those little gestures and words from her son gives her the strength to carry on. There is a mutuality of care in their interaction. They both mutually recognise what they can each do within their capacity to show love, friendship and appreciation for themselves and they do so.

Now, caring for persons with albinism in African traditional societies — at least for those who were not killed as infants — can be understood within these same lines of thought. The traditional and modern African society succeeds quite well, through its representations of albinism, in making caring for such persons a heavy and an unpleasant burden in many ways. First, there is no social support for caring for persons with albinism because the representations of their being as queer and harmful intensely discourages the development on the part of family and community members of the positive attitude toward care and discourages viewing caring for persons with albinism as a virtue. The burden of care for such persons falls solely on a mother, a father, a parent, a sibling, a friend or a schoolmate who has made the personal decision to care for a person with albinism against all odds. Such persons need to individually, deliberately and consciously develop the disposition to care for persons with albinism and consider doing so as a virtuous duty. Doing this, however, is a difficult task because a person who decides to impose on herself the duty to care for a person with albinism is standing at odds with the community. Hence, it is a common experience for the decision made by a mother to care for her child with albinism to bring a serious rift between she and the husband due to the fact that the latter disapproves of such care.[30] It is not uncommon for peers to wonder in awe why a schoolmate has formed bonds of friendship with another classmate with

86 *Ethics of albinism in African traditions*

albinism. It therefore takes a firm determination to care for a person with albinism in African traditional and modern societies.

But what exactly does the duty to care for a person with albinism entail? As already highlighted, it involves being disposed to do it and consider showing such care as a virtue. But furthermore, it also involves the labour of caring for such persons. And herein lies another difficult terrain that a caregiver must tread. Albinism is a health condition requiring certain professional knowledge about the condition. It is different from a mother caring for a child without disability. In traditional African and modern societies, however, the knowledge of the exact nature of the condition is either unavailable to the caregiver and the one being cared for, or it is obscured by deeply entrenched ideologies and representations of the condition that are unfortunately false. Within this context of individual and systemic ignorance, the disposition may be right, the duty may be viewed as virtuous, but the labour may be done wrongly.

Common experience has shown caregivers and those cared for that the sun is harmful to persons with albinism even when they are not sure of exactly what that may result (such as skin cancer). So, they try to avoid the sun but often with little or no success. The child with albinism still plays in the hot sun, walks in the hot sun to and from school without properly covering sensitive parts of the body, and goes to work under the sun for hours in the farm or other outdoor activities. In some cases, the effects of the sun on the skin is attributed to other factors that may have nothing to do with it. It is a common belief in Nigeria, for instance, that eating salt, even in little quantity, is the cause of the rough skin and freckles that characterises the body texture of a person with albinism. Motivated by complete love for, and disposition to care for, a child with albinism, a Nigerian mother then decides to ensure that the child does not take in any salt as part of her food right from the time of birth to adulthood when the child is grown enough to decide for herself.[31] As the one cared for grows up to see her siblings enjoy their meals with salt while she has to stay clear of it and eat 'tasteless' meals, it is difficult for her, but she understands that the mother wants the best for her and struggles to do as told. Unfortunately, however, while salt is avoided, the person with albinism deliberately and circumstantially remains exposed to sun every day of her life. The primary goal for avoiding salt remains unachieved. The skin becomes rough gradually, a numerous number of freckles — that could signal an impending cancer — are seen on the skin, and this brings frustration and pain to both the caregiver and the one being cared for. The same thing can be noticed even with personal hygiene. While persons with albinism have very sensitive skin that needs nothing harsh on it, many parents who decide to care for their children with albinism however believe that such children need to be provided with special soaps and body creams, which are mostly medicated, containing substances that would further damage an already fragile skin. Hence, it is obvious ignorance, systemic or individual,

Ethics of albinism in African traditions 87

that inhibits successful caring for persons with albinism, and the labour put into such care is often done in vain.

Therefore, without the relevant social support and adequate knowledge for caring for persons with albinism, the duty to care for persons with albinism would not be entrenched as a norm, and the care given by determined caregivers would become very burdensome. Suppose, for instance, when a baby with albinism is born in the hospital within a certain community in Tanzania, the parents are directed to a doctor or some unit caring for persons with albinism. Then they are thoroughly counselled and educated not only on why they had a baby with albinism, but also how they should care for her, including basic dos and don'ts. The couple would have, from the beginning, had adequate knowledge on how to cope with the condition of their child and would not depend on popularly held claims or deeply entrenched false consciousness in dealing with their baby. Unfortunately, the current state of things is completely different in many African societies. In Nigeria, for instance, there are no units in the federal, state and local government hospitals or centres dedicated to the care of persons with albinism. More often than not, healthcare workers bring their personal beliefs — religious, cultural and so on — into play in dealing with persons with albinism and their caregivers. They fail to provide the needed guidance for both the caregiver and the one being cared for. In many cases where a doctor is consulted, for instance, specifically to help with the sun-burnt skin of a teenage with albinism, one easily senses the lack of disposition to render the needed care and the conviction that it is a mere waste of time. The labour to care by the health worker becomes a forced labour and, of course, to care under duress is not caring at all.[32] But how can the quality of care for persons with albinism be improved upon in African societies? How can the burdensome duties of caregiver be lightened through support and accurate knowledge? What role can society play in these regards? And how can the one being cared for help?

Social justice, dignity and easing of the burden of care

Caring for persons with disability is not always an easy task and often requires much support from society and social institutions. A society and its institutions must recognise their duties and obligations to the persons with disability and their primary caregivers and should not shy away from fulfilling them. For, as Rawls says, 'justice is the first virtue of social institutions, as truth is of systems of thought.'[33] This eases the burden of the caregiver and provides a conducive environment for thriving for the disabled persons, but it must be done in ways that preserve the self-respect and worth of the individual persons. The extent to which the society recognizes or fails to recognise its obligation to disabled persons while preserving their dignity takes a central place in the perennial issues of social justice for persons with disability. But what is social justice?

88   *Ethics of albinism in African traditions*

Social justice takes a central place in moral and political discourses in philosophy and the social sciences. It has been variedly defined and employed in these discourses, but in the words of Jost and Kay:

> By synthesising the common elements of various philosophical treatments, it is possible to offer a general definition of social justice as a state of affairs (either actual or ideal) in which (a) benefits and burdens in society are dispersed in accordance with some allocation principles (a set of principles); (b) procedures, norms and rules that govern political and other forms of decision making preserves the basic rights, liberties, and entitlements of individuals and groups; and (c) human beings (and perhaps other species) are treated with dignity and respect not only by authorities but also by other relevant social actors, including fellow citizens... A theory of social justice need not address all three aspects, but it should address at least one of them. Conceived in this way, social justice is a property of social systems... A just social system is to be contrasted with those systems that foster arbitrary or unnecessary suffering, exploitation, abuse, tyranny, oppression, prejudice and discrimination.[34]

Notice that in (a), for instance, what is dispersed or distributed are not just benefits but also *burdens*. This is important because if only benefits are distributed, only a few in the society would bear the burdens and this, of course, becomes an unjust situation. Also, (c) places emphasis on the preservation of the dignity of individual persons in social interaction. In sum, social justice 'involves finding the optimum balance between our joint responsibilities as a society and our responsibilities as individuals to contribute to a just society.'[35]

Social justice for persons with disability in general and persons with albinism in particular therefore implies two major things. First, it implies fair treatment of such persons by a society and its institutions. This implies that a society, its institutions and its rules of allocation take into account the special challenges faced by those with albinism and allocate resources to assist them with those challenges. Take, for instance, the role of the society in ensuring that persons with albinism benefit from universal basic education. It would not be enough for a society to ensure that all children are in school. The society must put into consideration the challenges of children with albinism that may hinder them from benefiting from such arrangement and take conscious steps to address them. For instance, due to poor vision, persons with albinism find it difficult to cope in classrooms. They find it difficult to see what is written on the board and this affects greatly their learning process in general. If a society really wishes to actualise social justice for all, including persons with albinism, she must find ways to ensure that this challenge is taken care of so that such persons can learn. It may involve providing special visual gadgets or arranging special sitting positions in classes

Ethics of albinism in African traditions 89

for such persons. In this way, they do not miss out on the benefits of education. Consider also the scenario in the Nigerian education system. Students are involved in doing some maintenance work such as caring for the school compound by cutting grass for a reasonable amount of time under the sun. A just social system would put in considerations for students with albinism. Knowing fully well that persons with albinism should not be under the sun for even a short period of time since it is hazardous to their health, school heads ought to ensure that such persons carry out more indoor activities than participate in outdoor activities.

But currently in African societies, this situation is different and far from ideal. Students with albinism struggle to learn under the same conditions as students with melaninism. They are unable to see what the teacher writes on the board. In many cases, they have to get up from their seats and move very close to the board to see what has been written before going back to their seats to write it down in their notebooks. This is often stressful for them and they also have to deal with teachers and students making jest of them. Again, they participate fully as other students do in outdoor activities such as cutting grass and standing in assembly grounds for a long periods of time under the hot sun (long enough to cause sun burn) just like every other student, without consideration for their peculiar situation.[36] Hence the years of attending school become a means of developing skin cancer for many students with albinism because no attention is paid to their disability. Therefore, a society would not be just if the principles of allocation of benefits do not take into consideration the peculiar situations of its citizens with albinism in Africa.

Beyond the allocation of benefits, it is important for a society to fairly disperse burdens as well for it to be considered just. Caring for a person with a disability is not an easy task, particularly during the early years of existence. Accurate knowledge about the condition is essential. Provision of special healthcare and educational services by the relevant social institutions is also important. Unfortunately the situation in most African societies today is the exact opposite. The duty to care, and the accompanying burden, is left solely to the immediate caregiver — the mother, the father, the parent, a friend, or a sibling. The society does not only shy away from a fair distribution of burden, they play an important role in compounding the burden of the one who cares and the one being cared for. The social institutions in modern African societies reinforce and corroborate the traditional perceptions of albinism as not only queer but harmful. In 1994, I had written an entrance exam to gain admission to a reputable Catholic minor seminary in Nigeria for secondary school education. I had performed very well in the examination and then the forms and scores were sent to the school from the unit where I sat for the exam. Although being the best candidate from my unit — the then Parish Priest of the Catholic Church had publicly and proudly announced this in the Sunday mass service immediately after the examination, the school refused to take me on the basis that I had albinism.

90 *Ethics of albinism in African traditions*

I finally gained admission to a much more secular school. Interestingly, the proprietor of the school had a likeness for me and was happy giving me the admission. But the teachers weren't so friendly. For the years I spent in secondary school, I had to deal with a schooling system that in many ways perpetuated the beliefs of the old order about albinism. The discrimination and stigmatisation were open and obvious from both teachers and students. My Introduction to Technology teacher in my Junior Secondary School 3 told me once in class that if it were decades before, I would have been left in the evil forest to die because I was, to him, completely useless being in the class. These instances are merely a reflection of the larger picture. They showcase the precarious situations that persons with albinism go through on a daily basis in sub-Saharan Africa. The social institutions in Africa therefore have a long way to go in ensuring that the society is just and fair for persons with albinism. The lack of social justice for persons with albinism in sub-Saharan Africa has resulted in the establishment of a number of human rights foundations and activist groups for persons with albinism. These movements have, however, had little success because the deeply entrenched ideologies about albinism are still very much deeply rooted and in place. And in most cases, the agenda is never really clear. It is not enough to advocate for the rights of persons with albinism without stating clearly how the society can be involved in ensuring a just and fair society for such persons to live in.

Second, it is one thing to distribute benefits and burden in such a way that the person with albinism is treated fairly. It is another thing to ensure that such is done in ways that do not trample on the rights, dignity and self-respect of individual persons with albinism involved as well as their caregivers. The term *dignity* itself is one of the most essentially contested concepts in human history. In modern times, the contestation of the ethical, legal and biological meanings of the term has greatly increased.[37] But dignity, it seems to me, has to do with showing respect and recognising the worth of a person as an autonomous and valuable being. Hence, when someone says that she desires to be dignified or that she lost her dignity when she stole from the mall, she is say nothing more than, 'I love to be respected and valued' or 'I lost my respect and value when I stole. Hence, dignifying a person with albinism in the process of easing his burden and providing him with social benefits that take cognizance of his situation is to show respect and recognise the worth and value of such a person as a human being. It would be wrong, therefore, for society to provide for the needs of persons with albinism in a manner that further dehumanises and devalues them. It is important that the provisions made for persons with albinism to ensure just and fair treatment helps to enhance their dignity and autonomy such that in no distant time, as they reach adulthood, they can care for themselves and ease the burden on society. Hence, as has been observed in some African countries, it is wrong and not dignifying to bring children with albinism together in one place, providing them with their daily needs such as food and clothing, without helping them to become educated and acquire skills

Ethics of albinism in African traditions 91

to fend for themselves. They grow up not knowing how to live a dignified, independent life. Such societies are only concerned with protecting such children with albinism from predators seeking to kill them for their body parts that they completely forget to empower and dignify them. But this would simply be preventing one problem while ignoring others.

The challenge of an elitist virtue ethic

One major challenge to overcoming the maltreatment of persons with albinism is to be found in a firmly established elitist virtue ethics in African traditions. By elitist virtue ethics, I mean the evaluation of the permissibility or impermissibility of actions based on the perspective of the custodians of the traditions of the people, the elite. Virtue ethics, as an ethical theory, places emphasis on a person's character as the fundamental factor to consider in making moral judgements rather than normative principles of moral actions. As Rosalind Hursthouse puts it, 'An act is right if and only if it is what a virtuous agent would, characteristically do in the circumstances.'[38]

In traditional African societies, the virtuous agent is the elite group that, as we learned in the previous chapter, include such important social agents in traditional African societies as the elder, chief, king and chief priests. People in an African society look up to these virtuous agents for guidance on what is right and wrong on a daily basis. Suppose I bring a young, beautiful lady home to my father as the lady I wish to marry, but she has albinism. And my father says it is not right to get married to her for the reason that she has albinism. I insist and try to convince him that I do love this girl and I really want to marry her. But the more I insist, the more he stands his ground and provides reasons why he cannot bless my union with a girl with albinism. Some of the reasons he gives is that it is unfortunate that I am ignorant about the ways and culture of the people because he is aware that it brings nothing but bad luck to be close to a person with albinism. He goes as far as threatening me that if I insist on going ahead with the marriage, I should know that I am doing it without his approval. If I have always seen my dad as an important source of learning about moral values, about what is right and wrong, a role model, I am likely to call off the wedding plans with the girl because I live by an elitist virtue approach to morality, believing that my father's moral perspective is wise and reliable.

Many persons in Africa today live primarily by the alleged virtue of the elite group. They evaluate the rightness or wrongness of their actions, using the elite as a standard. Hence, many persons refuse to associate with persons with albinism and to treat them with dignity because the virtuous agents they look up to do the same. For instance, if a king in an African community suddenly gets married to a lady with albinism and provides to his people reasons for his actions such as that the marriage would bring him blessing and fruitfulness and that the ancestors had blessed the union, it will not take long for many other young men within the community to

92   *Ethics of albinism in African traditions*

start seeking out young girls with albinism for marriage because one of their most respected virtuous agents has done so.

As questionable as the virtue of the elite may be, the moral authority they enjoy remain a major challenge that must be tackled if the discrimination against persons with albinism must be dealt with. This implies that the elite class is an important group to focus on in any attempt to overcome the prejudice against albinism. If the elite class is properly enlightened about albinism, and their perspectives change due to new facts brought before them, it will go a long way in shaping the views of many in the community in which they belong. How exactly can the elite class be educated about albinism? We shall return back to this point in the last chapter of this book.

There are obviously many issues for the ethicist to grapple with regarding albinism in Africa. This chapter in no way exhausts the issues, but rather, it attempts to point readers to the paths of discourse to focus on. But the few issues examined in this chapter show very clearly that persons with albinism are in a precarious and unfair situation. They live in societies without justice and fairness to them. The systems in the society are structured in ways that immensely diminish their self-worth and dignity. Many persons with albinism strive every day to live beyond these circumstances and lead meaningful lives. Many fail due to the existential situations in which they find themselves. Very few succeed in overcoming these prejudices and make meaning out of their socially condemned existence. Many contemplate suicide; many withdraw from existing and become beings that are simply there, passively occupying space, waiting for death. How do persons with albinism react to the prejudice and discrimination they face? Why have some resulted to suicide? What peculiar existential experiences do females with albinism face? The next chapter focuses on these existential issues faced by persons with albinism.

Notes

1. Thaddeus Metz (2007). 'Toward an African Moral Theory'. *The Journal of Political Philosophy*. 15.3: 321–341.
2. Polycarp Ikuenobe (2006). *Philosophical Perspective on Communalism and Morality in African Traditions* (Lanham: Lexington Books). 65.
3. G. Setiloane (1998). 'Towards a Biocentric Theology and Ethics — via Africa.' Du-Toit, C. W. Ed. *Faith, Science, and African Culture: African Cosmology and Africa's Contribution to Science* (Pretoria: UNISA). 79.
4. Thaddeus Metz, 'Toward an African Moral Theory'. 326.
5. For a detailed analysis of U1 to U6, see Thaddeus Metz, Toward an African Moral Theory. 328–334.
6. Metz cites a number of such scholarly literatures including Benezet Bujo (2003) *Foundations of an African Ethic* (Kenya: Paulines Publications Africa); and Kwame Gyekye (1987), '*An Essay on African Philosophical Thought*' (Cambridge: Cambridge University Press).
7. Thaddeus Metz, 'Toward an African Moral Theory'. 331.
8. Cf. Metz's counterexample. 331–332.
9. Thaddeus Metz, 'Toward an African Moral Theory'. 332.

Ethics of albinism in African traditions 93

10. Thaddeus Metz, 'Toward an African Moral Theory'. 334.
11. P. Ikuenobe, *Philosophical Perspective on Communalism and Morality in African Traditions*. 65.
12. Desmond Tutu (1999). *No Future without Forgiveness* (New York: Random House). 35.
13. P. J. Nel (2008). 'Morality and Religion in African Thought'. *Acta Theologica* 2: 46.
14. Jack A. Aigbodioh (2011). 'Stigmatization in African Communalistic Societies and Habermas' Theory of Rationality'. *Cultura: International Journal of Philosophy of Culture and Axiology*. 8.1: 31.
15. KwasiWiredu (1980). *Philosophy and an African Culture* (Cambridge: Cambridge University Press). 6.
16. Jack A. Aigbodioh, 'Stigmatization in African Communalistic Societies and Habermas' Theory of Rationality'. 30.
17. Kwame Gyekye, 'African Cultural Values'. 58–59.
18. SegunGbadagesin, (1998). Yoruba Philosophy: Individuality, Community and the Moral Order. Eze, E. C. Ed. *African Philosophy: An Anthology*. Oxford: Blackwell Publishing. 130–141.
19. John Mbiti, *African Religion and Philosophy*. 36. V. Y. Mudimbe (1988). Has accused Mbiti of over-Christianizing the issue of the effect of religion on morality in Africa in his book *The Invention of Africa: Philosophy and the Order of Knowledge*. London: James Currey.
20. Bolaji Idowu (1966). *Olodumare: God in Yoruba Belief.* New Jersey: Prentice Hall Press. 144–146. This view is also shared by Akin Makinde (1988). *African Philosophy, Culture and Traditional Medicine*. Ohio: Ohio University Press.
21. Kwame Gyekye, *African Cultural Values: An Introduction*. 57.
22. John Mbiti, *African Religion and Philosophy*. 38–39.
23. Infeanyi A. Menkiti, 'On the Normative Conception of a Person'. 326.
24. Olusegun Oladipo (1996). *Philosophy and the African Experience: The Contributions of KwasiWiredu* (Ibadan: Hope Publications). 58. See also KwasiWiredu, Philosophy and an African Culture. 53.
25. ElechiAmadi (1982). *Ethics in Nigerian Culture* (Ibadan: Heinemann Educational Books Ltd.). 6; the emphasis is mine.
26. Eva FederKittay (2011). 'The Ethics of Care, Dependence and Disability'. *Ratio Juris: An International Journal of Jurisprudence and Philosophy of Law*, 24.1: 52–53.
27. See Barbara H. Andolsen (1993). 'Justice, Gender and the Frail Elderly: Reexamining the Ethic of Care'. *Journal of Feminist Studies in Religion*, 9.1: 135–137.
28. Barbara H. Andolsen, 'Justice, Gender and the Frail Elderly'. 137.
29. Barbara H. Andolsen, 'Justice, Gender and the Frail Elderly'. 137–139.
30. I have experienced real-life situations where this happens. I know of a man who refused to support the care given to his two daughters with albinism by his wife. This consisted of his refusal to pay their school fees, provide for their clothing and attend to their needs in general, except allowing them to eat from the meal in the house. The wife had to work very hard to provide these things for the girls, including paying their school fees. But he pays regularly the tuition fees of the other three children without albinism. He tell his friends that it is a waste of money to send a child with albinism to school or spend money on the child training. Although he lives in one of the cities in Nigeria with his family, where there are no more killing of infants with albinism, it is obvious that if it was in the time past, he would have definitely supported killing the girls after they were born.
31. My parents did this to me as well. And denying a person salt intake, particularly a growing child, is not always best for her health. But as my mum always

94　*Ethics of albinism in African traditions*

told me when I was young, it was the best way to keep my skin clean and neat. Thus, even when I didn't like the food I ate, and I felt cheated that my other siblings enjoyed their food with salt, I had to understand that my mother was trying to do her best for me.

32. A friend of mine had such an experience with health workers in a federal hospital in Nigeria. He had sores on his face due to exposure to sun. He had gone to the hospital to see if he could be treated, but the team of doctors that attended to him treated him so badly that he left the hospital in tears, and without any medical assistance, of course.

33. John Rawls (1971). A theory of Justice.

34. John T. Jost and Aaron C. Kay (2010). 'Social Justice: History, Theory and Research'. In S. Fiske and D. Gilbert (Eds.), *Handbook of Social Psychology* (New Jersey: John Wiley and Sons). 1,122. In this quotation, Jost and Kay state that the three aspects mentioned as (a), (b) and (c) each correspond to three forms of justice — namely distributive, procedural and interactional justice. Social justice, therefore, encompassed these various forms of justice.

35. Leanne Ho (2011). 'What is Social Justice: Occasional Paper #1' *National Pro Bono Resource Centre Occasional* Papers (Australia: The University of New South Wales). 2.

36. The first major sunburn experience I had was in Senior Secondary School. My entire class was made to cut grass for about four hours under a relatively hot sun. When I got back home from school, I could not really explain what exactly was going on with my body because it was my first time. I felt extreme pain and was hot all over my body, as if chillies was rubbed on my skin. A neighbour gave my panicking mum a bottle of honey to apply on my skin, and as it was applied to my skin, my body was literally smoking. In the next few days, my skin started peeling off completely in the same way the skin of someone who had a fire burn would. I wasn't able to go to school for a few days. My father went to school to ask the class teacher why he allowed me to participate in the exercise. The simple answer was that he wasn't aware that my participation would result in the obvious consequences, another tale of ignorance.

37. See, for example, these recent essays on the essentially contested nature of the concept of 'dignity': David J. Mattson and Susan G. Clark (2011). 'Human Dignity in Concept and in Practice'. *Policy Sciences*, 44.4: 303–319; Ruth Macklin (2003). 'Dignity is a Useless Concept: It Means No More Than Respect for Persons or Their Autonomy'. *British Medical Journal*, 327.7429: 1419–1420; Richard Ashcroft (2005). Journal of Medical Ethics, 31.11: 679–682; and Ghan Shaoping and Zhang Lin (2009). Human Dignity as a Right. *Frontiers of Philosophy in China*, 4.3: 370–384.

38. Rosalind Hursthouse (1999). 'Virtue Ethics and Human Nature'. *Hume Studies*, 25.1&2: 67.

5 Albinism in Africa: Some existential issues

Beyond the general notions of the being of persons with albinism in African traditions, the question of how such notions are acquired and become deeply entrenched knowledge claims and the moral issues that emerge therein, a philosophical analysis of albinism in Africa would be incomplete without shifting the horizon of discourse to the existential perspective on the matter. This involves encountering the intricacies of existence of persons with albinism in African societies, not from the standpoint of the community, but from the personal experiences of persons with albinism themselves. To be sure, their personal experiences and their perceptions of existence are not clear cut from the ideas and knowledge claims about their beings that we have spent more than half of this book discussing. In fact, such ideas and knowledge claims inherent in the communities in which they find themselves have strong effects on their everyday existences. But it is important to see beyond these and get into the skin of a person with albinism to see the extent to which she is overwhelmed by the socio-cultural understanding of albinism and the possibilities of making meaning of her existence within such contexts. It involves understanding her pain, suffering, frustrations demands, fears and anxieties; her joy, choices, exercise of freedom, boldness, projection and possibilities. It consists of analysing the extent to which society has determined the meaningfulness and meaninglessness of her existence, and the extent to which she has done so on her own terms. Thus, an existentialist analysis of albinism in Africa is an attempt to encounter a person with albinism as she exists, dwells within and occupies an African place and how she makes meaning out of her encounter of such an existential space.

Perhaps an appropriate point to begin contemplating the existence of a person with albinism, or, indeed, every human being, is to be found in Martin Heidegger's German concept of *Geworfenheit*, best translated as 'thrownness' according to William J. Richardson.[1] A purely ontological fact of our being is that we are all thrown into existence. No human being plays an active role in deciding how, when, where or under what and what circumstances she would come into being. We simply, at some point, become conscious that we exist. We have no say over the days we should be born, where

96 *Albinism in Africa: Some existential issues*

we would love to be born, the physical qualities we would love to have and other aspects of our being. The families we are born into, the communities in which we find ourselves and our physical appearances are completely out of our hands. We come into this would finding ourselves to be black, white, short, tall, disabled, non-disabled, rich, poor and so on. Our thrownness into the world reveals our finitude and limitations. More so, the place in which our thrownness occurs and in which we become conscious of our existence immensely determines how we exist. The families and communities in which we are brought up decide our values, our understanding of the world and things around us, our perception of ourselves and other beings including fellow humans. Whether we continue to live by such socially infused values and meanings or we grow up to choose to war against them and make our own meanings of life, they remain the determinant of how we live, how we fight, what we fight for and what we fight against.

Hence, two things stand out from the very moments we become existentially conscious: the ontological fact of our thrownness and the ontological priority of the community. The latter is often so intensely felt that it does well in veiling the former. The ideas about where we come from and how we develop within the cultures and societies we are thrown into remains a reliable veil that covers the very fact of our thrownness, for many from the day they become conscious to the day they die. Hence, due to socially infused values and beliefs, many do not consider themselves as thrown into existence; many live by the concealing idea of coming from an other-worldly existence with a destiny of some sort. The moment they accept this notion of their being, they become bound to live by social standards for the rest of their being. Only few have risen above such bedtime stories and confronted their existence as it lay bare to them, not shrouded in any myth or tale of some other-worldly existence. And going against already established social systems and values remains one of the most difficult tasks any human being can engage in, no matter how convinced she is that it is the right thing to do.

Now, persons with disabilities and queer beings are thrown into much more perplexing and difficult circumstances. Every place of human dwelling already has certain established facts, assumptions and myths about disabilities and queerness. Every person with disability or queerness thrown into each particular world is confronted from the very day she becomes conscious of her existence with these established notions of her being, which are in many cases harmful and discriminatory. The conventional though unpleasant path to follow for a person with disability is to struggle and endure within the established representations. A few however would take the more difficult and narrow path, which is to live outside such representations and attempt to forge out a meaningful existence. In this chapter, I am primarily concerned with how a person with albinism in African societies is confronted with the former and what is involved in attempting the latter. I begin by examining how fear becomes an integral part of the existential ontology of a person with albinism in African societies due to established notions about his being within such places. I examine also how difficult it is for such a person to build courage and overcome fear. I then proceed to examine how the major features of the deeply entrenched ideas about albinism — stigma, discrimination and isolation — result more often than not in the contemplation of suicide. It remains a difficult task for persons with albinism to find hope to stay strong and alive. This is followed by an examination of certain existential situations faced peculiarly by females with albinism due to beliefs and ideas about their beings that are engrained in African societies. This includes the issue of rape, which has been increasingly perpetrated on women with albinism in recent time. What becomes obvious from these analyses is that although a difficult task to achieve, the person with albinism can rise above the socially infused absurdities and arbitrariness of life. Many persons with albinism have risen above such representations and have made existence to be a meaningful one for themselves, earning respect and honour from members of the community.

Fear and dread

To understand why fear, dread, anxiety and a general feeling of angst is a defining quality of the existential experience of persons with albinism in African societies, it is perhaps fitting to begin by saying a few things about existence itself, that is, what it means to say an entity exists. To exist consists of the ability of an entity to occupy or inhabit a here, a region of being, a sphere of events, happenings and situation at any given point in time in a manner that it is able to make meaning out of the here that it occupies. By implication, in inhabiting a here, an existent inhabits a sphere of meaning where other beings reveal themselves to it and influence its meaning, and where it is able to find and create meaning for itself.[2] As Heidegger explains throughout his works, existence is being there in the sense of openness to itself and others in a manner that is fluid and dynamic.[3] Thus, to exist is to be in the world — occupy a here and to be with and interact with others.[4] In existentialist thought, only human beings are qualified as existing. Other beings merely are. This means that only human beings have the capacity to inhabit a here in the actual sense because in their being there, they reflect on and make sense of the here they occupy and choose — even in difficult situations — to either transcend the meanings inherent in the here they occupy and create new meanings for themselves.

In their being there, human beings find themselves thrown into a world of multifaceted and perplexing experiences, events and happenings, some of which we have no control over. More so, a human being finds herself with her kind, who collectively try to impose meaning on her being. In this eventing of existence, particularly in her confrontation with perplexing experiences, she is bound to have phases of fear, dread, anger, frustration, pain, suffering and angst. However, these are in many cases momentary and temporal.

98 Albinism in Africa: Some existential issues

There are also times of joy, peace, happiness, courage and boldness. Human existence is therefore conventionally characterised with a mixture of such contrary experiences as anxiety and calmness, fear and courage, dread and boldness, suffering and joy. But what is of interest to us here is the unconventional nature of the experience of fear, anxiety and dread by the majority of persons with albinism in African societies.

Although fear and dread is conventionally momentary, it becomes a defining quality and an essential feature of the being of persons with albinism in many African communities. Their existence is intrinsically characterised by persistent fear and dread; the dread of being hunted and killed for their body parts; the fear of going out and walking on the streets due to name calling and mocking; the fear of going out when the sun shines due to the hazards of consistent sun burn; anxiety of going to school due to consistent mocking by school mates and the difficulty to see; angst about never being able to get married, raise a family, get a good job and live a normal life. It is an everyday existence characterised by fear from the day the person with albinism is conscious of her existence to the day she dies. A CNN graphic and quite disturbing 2016 report on the hunting of persons with albinism in Malawi aptly captures the being-with-fear existential nature of persons with albinism:

> For Agness Jonathan [a mother with two daughters with albinism], every day is a gamble with her children's lives. Simple questions like whether they should go to school carry an unimaginable risk of death and dismemberment to satisfy a barbaric demand. This is because her daughters are living with albinism… And this makes them a target. It is children like Agness who … are being hunted like animals in Malawi where their bones are sold in the belief the body parts bring wealth, happiness and good luck. The bloodiest month was April this year, when Amnesty says four people were murdered, including a baby. One of the victims was 17-year-old Davis Fletcher Machinjiri, who left his home to watch a soccer game with a friend, but never returned. The Malawian police say he was abducted by "about four men who trafficked him to Mozambique and killed him." Describing his gruesome death, they say "the men chopped off both his arms and legs and removed bones. They then buried the rest of his body in a shallow grave."[5]

The report adds that:

> Attackers are known to sell body parts to witch doctors in Malawi and neighbouring Mozambique, hoping to make quick money. Amnesty says "thousands of people with albinism are at severe risk of abduction and killing by individuals and criminal gangs," while the United Nations warns that Malawi's albinos are at risk of "total extinction."… Grace Mazzah, a board member of the Association of People with

Albinism in Africa: Some existential issues 99

Albinism in Malawi, is always aware of the price on her head. "It really raises fear," she says. "Why should people hunt me like they're hunting for animals to eat?"[6]

The kind of fear and angst that persons with albinism go through in Africa is thus caused by both physical and social factors. The physical factor consists of biological and environmental factors of persons with albinism. In terms of the environmental factor, there is always an anxiety about carrying out activities in the open sun without getting harmed. Concerning the biological factors, many persons with albinism suffer greatly from poor vision. It affects class performance and other activities. Many drop out of school because of the fear of not being able to cope, and many beg on the street to survive, particularly when family fails to give the needed support. This sort of fear never goes away. By the very nature of persons with albinism, they cannot completely overcome such fears and anxieties. Living an authentic life for such persons does not include doing away with the fears and anxieties about the hot sun and poor vision and living as if such concerns do not exist. Living an authentic life, rather, involves coping with such anxieties, being deliberately and actively concerned about them, and devising means of leading a meaningful and fulfilling life even with the presence of such anxieties. Coping with this fear of the sun involves taking conscious efforts to protect oneself from it and avoid it as much as possible. Many persons with albinism do not consciously attempt to cope with these anxieties and it is often not deliberate. They and their caregivers are often not aware of the problem until it is too late. They often learn the hard way from the experiences of the problem (the sun and the effects of poor vision) and the anxieties that ensue from them. The few well-informed persons with albinism and their mostly educated families (primary caregivers) deliberately reduce the anxieties by reducing contact with the sun and providing aiding glasses at an early age. In this way, their fear of the physical factor is reduced and they are able to focus on living meaningful lives.

The social factors that cause anxiety and fear have been discussed many times in this book. They have to do with the representations of albinism in African communities and the consequences of such representations. Again, this anxiety is not what any person with albinism living in some part of sub-Saharan Africa can ignore. In fact, to be able to live a meaningful and authentic life, a person with albinism must acknowledge these representations not as true representations of their being, but as representations and ideas that can harm their being if not tackled. To be sure, the anxiety caused by social representations is real. I fear going to many parts of sub-Saharan Africa — particularly the Eastern part — to live, work or even to attend a conference. I am anxious about how long I would survive without someone remembering one day that I would fetch him a good deal of money. For instance, I wanted to send a proposal to attend a conference in Tanzania and certain disturbing questions made me refrain from applying. What if

100 *Albinism in Africa: Some existential issues*

I arrive at the airport at night and the taxi driver I pay to take me to the hotel decides to take me somewhere else? When I get to the airport in Lagos, Nigeria, particularly at night, I am not only worried about being robbed; I am also worried about getting into the taxi of someone who believes strongly in the social representations of my person. So, I make arrangements for a friend to meet me at the airport so that I am not alone. When I am about to leave my house everyday, I am worried about how many children and adults, who I do not know in any way, will hoot at me the moment they see me, how many embarrassing situations I might face on that day.

This angst and anxiety does not go away during the daily existence of a person with albinism. It means that it requires a higher form of perseverance, determination and resilience and an accurate knowledge of albinism as a human condition for a person with albinism to survive and lead a meaningful life. A strong sense of security and consciousness for survival is needed. Many persons with albinism have fled their homes due to the fear of being killed.[7] Others take other forms of precautions to stay safe. Unfortunately, many have been overwhelmed with the fear that arises from these social factors. There are a number of reasons for this. Many persons with albinism (and their caregivers) do not have the accurate understating of the condition and, thus, live by the representation of the condition present in the societies in which they live. This overwhelms them and they live every day in pain and fear. Again, many live in remote villages and rural areas where the hunting for body parts of persons with albinism is much more pervasive than in others. In February 2017 a Malawian lady with albinism, Femia Tchulani, who had already survived an attempted kidnapping by people wanting to kill her for her body parts, said she is scared to sleep at night. She adds that:

> Before the incident, I could go to the place where we buy vegetables in bulk, and I would go door to door selling them. Now I am always afraid to move deep into the township. So all I'm left with is the bench at the market, where I sell from. As a result, I cannot make enough money for my children's school fees, uniforms and even for food, because I have to restrict myself to the market stall. Now some of our children have been sent home from school. I don't feel that the police or government are doing anything to protect people with albinism like me.[8]

Hence having accurate knowledge about the conditions, taking measures to protect oneself and being firmly resilient and determined to survive are essential for coping.

Therefore, this fear and dread cannot be completely overcome. They always remain present, and a person with albinism can only be firmly determined to cope with them by first recognizing and acknowledging that they exist and that they cause her angst. Having accurate knowledge of their nature and taking necessary precautions to cope with them is fundamental to leading a meaningful life.

Alienation, suicide contemplation and authentic living

In the words of Ramakant Sinari:

> The phenomenon of human alienation has today become so complex and multidimensional that any amount of analysis, from whichever aspect one can think of, is inadequate to exactly tell us where to locate its causes and how to avoid its undesirable effects... like every concept that grows intentionally as more and more akin forms of experience are brought under it, the concept of alienation has growAn in its meaning-content.[9]

This is true because alienation has become an important concept that assumes different meanings in different contexts such as political, philosophical, religious, educational, social-scientific and existentialist discourses. Sinari identifies seven senses in which we can talk of someone as alienated in different contexts:

1 alienation of an individual from an object or objects to which he is attached;
2 alienation of one from society 'in the event of one's belonging to a minority — religious, ethnic, linguistic, occupational, etc. — in a place where affairs are determined by the majority;
3 alienation of one who shows dissension with regard to the values and ideals society stands for; from such a dissension might, emerge ethical rebels and social reformers;
4 alienation of a person who disapproves of his self and thus experiences a peculiar sort of self-estrangement; this self-estrangement might occasionally give rise to neuroses, but if properly manipulated by the rational censor may produce creative genius;
5 alienation of one who in a highly industrialized and technologically oriented society as in the U.S. gradually ceases to use one's body; more and more use of buttons and switches deprives one from the natural physical operations; this eventually causes a rupture between man and Nature;
6 alienation of those who are uprooted from their cultural habitat; this peculiar form of estrangement can be witnessed in all those countries where, as a result of prolonged Western influence, people experience isolation from their original ethos;
7 alienation of a person or of a class that is exploited, or whose interests are downtrodden, by another person or class; it is this form of alienation that figures as the central issue of Marx's, Engels's, and of all socialists' thinking.[10]

102　Albinism in Africa: Some existential issues

These senses of alienation are, however, subsumed under the broad under-standing of alienation in existentialism. This is because, in existentialism, alienation consists of the estrangement or isolation of a person from him-self, others or the world due to systemic representation of himself to others and the world. Thus, whether the person is estranged from an object, social group, class or a value system, the estrangement is caused by already exist-ing social structures and representations into which one is thrown. Hence in existentialism, alienation is seen as a state of inauthenticity because it implies living not by one's choices and convictions but rather by social struc-tures and values. For Heidegger, for instance, this is the conventional way we all live. In his word, it is 'that kind of Being which is closest to *Dasein* and in which *Dasein* maintain itself for the most part.'[11] Hence it takes a strong will and determination to live outside such a box of existence.

It is within this context of the existential understanding of alienation that I wish to examine the alienation of persons with albinism from self and others, an alienation caused by the representations of their being in the society in which they are thrown into and the consequent stigmatisation and discrimination. When a person with albinism becomes conscious of her existence in an African community, she also gradually becomes conscious of how the world in which she finds herself perceives and understands her being. While in childhood innocence, she relates with the world and others with openness and without boundaries. In this relation with the world and others, over time, she gradually becomes conscious of the hatred, disdain, social stigma, ill-treatment and discrimination the system and those in it has for her. The debasement of her personhood steadily becomes vivid to her. So, while she struggles to relate with the world and with others — a nec-essary outcome of her ontological nature of being a being-in-the-world and a being-with-others — the world by its very structures and value systems struggle to isolate her and cut her off, and they succeed quite well in doing this, turning her into a being-to-herself.

A young girl with albinism is excited because she is going to school for the first time. She puts on her school uniform and feels on top of the world. He parent drops her off at the school gate and a drama begins to unfold right in front of her, probably for the first time. Fellow schoolmates stare at her in awe, call her derogatory names, some of which she understands, others she does not, but she recognizes that it is name-calling. The class begins and she tries to write down in her book what the teacher has written on the board and asks the pupils to write down. But it dawns on her that she can-not see what is on the board. Others are writing, but she is unable to. Then the teacher comes to her desk and sees that she is not writing. Rather than offering help, the teacher scolds her and calls her names and the entire class makes jest of her. So, although leaving home that morning for school happy and full of life, she returns home sad and dejected. This debasing experi-ence continues day after day, month after month, year after year, in different spheres of her existence, at school, in the market place, in the church, on the

Albinism in Africa: Some existential issues 103

streets and other places of coexistence. It continues until she assimilates the unpleasant facticities of life into her subconscious being: 'I am not wanted around; people do not like me; I should be on my own.' Hence, at her teenage and adult years, she may be in pain but she is no longer surprised that people refuse to sit on the same row with her in the church until there is no other seat left to use; that her seatmate in school is not comfortable sitting with her; that when she sells things in the market, many turn the other way when they see her; that when she gets into a bus, no one wants to sit close to her, except there is no other seat around and some would even prefer to wait for the next bus than take the only seat left since it is close to her. These moments become the life she is used to, even though she may not like it.

The unpleasant facticity of her being becomes even more difficult to live with when it comes from her immediate family members. She slowly gives up inside of her when she sees her mother struggling alone to care for her and her father wants absolutely nothing to do with her. She cannot run to him and hug him when he returns from work because he would scold her and turn her away. Although her immediate elder brother loves her and cares for her, her other siblings make jest of her and refuse to play with her. It is difficult to bear the degradation and debasement of her person in school, church, bus, market places and so on; it is much more difficult and almost unbearable to cope with the same attitude under the roof she lives . Some persons with albinism have left home because of the pain that results from being turned away by family members who do not care about their well-being, and they have turned to begging and scavenging as the only means of survival.

The facticity of existence for a person with albinism is even more compounded when it dawns on her that she is not even considered by many others as having the same status of a human being as others do. So expecting to be treated and dignified as a human being would be to be expecting too much for her. In Cameroon and many other Western and Eastern African countries, for instance, persons with albinism are considered not as human beings but as divine gifts to men to be sacrificed for certain ends. Stephane Ebongue succinctly puts it in an interview that:

It has always been this way; they consider that albinos are gifts, sources of protection: a politician who wants to win elections, a national football team that wants to win a competition that will give glory to the entire nation, a military head who wants to become invisible or [have] the power to defeat or have to become invulnerable to bullet. At times, a woman will want to seduce the rebellious heart of a man who does not return her affections, so she asks for albino hair to mix into a love potion — the minimum. Sometimes it is believed that when fishermen weave the hair of an albino into their nets, it brings an abundance of fish, but this is still the minimum, hair, nails etc. However, to win the elections you need an albino heart, to prevent a natural catastrophe

104   *Albinism in Africa: Some existential issues*

you need the head, the body, the entire albino. It is believed that only the blood of one or more albinos could placate the god following the eruption of the volcano. And so these things are not at the same level.[12]

He adds that:

… on the eve of Election Day, politicians will make human sacrifices to win. When a politician has not won a government seat he thinks that maybe his witch doctor was not capable or strong enough to properly use the sacrifice — the next time he turns to a stronger witch doctor. When you have elections only two outcomes are possible, someone wins and someone loses, the winner had a stronger witch doctor and the loser will turn to a stronger witch doctor the next time. Football matches are also occasions for which albinos are murdered. Albinos can be sacrificed to go as far as possible in the competition. Again, when a team loses they believe that the witch doctor was not skilled enough… the next time you take another and so the cycle perpetuates itself.[13]

Confronted with the facticities peculiar to her existence, the person with albinism shrinks away from everything including her own being. As it is with the existential ontology of a human being, she fits into the isolating system, accepting and recognizing herself as different, unwanted and despised and on the basis of the cultural conception of her being, she begins to isolate herself from her own very nature, taking herself to be cursed, inferior, not deserving of relations and possessing supernatural powers which the *real* human being are wont to harness from her. The isolation and withdrawal tears her apart. Every day becomes a struggle to keep living while waiting for the inevitable, death. Death for many persons living with albinism becomes the most meaningful and sought after event life can offer, something to long for that would bring an end to the pain and suffering. While many persons with albinism contemplate not to wait for too long for death to come by committing suicide, a few decide to actually take their lives and end the suffering. The Nigerian *Vanguard Newspaper* reported on August 17, 2015 how a twenty-three-year-old man with albinism committed suicide due to discrimination and stigmatisation. According to the report:

A 23-year-old man, Ugochukwu Ekwe, yesterday committed suicide at Festac Town, Lagos, over the colour of his skin being an albino. His dangling body was discovered in an apartment… where he lived with his parents and siblings. *Vanguard* gathered that the deceased refused to eat since Saturday in protest of what he said was people's rejection and stigmatisation because of his skin condition. He was also said to have refused to go to church with other members of the family yesterday. When the family returned from church, Ugo, as he was fondly called,

Albinism in Africa: Some existential issues   105

was dangling at the end of a rope tied to the ceiling fan... Vanguard gathered that the deceased had attempted to take his life before now.[14]

On November 2, 2016, the website Malawi24 reported that a lady with albinism, Tiyamike Robson, committed suicide the same way, by hanging herself in the house. The police, the news reported, were still carrying out an investigation at the time but advised people who had problems to speak up.[15] These instances show how some persons with albinism resort to suicide due to alienation and withdrawal from self and others. They consider it as the only means to release themselves of their existential burdens.

This withdrawal from self and others faced by persons with albinism appears to be a withdrawal from existence — attempting to cease to exist, which, as we have seen, results in suicide in some cases — but, in the real sense, it indicates that the person with albinism is existing in the exact way the society wants her to. Hence, in existentialist terms, the person with albinism is living the way we all live our lives for the most part of it, living in accordance to how the society expects us to, living an inauthentic life. And existentialist philosophers have always and rightly emphasised the fact that living simply by conformity to social rules and expectations or suggestions and recommendations by others without a personal conviction on the matter is not only to live an inauthentic life, but a life devoid of meaning. Hence Heidegger characterises a person living an inauthentic life as *Dasman*;[16] Karl Jasper refers to such a person as the mass man;[17] and Jean-Paul Sartre characterises inauthentic existence as bad-faith.[18] To live an authentic life and create meaning into one's life, a person must find his own way and be convinced about it. This does not in any way imply that persons cannot live by social norms and still find meaning; it only implies that if one must live by social norms, it must be that she is convinced that it is worth living by and deliberately decide to live by such an authentic life. Authentic life in existentialist thought therefore involves discovering and defining oneself, displaying originality even within an ontologically necessary social space.

Now, for a person with albinism to live a meaningful, authentic life that seems to elude her in her conformity to social systems, she needs to play a crucial role in discovering and defining that life. This, to be sure, is the most difficult task that any person with albinism would ever embark on. It would involve a determined and consistent effort to ignore the mocking and jesting, name-calling, hatred and discrimination; it would involve developing a positive outlook and being around those who encourage that positive outlook; it would consist of going against all odds to keep oneself safe and unharmed, educated and enlightened, healthy and beautiful. Like every other quest to find a meaningful existence, getting these done will not be easy. It would require perseverance and determination. A few have done it and have no regrets. They have gone against all odds, suppressed social stigma and discrimination and have been able to lead meaningful lives where the contemplation of suicide is not called to mind. Interestingly, when a person with albinism, like any other person, rises above the challenges and makes meaning out of life for herself, she earns the respect of people around her, of her community. Hence, whereas human beings are generally seen as beings to be dignified by their very nature as human beings and their self-worth recognised, a person with albinism has to earn it for herself.

Today we know of Salif Keita, the Malian artist who was once ostracised by his family and his community because of his albinism, which is considered bad luck in the Mandinka culture, but still made his way to stardom. We know of his adopted daughter, Nantenin Keita, a Paralympian athlete with albinism who has also done very well for herself.[19] Ikponwosa Ero, a young Nigerian girl, has risen beyond all challenges and stigmatisation to become the current independent expert on albinism for the United Nations.[20] Beyond these examples of persons with albinism that have risen to stardom, every community in Africa with persons with albinism has a few examples of such persons rising above the peculiar challenges faced by persons with albinism to become successful medical doctors, tutors, journalists and the like. It is definitely difficult to do this, but it is not impossible. Persons with albinism need to take the meaning of their lives in their own hands rather than wait for society to provide them with the meaningful life that they need. That is the only way they can rise above the current existential facticity of their being.

Peculiar feminine experience of albinism

The existential experiences faced by persons with albinism, some of which have been discussed above, affect both male and female persons with albinism, and both young and old. The stigma, discrimination and ill-treatment are felt by allpersons with albinismin African societies. The degree of discrimination and stigmatisation may vary from society to society, but the effect on persons with albinism within such societies remains the same. The few cases where a person with albinism may be treated differently from others of her kind arise when she strives to live an authentic life. In other words, she has not allowed the society to define her existence; rather she has risen above the challenges and has become someone admirable in the society. Hence, although she has not been dignified by virtue of the fact that she is human, she has earned her dignity through deliberate efforts to distinguish herself in the society in which she lives. Another instance where a person with albinism is able to earn dignity and respect from members of the community and reduce the insults and discrimination against her person — these can only be reduced and not eliminated, and the problem of fear of the insecurity of life remains there — is through the beauty of her visibly different skin. This is often achieved if her caregiver(s) are knowledgeable enough to be able to care for her skin from a very tender age. Hence, as I have experienced in many public spheres in many African societies, a person with albinism would be hooted, jested and insulted more

Albinism in Africa: Some existential issues 107

if her skin is rough looking, and she will be told to imitate another person with albinism whose skin looks clean and well maintained. However, these scenarios of living an authentic life and distinguishing oneself from other persons with albinism through care for one's physical appearance applies to both males and females as well. A male or female with albinism can distinguish himself or herself in these ways. But my concern here is to identify certain existential experiences that occur only to the female folks due to the facticity of albinism in African societies.

There are two main existential experiences that are peculiar to females in the experience of albinism in African societies. The first concerns not the female with albinism, but the black woman who gives birth to a child with albinism. When a black woman gives birth to an infant with albinism in some African traditional community, the child is seen as a divine sign of infidelity or some other form of culpability on the part of the woman. The husband, who is never to blame for the child's pigmentation, may, on the basis of this understanding, make any of the following decisions with the support and backing of his kin: He may decide to send the wife and the child away on the basis of infidelity confirmed solely by the visible appearance of the child. The United Nations Independent Expert on the Enjoyment of Human Rights by Persons with Albinism Ikpomwosa Ero, aptly presents this quagmire thusly:

> A significant lack of awareness on how albinism occurs - that it is a genetic condition transferred by both parents - has a detrimental impact on parents of children with albinism with a disproportionate impact on the mother. The mother is often blamed for causing the pale colouring of the child with albinism. She is often accused of infidelity in her marriage or having contracted a curse embodied as the child with albinism. Consequently, mothers are often abandoned by their husbands on grounds that they have been unfaithful since the child is of a different skin colour. Isolation and expulsion from the community is also commonplace due to the belief that the child with albinism is a curse upon the community. Self-removal from the community also takes place in some cases to avoid hostility from the community.[21]

Also, the husband may decide not to send the wife away but comply with the tradition obtainable in his community of what should be done to the child. In any case, the mother is left traumatised and may become solely responsible for the care and upkeep of the child, which she does with the limited knowledge that she has of albinism.

The second feminine experience of albinism has to do directly with the female with albinism — not the mother. This peculiar existential challenge that has become common in places such as Malawi and Tanzania has to do with the claim by witch doctors that having sexual relations with a girl or woman with albinism would cure a person of the HIV/AIDS virus.

108 *Albinism in Africa: Some existential issues*

A BreitBart news report in 2016 explains the precarious situation for females with albinism thus:

> The pervasive myth that having sex with a person with albinism... can cures AIDS has made rape and sexual assault of women and girls with albinism a commonplace threat in places like Malawi. An Amnesty International report released this week ... exposes the pervasive violence against albino people in Malawi, though the killing, kidnapping, and rape of albinos have long been common in neighbouring countries like Tanzania, as well. These nations have an outsized population of albino people, whose appearance is particularly striking in black villages.[22]

According to the news report, the Amnesty report notes that:

> ... the dangers facing albino women are even higher than that for men... Predatory men would begin a relationship with a woman with albinism with the intention of killing her or selling her for body parts... It is also commonplace for catcalling men to yell the word "cure" at albino women, an indication they seek sex with them because they are HIV positive. Amnesty is clear to note that they were unable to confirm any incidents of rape of albino women, though they attribute this to cultural factors. 'A medical doctor told Amnesty International researchers that generally in Malawian society a woman is blamed for rape, making it more difficult for a woman from a group that experiences extreme marginalization to report the crime,' the report notes. 'Amnesty International... believes that such violations may be taking place without being reported because of victims' fear of stigmatization.'[23]

This experience is peculiar to women with albinism. It is a traumatic existential experience that never goes away, even when a woman with albinism distinguishes herself and earns the respect of community members. This is because the predators are always lingering around looking for an opportunity to attack a girl or woman with albinism. It therefore requires complete vigilance on the part of the women and girls with albinism and more effort to arrest the situation on the part of the state.

Ikponwosa Ero summarises the peculiar existential challenges faced by women and girls with albinism thusly:

> Women with albinism are reportedly victims of targeted acts of sexual violence spurred by the myth and misbelief that sexual intercourse with a woman with albinism can cure HIV/AIDS. Furthermore, women who give birth to a child with albinism may face ostracism and discrimination. They are also exposed to rejection by their husbands or partners, accused of adultery or infidelity and blamed for giving birth to a child

Albinism in Africa: Some existential issues 109

who is generally seen as a curse or a bad omen. The rejection of mothers of children with albinism exposes them to poverty and isolation and increases the vulnerability to attacks of both mother and child with albinism.[24]

Hence, by virtue of being a woman and having the condition of albinism, these persons go through more difficult and traumatic situations that require even more resilience, alertness and determination to overcome. Any attempt by the state, non-governmental organisations and human rights movements to help persons with albinism must take into recognition these peculiarities with the feminine situation.

A key foundation for existentialist thought is the claim that existence precedes essence and not vice versa. Human beings have the capacity to make meaning out of existence. But this is not always an easy task. This is because a socially infused essence precedes our existence. As history shows, the socially constructed essences of black people, Jewish people, White people, Muslims and such categories of persons have preceded them, and the precedence has had consequences for persons within these categories, both positive and negative. Hence to claim that deeply entrenched social representations play no part in the unfolding of a person's existence is to deny the very facticity of existence. As we have seen in this chapter, the socially constructed essences of albinism that have been deeply waxed into African societies have had and continues to have dire consequences for persons with albinism. What does not precede a person's existence is the self-constructed and deliberately developed essence that every human being has the potential to showcase, only if she can look beyond the socially constructed essences and forge one for herself. Perhaps this is the starting point for persons with albinism to live an authentic, meaningful and less dampened life. But this would be an extremely difficult task to achieve if well-meaning stakeholders do not play their part. The final chapter of this book focuses on how this can be done.

Notes

1. William J. Richardson (1963). *Heidegger through Phenomenology to Thought* (New York: Fordham University Press). 37
2. See Gregory Freid and Richard Polt (2000). Translators' Introduction to Martin Heidegger, *Introduction to Metaphysics* (New York: Yale University Press). xi-xii
3. See Frank Schalow and Alfred Denker (2010). *Historical Dictionary of Heidegger's Philosophy,* 2nd Ed. (Lanham: The Scarecrow Press). 107.
4. See Martin Heidegger (1962). *Being and Time*, trans. J. Macquarie and E. Robinson (Oxford: Basil Blackwell, 1962). 60
5. Dominique van Heerden (2016). 'Hunting for Humans: Malawian Albinos Murdered for Their Bones'. CNN. Accessed May 20, 2017 from: http://edition.cnn.com/2016/06/07/africa/africa-albino-hunted-bones-malawi/
6. Dominique van Heerden. 'Hunting for Humans: Malawian Albinos Murdered for Their Bones'.

110 *Albinism in Africa: Some existential issues*

7. In an Interview conducted with him by the Italian *Freedom from Fear Magazine* (Issue 9), Stephane Ebongue Kouube, a Cameroonian with albinism, gives a detailed explanation why he ran away from home to Italy. Briefly put, his brother Maurice, who had albinism, also had already disappeared obviously due to hunters for body parts of persons with albinism. He had also become their target and had to do something quickly to save his life from such persons. For details of the interview, see http://f3magazine.unicri.it/?p=609#

8. 'Malawi Albino Attack Survivor: "I am too Scared to Sleep." ' Interview by Patience Atuhaire, BBC News Africa, February 21, 2017. http://www.bbc.com/news/world-africa-39026482

9. Ramakant Sinari (1970). 'The Problem of Human Alienation'. *Philosophy and Phenomenological Research*, 31.1: 123–124.

10. Ramakant Sinari (1970). 'The Problem of Human Alienation'. 125

11. Martin Heidegger, *Being and Time*. 220

12. Stephane Ebongue, 'Albinism in Africa: Interview with Stephane Ebongue', *Freedom From Fear Magazine*. Accessed on April 13, 2017 from: http://f3magazine.unicri.it/?p=609#

13. Stephane Ebongue, 'Albinism in Africa: Interview with Stephane Ebongue', *Freedom From Fear Magazine*.

14. Evelyn Usman and Esther Onyegbulam (2015). '23-yr-old Albino Commits Suicide Over Condition', *Vanguard* newspaper. Accessed April 14, 2017 from: http://www.vanguardngr.com/2015/08/23-yr-old-albino-commits-suicide-over-condition/. On the same day, other newspapers in the country carried the news under such headings as: 'Albino Commits Suicide over Discrimination' (*The Nation* newspaper); and 'Albino Commits Suicide over Skin Condition in Lagos' (The Trent: Nigeria's Online Newspaper).

15. 'Albino Lady Commits Suicide'. Malawi24. Accessed on April 14, 2017 from: https://malawi24.com/2016/11/02/albino-lady-commits-suicide/.

16. Martin Heidegger, *Being and Time*.

17. Karl Jaspers (1957). *Man in the Modern Age* (London: Anchor Books)

18. Jean-Paul Sartre (1957). *Being and Nothingness* (New York: Philosophical Library Press).

19. For the biographies of both Salif Keita and his adopted daughter Nantenin Keita, see these entries in Wikipedia: the Free Encyclopedia: https://en.wikipedia.org/wiki/Salif_Keita and https://en.wikipedia.org/wiki/Nantenin_Ke%C3%AFta.

20. For more information about Ikponwosa Ero, see the article: 'New Independent Expert on Albinism Take Up Post'. United Nations Human Rights: Office of the High Commission. Accessed on May 20, 2017 from: http://www.ohchr.org/EN/NewsEvents/Pages/IndependentExpertOnAlbinism.aspx.

21. Ikponwosa Ero. 'Women With Albinism: Intersecting Social and Gender based Discrimination'. (Inputs from the Special Rapporteur on Albinism — Mandate of the Independent Expert on the enjoyment of human rights by persons with albinism, Human Rights Council Resolution, Special Procedures Branch. Accessed May 20, 2017 from: www.ohchr.org/Documents/Issues/Women/WRGS/Report/.../albinism.docx. 2

22. 'Africa: Myth of Magical AIDS Cure Fuels Sexual Assaults on Albino Women'. BreitBart. Accessed on April 12, 2017 from: http://www.breitbart.com/faith/2016/06/08/witchcraft-fueled-albino-killings-reaching-record-levels-africa/.

23. 'Africa: Myth of Magical AIDS Cure Fuels Sexual Assaults on Albino Women'.

24. Ikponwosa Ero. 'Women With Albinism: Intersecting Social and Gender based Discrimination'. 1

6 Overcoming the violent othering of albinism in Africa today

The issues that have been raised and discussed in the previous five chapters expose the sour state of the experience of persons with albinism in many African societies. They penetrate into the deeply harmful internalised and institutionalised othering of albinism and the adverse effects that othering, or the conception of difference of albinism, has had, and continues to have, on persons with albinism. Such violent othering of albinism as an other is continually perpetuated and sustained in societies by individuals and institutions, including educational, religious, political, health and cultural institutions. Hence, it is imperative that we map out ways that are crucial for overcoming the violent perception of, and consequent violent treatment of, persons with albinism in African societies. To be sure, there have been a number of deliberate efforts in recent times — particularly in the last decade or so — to overcome the discrimination against and maltreatment of persons with albinism. These well-meaning efforts have been in the form of research, conferences, human rights activism, minimal governmental involvements through policies, roles of non-governmental organisations and the media. For instance, the belated First Pan-African Albino Conference, hosted by Under the Same Sun (UTSS), an international organisation advocating for the rights and protections of persons with albinism, was held in November of 2015.[1] This was followed by another belated intervention by the United Nations that organised the United Nations Consultative Forum — Action on Albinism in Africa, which was held in June of 2016 in Tanzania.[2] There are now many active advocacy groups for persons with albinism in different African countries, advocating for the rights of persons with albinism. These include The Albino Foundation, Nigeria, The Albinism Society of South Africa, Albinism Society of Kenya, Tanzania Albinism Society and the international advocacy group Under the Same Sun. There was an interesting twist in the advocacy for the rights of persons with albinism when the Albinism Society of Kenya and other organisations hosted the First Albino Beauty Pageant in October 2016.[3] African governments have also made some efforts to improve the safety and well-being of persons with albinism. We recall, for instance, the unfortunately unsuccessful ban of witch doctors in Tanzania in 2009, due to the role they play in encouraging the killing and

112 *Overcoming violent othering of albinism*

dismembering of persons with albinism, which they use for sacrifices and rituals for interested persons.[4]

As well-meaning as these efforts and ones like them have been, they have not been very successful in minimising the stigma, discrimination and harm against persons with albinism. And this, to me, has been the case for a number of reasons. First, many of the efforts of non-governmental organisations and governmental policies have been non-deliberately insensitive to the plights of persons with albinism. For instance, all persons with albinism — at least all those I have come in contact with — passionately hate being called 'albino' for obvious reasons. Besides being a Portuguese blank labelling of a reality they were not used to, the word *albino* concentrates on the disability of persons with albinism without first recognizing that they are persons, which continually perpetuates the idea that they are not persons. Hence, throughout this book — except in quotations, 'persons with albinism' is used rather than 'albinos'. However, in most of these efforts, the fact that persons with albinism hate being called 'albinos' is ignored. The word *albino* continually resurfaces, which plays a key role in setting them further apart from their personhood. In Nigeria, for instance, The *Albino* Foundation does not even recognise that by the very labelling of the advocacy group, it further stigmatize persons with albinism. Second, there is too much focus on the clamour for human rights for persons with albinism, which focuses only on the immediate needs for the rights and ignores without notice the very latent reasons that gave birth to the clamour in the first place. There are more latent and fundamental reasons why persons with albinism are denied their human rights and dignity such as the unavailability of accurate information about the condition. Now if such fundamental issues are not dealt with, the clamour for human rights for persons with albinism would not yield the desired results. Third, the primary objective of these activities and efforts is often not clear to me. Are they meant to concretise and establish firmly the contested personhood of persons with albinism or simply meant to give rights and privileges to entities that the African societies do not consider persons? If the former is the case, the efforts made are not sufficient enough or they reinforce the latter non-deliberately rather than the former. Take, for instance, the beauty pageant organised by the Albinism Society of Kenya. The formal objective of the conference was to reduce stigma and discrimination against persons with albinism. But what seems to stand out during the pageant and what seems to be on the contestants' and organisers' lips, which for me is worrisome, was that 'albinos can do what other persons can do'. Now, does this reduce the violent othering or does it further perpetuate it? Must persons with albinism act like coloured persons with melaninism for them to be regarded as human beings? It often seems that the main objective is left out, and this, to me, is educating and enlightening the people, helping them see reasons why they should do away with the false ideas about albinism and embrace the facts about it. Once this is done, the respect for persons with albinism will naturally ensue. Fourth,

Overcoming violent othering of albinism 113

the primary audience are not targeted in the activities of these institutions, both governmental and non-governmental. The persons on the streets in my town who call me names and stare strangely at me when I walk past are not aware of the conference held in Tanzania or the pageant held in Kenya and the results and findings from those forums. They are not aware of some United Nations report on the matter. They will not deliberately go online and seek for such information even when it is available. And I speak for many persons with albinism in many villages, towns and cities in Africa. This information — accurate information about albinism — needs to be brought to the ten-year-old girl in school, the market woman in the town, the village head in the village, the medical doctor in the hospital and the school teacher in the school. There must be some way of targeting these persons and disseminating the information to them. More worrisome is the fact that there has been very little done in these fora to educate not only the persons prejudiced against persons with albinism, but persons with albinism themselves and their caregivers who struggle to fulfil their responsibility of care for persons with the condition. There is so much ignorance about skin care and the like on the part of persons with albinism and their caregivers. And yet there is little or no effort to overcome this significant problem. It is not enough to fight for the rights of persons with albinism and prove that they are persons when they are not empowered to care for their personhood both physically, psychologically and otherwise.

Thus, there is much left to be done in the areas of overcoming deeply entrenched falsehoods and the enlightenment of all stakeholders including persons with albinism and caregivers. I intend to fill the gaps and focus on these areas as much as I can in this last chapter of this work. I focus mainly on the role of education and research as the most fundamental long-term approach to employ in achieving these goals. In doing this, I begin by developing a blueprint for a reconstructive and awareness education and training exercise for key social institutions in African societies. This is followed by a discussion of how a reconstructive and awareness exercise is also essential for persons with albinism. I then proceed to identify important social structures that must be put in place to improve the quality of care for persons with albinism and minimise the burden of care for primary caregivers such as family members. Lastly, I examine the prospects and implications that recent advancements and research in gene therapy could have for albinism and persons with albinism in African societies today.

Reconstructive and awareness education and training for key social institutions

Education consists of the systems, processes and procedures of knowledge transfer. In education circles, a number of philosophies or theories on what should constitute the primary objective of education has gained prominence. They include perennialism, essentialism, progressivism, eclecticism

114   *Overcoming violent othering of albinism*

and reconstructionism.[5] Of particular interest to me here is reconstruction-ism, or what I would preferably call reconstructive philosophy of education. Reconstructive philosophy of education is the view that the goal of educa-tion is to assist the educated to address social questions through a curricu-lum that focuses on social reforms and a constructive criticism of ideologies and beliefs inherent in societies. Reconstructive education is attributed to the twentieth century philosopher of education, Theodore Brameld, who pioneered the philosophy of social reconstructionism in education. After the Second World War, Brameld had recognised the role of education in social reforms that would prevent humans from annihilating themselves through technology and human cruelty that had become prominent. His ideas were similar to those of critical theorists that had also become poplar at the time.[6] In fact, reconstructive philosophy of education can simply be called an educational critical theory.

Like reconstructionists, critical theorists — such as those of the Frankfort School — were convinced that systems must be changed to overcome oppres-sion and improve human condition. For instance, Max Horkhiemer, during his leadership of the Frankfurt School, drew a blueprint for critical theory — what he might have arguably called social philosophy[7] — as a theory that must be interdisciplinary, critical, reflective and dialectical, and fulfil the Enlightenment project of emancipation.[8] For instance, a critical theory must be critical in a number of ways. Generally the task of the theory must be prac-tical, not just theoretical: that is, it should aim not just to bring about correct understanding and knowledge, but to create social and political conditions more conducive to human flourishing than the present ones. Thus, critical theory is 'a *theory* of society conceived with a *practical* intention.'[9] It must establish a strong relation between the ideals of critique and praxis.[10] More specifically, it means that the theory had two different kinds of normative aim, diagnostic and remedial. The goal of the theory was not just to deter-mine what was *wrong* with contemporary society at present, but, by identify-ing progressive aspects and tendencies within it, to help transform society for the better.[11] Hence, it is not just enough to identify the bad or negative aspects of society; one must also identify and develop positive aspects of society that could help remedy the negative aspects that have been diagnosed.

The educator and author of *Pedagogy of the Oppressed*,[12] Paulo Freire, thought and theorised along these same lines of critical theory in education. His lived experiences of oppression and poverty led him to champion edu-cation and literacy as the vehicle for social change. In his view, humans must learn to resist oppression and not become its victims, nor oppress others. To do so requires dialog and critical consciousness, the development of aware-ness to overcome domination and oppression. Thus, rather than teaching as banking, in which the educator deposits information into students' heads, Freire saw teaching and learning as a process of inquiry in which the learner must invent and reinvent the world. Hence, for reconstructive education the-orists cum critical theorists, curriculum focuses on student experience and

Overcoming violent othering of albinism   115

pays attention to real problems, such as violence, hunger, international terrorism, inflation, inequality and discrimination. Strategies for dealing with social issues.

Awareness education on the other hand consists of education targeted at providing reliable and current information and knowledge to the educated. It is not just about providing information, but the information must be factual, current, reliable and heuristic. Most education systems provide information and knowledge. In fact, they are like a bank of information. But only a few truly meet up as an awareness education system because that would require consistently and diligently updating the information that one has stored up in the information bank. Now, awareness education needs reconstructive or critical education to flourish and be useful and vice versa. One cannot be successfully critical of a system that one is not well-informed about, and one cannot become well-informed about a certain subject matter if one remains in the comfort zone of what she already knows without raising questions and seeking out new information.

The critical reconstructive and awareness approach to education is, to me, fundamental in dealing with the oppressive and precarious situations that persons with albinism face in many African societies once they are reflective in the key social institutions in such societies. One of the most important social institutions where this critical and awareness attitude to learning, teaching and training must reflect is the education sector — and this means charity must begin at home. The education systems in African societies must actively stay informed and participate in the diagnosis of social ills and mediums of oppression in the society in which they exist. Then they must incorporate such diagnosis and possible remedies into their programs, curricula and literature. The education institution and its personnel must never be seen as furthering such ills and oppression in one way or another. Unfortunately, the ministries and departments of education in many African nations are still largely organised round the idea of teaching as banking, where the educated are merely loaded with information, useful or not. Many of these institutions of learning and knowledge transfer still operate mainly on outdated and anachronistic curricula still largely reflecting the realities of the nineteenth and early twentieth centuries when they were formulated by the colonial masters. Such curricula are yet to be decolonised and updated to reflect current experiences and challenges. They are neither meant to be diagnostic nor remedial but merely a storage of knowledge and information, most of which are outdated. These institutions are therefore neither effectively critical nor effectively informative of the society in which they are found. Philosophy students graduate from philosophy departments in African universities knowing so much about European philosophical theories and so little about African philosophical theories. Literature that students read include so many works by renowned Western artists and so little by African artists. The same is true in economics, sociology, medicine, engineering, and education.

116 *Overcoming violent othering of albinism*

With particular reference to albinism and the problems that persons with albinism continue to face even in very recent times, the departments and ministries of education have failed to live up to their expectations because they are largely not reconstructive and aware — or at least pretend not to be aware — of disability experiences in African societies and the actual facts about such conditions of disability including albinism. And I say this for a number of reasons. First, the education structures and institutions of a country that is effectively reconstructive and well-informed of the facts about disability and the experiences and challenges of disabled persons would introduce, entrench and sustain in its structure and curriculum glaring evidences that the institution is not only well-informed of the subject-matter but also making efforts to reduce the ill-treatment and oppression of disabled persons. If this was the case with many African nations with particular reference to albinism — and, of course, this applies to other forms of disability and the consequences of the oppression of such persons with disability in Africa — young African students would be taught from an early age to refrain from using terms that are derogatory in addressing persons with albinism, facts about albinism that are accurate and up to date, wrong notions about albinism, how they evolved and were sustained by ignorance, and how holding on to them show ignorance on their part, and measures to be taken by and for persons with albinism to ensure that they are cared for both physically and otherwise. This can easily be done in a general introductory course on disability studies that runs through a number of years from primary to secondary schools.

Consider this scenario: As a six-year-old child, I am enrolled in Primary 1 class by my parents in a town in Southern Nigeria. One of the courses I will be taking in the class is titled 'Difference'. I go through the accompanying book with the help of my parents and my teacher and find such subjects as ethnic differences, religious differences, language differences, and physical differences. When my teacher starts the course, he reads the introduction, and I remember he says we cannot all be the same and being different does not make the one superior or inferior to the other. I enjoy the course through the class year, get a good grade and move on to the next year. All through my primary and secondary school, I encounter the same course four different times with more details at every higher stage of education, and then I encounter it for the last time in my first year in the university under the general studies program. There is no doubt that after these years of studying differences, I would be more tolerant of difference even if it is caused by physical disabilities, religion or ethnicity. This scenario is unfortunately only imagined. Nothing of such is available at the primary, secondary or tertiary levels of education in Nigeria and indeed many African countries. But departments and ministries of education in African countries need to start thinking along these lines to facilitate the enlightenment of people about albinism and other forms of disability.

Overcoming violent othering of albinism 117

Second, a reconstructive and well-informed education system, which intends to stay so, would regularly and periodically train its personnel. Training of education personnel at all levels is essential because these persons come into the system with their beliefs and biases, which may foster the oppression of disabled persons rather than ease it. Also, many personnel are not well-informed of the facts, nature and ways of caring for disabled persons as well as methods of reconstructive and critical engagements with those they educate; the points of information they have may be the popular ones that have become entrenched into their various communities but are untrue. Hence, they need to be trained to be able to pass the accurate and updated information on to those they educate. In African societies, such training on albinism and other disability matters in the education sector are either minimal, inconsistent and non-informative, or completely absent. Hence, personnel in the different sectors of education are unable to provide proper information for their students and the students are left with no other option than to deal with persons with albinism in the way they have become accustomed to. If teachers are randomly picked around primary, secondary and tertiary institutions in Nigeria and asked questions concerning the cause of and ways to care for albinism, more than ninety percent would have no idea of the information required. But virtually all of them would be able to provide details of how persons with albinism are perceived within their respective communities. Hence, when they have a person with albinism in their class they are unable to adequately cope with her. Hence, the departments and ministries of education in different African nations must regularly organise training programs for personnel to help them deal with these issues.

It is in this aspect of the training of personnel, to be able to foster and support actively an education and enlightenment process that is both reconstructive and well-informative, that other key social institutions must be brought into the picture. These include, but are not limited to, the health sector, unions, such as the trade and worker unions, media sector, religious institutions and, very importantly, the traditional elite class. For instance, the health sector is very key in providing an accurate understanding of albinism, and the appropriate information, for persons with albinism and their caregivers. It is, in fact, the very first institution that comes in contact with persons with albinism at the time they are put to birth. In this regard they have two key responsibilities: First, they must educate and provide accurate information for parents who have children with albinism, not only during the time of birth but consistently through an ongoing support in the early stages of the growth of the child. Such information is, of course, reconstructive and critical in itself, as it challenges the oppressive falsehoods and ignorance inherent in the society. The information must be positive and reassuring for such parents, caregivers and for persons with albinism themselves as they grow. The information must be heuristic, practical and reliable in solving problems associated with the condition of albinism.

118   *Overcoming violent othering of albinism*

Second, and this is important for the first, there must be regular training of healthcare workers, specifically those specialising in aspects of healthcare, such as dermatology, that are especially relevant to persons with albinism. A medical doctor who is trained as a dermatologist and lives and works in Tanzania but knows very little about caring for the sensitive skin of persons with albinism is not educated enough to deal with the challenges of the environment in which he lives. Healthcare workers also need to be trained on how to be positive and reassuring when dealing with or counselling persons with albinism and their caregivers. Now, there are no indications that these two key responsibilities of healthcare workers is standardised in the health sector in any African country. Basically, what is obtainable now is that a healthcare worker uses his discretion in dealing with persons with albinism as they encounter them and personal discretion may reduce or increase the challenges faced by persons with albinism and their caregivers. The lack of standardised, accurate and up-to-date information from healthcare workers for a mother who just put to birth a baby with albinism, for instance, puts the mother and the baby in a dilemma that may last a life time. There is therefore an urgent need for ministries and departments of health in different African countries to standardise how person with albinism and their caregivers are supported, treated and cared for in health institutions.

Also, a significant part of the discrimination and stigmatisation that persons with albinism face in life come from many of the unions in the society — certainly not all. It is members of these unions that continually isolate persons with albinism by, for instance, refusing for no reason to give them employment or allowing them to be active members of such environments due to the fact of their visible differences and the ideas about them in society. Trade unions, industrial unions, academic unions and corporate societies in African societies can ease the challenges faced by persons with albinism, rather than adding to them, by developing and actively pursuing an inclusive policy that ensures its members employ and allow active participation of disabled persons in general and persons with albinism in particular as long as they qualify. Failure to follow such policies by members should attract penalties. There have been too many cases all over Africa where qualified and intelligent persons with albinism are denied jobs and excluded from holding key positions in corporate societies and unions simply on the basis of their disability. And these bodies do nothing about it even when such victimised persons cry out for help. Persons with albinism do not often have equal opportunities, or a level playing field as other black persons in African societies do, to get employed or to be actively included in the activities of these bodies and unions. These problems will continue until corporate societies and unions take deliberate steps to standardise how their bodies treat disabled persons in African societies. The tedious task should not only be left for the government. Again, if these bodies want to make inclusivity of disabled persons an important part of their policies, it cannot be achieved without the needed training programs for members and

Overcoming violent othering of albinism 119

personnel. This is very crucial. Each union or corporate society must carry out intensive training programs and workshops for their members to help them gain accurate knowledge about albinism and other forms of disability and how they are cared for. This, for instance, would help the manager of a company that produces what needs to be marketed outdoors to make the right decision when allocating duties to her workers that include a person with albinism. By the knowledge she would gain from such workshops, she would know that it is unwise to give the worker with albinism the outdoor marketing job if she can be effective within the company building.

The media is also another very effective tool in promoting an education and enlightenment process that is reconstructive and accurately informative of what has already been known of albinism. It can, therefore, play a key role in combating the prejudice against persons with albinism. This can be done by airing programs and writing about things that correct the wrong notions about albinism in African societies. It can also be done by exposing sectors and aspects of society that continuously encourage the harming and stigmatisation of persons with albinism. It must do all of these in a manner that is positive and reassuring to persons with albinism, their caregivers and the entire society. But it can only carry out these duties and responsibilities if its personnel is also well-informed and trained to take up such duties. Hence, heads of media must take the forefront in ensuring that those under them get the needed training and support to carry out these duties. The media in African societies, specifically the news media, has made efforts to expose the violence that persons with albinism face but have done little in addressing the issue of care. The movie industry in Africa has failed in reducing the challenges of persons with albinism. They have, however, succeeded in increasing the burden such persons already bear. This is the case with the Nigerian Nollywood that has become notorious for depicting disabled persons, such as persons with albinism and persons with muscular dystrophy, as evil. And because personnel at media houses and regulatory bodies are not properly trained to recognise the harm such movies cause, the movies are then aired for the general public to see, thereby reinforcing the circle of violence.

Another very crucial institution of African societies to target in the reconstructive, critical and awareness education process is the indigenous elite class. The member of this elite class — the community head or king, the community elder, the head of a kin or family, the chief priest, and other custodians of the people's culture — continue to exert strong effect on how individual persons within their communities think and behave about various matters in various circumstances. They still have a strong hold on what is taken as right or wrong in such communities. If they do not frown at the maltreatment of persons with albinism within their communities, many others would follow their footsteps. Hence the elite class is an important class to target because if they can be convinced through deliberations, dialogues and persuasive arguments that the inherent notions about albinism

120 *Overcoming violent othering of albinism*

they have met within their cultures and have thus protected as the custodian of the culture are wrong and unjustified, it would imply that a much more larger number of persons have been in effect convinced since they follow the footsteps of the few in the elite class and would listen to them when they give directions. It is therefore important to educate these people on the facts about albinism in a manner that is respectful but persuasive. Meetings could be held by concerned bodies, such as non-governmental organisations or health workers, with the elite class in a forum appealing to them. Such fora could include the popular town hall meetings, village square meetings, or meetings at the king's palace. Here, persuasive, positive and reassuring dialogues can be entered into with members of the elite class, which would help them see reasons why their dominant perspectives about albinism need to change and reassure them that persons with albinism can be cared for to live normal, healthy, responsible and autonomous lives.

The measure discussed above, on promoting reconstructive and awareness education and the institutions instantiated, are definitely not exhaustive. But they point in the right direction, and African societies and all concerned stakeholders must follow to achieve positive results. But attention still needs to be paid to the education and enlightenment of persons with albinism.

Reconstructive and awareness education for persons with albinism

The last section focussed on mapping out a blueprint for education and enlightenment of people in African societies on matters relating to albinism and emancipating them from the deeply entrenched false beliefs that currently determine the attitudes and actions of many in African societies toward persons with albinism. In this section, the focus of my discussion of ways to achieve the much needed reconstructive and awareness education shifts from the community of beings in general to persons with albinism in particular. Hence, although the suggestion made above is relevant of persons with albinism as it is for persons with melanin in African communities — since they are all part of the human community that needs the emancipation and enlightenment — I wish to explore certain other important considerations that are peculiar to persons with albinism.

Now, in Africa, persons with albinism find themselves thrown into existence in communities that are already saturated with ideas about who they are, how they originated, of what use they are, and all such notions about their being, notions that have acquired the status of objectively given truths. Once confronted with existence, a person with albinism comes face to face with her own glaring visible difference, which causes her to question her being and identity and may lead her to alienate herself and retract from others. Worse still, she is gradually confronted with the discriminating and stigmatising ideas about her being and with people's attitude toward her

Overcoming violent othering of albinism 121

based on such ideas. Her experience of stigma and isolation is a recurring one. Of course, she still has friends and family, some of whom may genuinely love her, but the experience of stigma and discrimination from the society in which she lives tend to overwhelm and suffocate the love and attention she receives from a few. The name-calling when she walks on the street, the gap people put between themselves and her in a church seat row or a bus, the starring and whispers, and the fear at night does not go away. They hit her again and again on her face and nearly suffocate her. Gradually over time, many persons with albinism resign to this suffocating social system and allow the contaminated ideologies effortlessly choke them. Choice seem to be out of the question and destiny rules. Many persons with albinism actually come to believe all that is said in the society about them. They accept that they are inferior to others, a curse, something waiting to disappear, and a being have magical powers that is in high demand. They accept that they can do well in school and so they drop out and become beggars. They generally become what society has expected them to be — one that cannot actively live as part of the society.

Hence, persons with albinism need to be primarily targeted in African societies by stakeholders and interested parties for emancipation from the ideas about their being that their minds have become filled with, and for enlightenment on how to cope with their condition. They require a comprehensive education scheme that is reconstructive, corrective and critical, highly and relevantly informative, and empowering. An education scheme for persons with albinism is effectively reconstructive, critical and corrective if it aims at correcting the wrong notions about the being of persons with albinism inherent in human societies and restore dignity, self-esteem and confidence to the educated — the persons with albinism. This can be achieved through a number of the channels already discussed in the previous section. However, in addition to this, they may be needed for professional counselling for persons with albinism to help them regain and increase self-esteem and confidence in their being, contrary to what the society has offered. This can be done by professional counsellors in hospitals or in private practice. Unfortunately, in many sub-Saharan African societies, professional counselling is still very much perceived as a strange activity viewed with suspicious eyes by community members. Hence, one may find very few or no professional counsellors in practice in many African communities and towns. Therefore, well-meaning stakeholders such as the government and non-governmental organisations can provide counselling units, centres or workshops for persons with albinism.

An education scheme for persons with albinism is highly and relevantly informative. It not only provides up-to-date information on the nature and cause for persons with albinism but also detailed information on how persons with albinism can care for themselves such as skin care, personal hygiene and security tips. For instance, information about skin care is not just essential for the general well-being of persons with albinism, but it is in

122 *Overcoming violent othering of albinism*

fact life-saving. It is a fact that the lack of such information results quickly in loss of beauty and life threatening health challenges such as skin cancer. This leads to more expressions of disgust and isolation from other community members. It is common experience in African communities that even with the many falsehood about albinism, black persons feel comfortable, relaxed and attracted to persons with albinism who have managed to keep their skin neat, beautiful and clean, while they withdraw from and feel nothing but disgust for those who do not. In fact, skin care for persons with albinism may break the ice of ignorance faster than any other method employed to do so. It may not deal with all the issues of discrimination and stigmatisation but it would certainly go a long way in minimising them. A person with albinism and her caregiver need to be properly equipped to care for her skin right from infancy. This is because beyond the feeling of disgust, hatred and isolation from community members that result from skin not properly cared for, a much more dire implication is that rough-looking skin convinces the ordinary black person that a person with albinism cannot really be a person.

Hence, informative education on skin care is one of the most important and heuristic things that a person with albinism can receive. Interestingly, they are simple but effective facts that can save lives, guarantee beauty and reduce stigma, but unfortunately, they are not widely available or known or are veiled with ignorance and other popular but false ideas. It includes the following information for instance: (i.) persons with albinism should avoid the sun as much as possible; they should always cover their bodies properly when they walk or work in the sun with hats long sleeves and the like. To be sure, this can be done while being beautiful; (ii.) persons with albinism should avoid making their basic job an outdoor job such as fishing, farming or selling in an open market; (iii.) they should use soaps and body creams with little or no artificial chemicals, perfumes and fragrances such as most dermatologically approved soaps and creams for sensitive skin; medicated soaps and creams can easily burn the delicate skin of persons with albinism; (iv.) a person with albinism should always have some sunburn remedies on hand just in case she suffers sunburn. These should be preferably natural remedies such as coconut oil, Aloe Vera juice, honey and, perhaps, if affordable, sunscreen with little or no artificial perfumes and fragrance; (v.) a person with albinism must be selective of her clothing. Her clothing must be cool and comfortable and should not attract too much heat; (vi.) to avoid too much sensitivity to light, a person with albinism should use sunshades when outdoors and consult a qualified optician to determine and provide the appropriate lenses to help with her vision; and (vii.) a person with albinism should always consult a professional health worker, rather than following popular views, if she has any health concerns.

These skin-care tips are definitely not exhaustive, but they highlight the fact that a person with albinism can have healthy, beautiful skin and lead a meaningful, fulfilling life by following simple tips to get such relevant

Overcoming violent othering of albinism 123

information on skin-care and other matters — such as how to do well in school with poor vision — well-meaning bodies and institutions including the government can organise, workshops, training centres, produce easy-to-read pamphlets or books written in the language commonly used in the area, and, as we shall discuss further in the next section, establishing care units in hospitals and other locations.

The education of persons with albinism is empowering if its objective is to provide practical knowledge that a person with albinism can employ in living an autonomous, dignifying and independent life. Since it is not healthy for persons with albinism to be fully involved in jobs done outdoors, well-meaning organisations can provide training programs and workshops specifically designed to recognise the limits of persons with albinism and to train them to be economically stable and independent with basically indoor jobs. This is important in cases where persons with albinism are unable to afford higher education that may provide the means of getting a white-collar job or in cases where persons with albinism have successfully obtained higher degrees but are unable to secure jobs due to the inherent discrimination against them in the job market. Hence, such training and workshops would afford them the opportunity to learn skills to establish small businesses to help them fend for themselves. Such an approach to educating persons with albinism would be truly empowering if the organisers, governmental or non-governmental, provide soft loans or business grants to help such persons pursue their dreams and become financially stable and independent.

Hence, reconstructive and awareness education for persons with albinism must have as its primary focal point the goal of improving the life conditions of persons with albinism by targeting the removal of the barriers that impede their dignity, autonomy, health and general well-being. But the emancipation and enlightenment of persons with albinism as well as others in African societies would be difficult if African governments and non-governmental agencies do not establish the needed structures, legislations and institutions. In the section that follows, I make some suggestions along this line of thought.

Establishment of social structures and institutions

The recommendations made so far in the previous sections to improve the quality of life for persons with albinism in African societies may be difficult to achieve if African states and other stakeholders fail to put into place and sustain certain key structures and institutions that would be sensitive to the needs of persons with albinism. Here, I examine four key structures that the government or concerned non-governmental organisations of any African state must put in place and actively maintain in the health, education and social welfare sectors: the establishment of special health units of departments for albinism in the healthcare system; the revision of regulations

124 *Overcoming violent othering of albinism*

guiding the education system to take cognizance of persons with albinism and other disabled persons; the establishment by African nations of an institute or centre for the research on, or study of, albinism in Africa, one that is long overdue; and the enactment of a social welfare system for persons with albinism, in particular, and persons with disability in general.

There is an urgent need for African governments and non-governmental organisations to prioritise the establishment and sustenance of albinism healthcare units or departments in key hospitals across sub-Saharan Africa, particularly targeting areas where there are a number of persons with albinism. This healthcare unit would provide services related to caring for the health of persons with albinism, many of which have been discussed above. For instance, the unit — one I may call the 'White African Health Unit' — would provide counselling for parents who had babies with albinism in the hospital or nearby health centres immediately after the baby is delivered and consistently thereafter. This implies that nearby health centres or facilities without the unit would make it mandatory for parents who had their babies in their centres to visit the nearest White African Health Unit and follow up the case to make sure they do. The unit would also be responsible for paying visits to the family or primary caregiver(s) of the child with albinism to ensure that the instructions given them are properly followed and to provide updates, reminders and encouragements. The unit would also care for any health challenges of persons with albinism related to the condition itself such as sunburn, solar keratosis, skin cancer and impaired vision. It would provide positive and practical counselling and advice for persons with albinism on how to stay healthy and well. With the aid of the government, non-governmental organisation and corporate bodies, it would provide subsidised or free healthcare products such as effective sunscreens and other dermatological products and eye lenses for persons with albinism, as many families with children with albinism may not be able to afford these products. But to make such a unit effective and functional in carrying out these and other activities, the unit would need to have professional healthcare workers trained to care for persons with albinism. Thus, it is not enough to have qualified dermatologists or opticians in this unit, but they must be specialised in caring for conditions such as albinism. The White African Health Unit is therefore a very essential structure in to include in the healthcare sector for the well-being of persons with albinism.

There is also an urgent need for the revision of laws and regulations guiding the education system to take cognizance of persons with albinism. At the moment, what is obtainable in many African societies in an education system that does not take cognizance of albinism as a disability. To be sure, existing education systems in African societies have established within its structures special schools and institutions mainly for people with physical disability, such as inability to hear, speak or see. Even in this regard, there are a lot of issues, and so much more to be done. But this is not the space to elaborate on these issues and concerns so as not to deviate from the primary

Overcoming violent othering of albinism 125

focus here, albinism. The concern for persons with albinism is hardly felt in the education sector. This is largely due to lack of understanding and awareness of the nature of the condition. This, of course, is not a a call for the establishment of special schools for persons with albinism. Some African states such as Tanzania have often made the mistake of sending children with albinism to special schools for persons with physical disability rather than providing ways of dealing with them in the normal education system. And there are a number of things wrong with this approach. Albinism is not a disability that requires special schooling structures. In fact, current debates in disability studies call into question the whole idea of having special schools for persons with physical disability when they can be accommodated in the standard schools by simply revising certain part of the laws and regulations guiding the education system. Agreed, special schools are needed for some form of disability such as learning and mental disabilities, but certainly not for all forms of disability. For instance, persons born with the inability to walk do not need to be sent to some special school to learn. That would only further isolate them and perpetuate the cycle of stigmatisation and discrimination.

With regards to persons with albinism, creating special schools for them or sending them to already existing special schools would only further perpetuate an already existing and strongly felt social exclusion. This in no way helps with the discrimination and stigmatisation that is already deeply rooted in society. Tanzania has often depended on this form of isolation of persons with albinism to care for their education and security needs. Aislinn Laing gives a sad and painful but factual report in the *Telegraph* of how one of such schools or centres completely isolates young persons with albinism — as young as two years of age — from their family members and from the entire community in a bid to educate them and secure them from those hunting for body parts of persons with albinism. Buhangija, which Laing reports about, is one of 33 centres set up by the government to serve as a protection and education base for persons with albinism. Parents who feel that their children are not safe because of having albinism send their children there. Unfortunately the government that established these special centres initially for people with other forms of disability provide little or no funding to care for such persons there.[13] The centres completely isolate these persons from their families and the community. As Laing says:

> Separated from their families and forced to largely stay indoors because of the effects on their skin of the harsh east African sun, they sleep three or four to a bed. They survive on basic food strictly rationed by their head teacher because of erratic government funding that sometimes dries up for months at a time.[14]

In Buhangija, for instance, at the time of the report, there wear two-hundred, ninety-five persons with albinism, forty persons who were

126　*Overcoming violent othering of albinism*

blind and sixty-four persons who were deaf, and this was way beyond the capacity that the centre could handle since it was initially built for just forty students. So its head teacher has been compelled to turn the library and a classroom into dormitories.[15]

Special schools for persons with albinism are therefore not the way to go, even when they are properly organised and supervised — and this of course is not the case with many African societies. What needs to be done is in the manner of regulations and legislation. For instance, there is the need for it to be enacted in the education system regulations that persons with albinism in any school need to be provided special seating positions akin to the way special parking spaces are provided for persons with physical disabilities. In the same way, it needs to be clearly reflected in the regulations of the education system that persons with albinism must not be compelled to work in the sun or attend assemblies in sunny weather. Hence, as it is common is many West African schools, when it is Labour Day and students are expected to participate in outdoor duties, persons with albinism should, by law be permitted to forgo the activity. In this way, governments would be showing sensitivity to the plights of persons with albinism. Christine Peto summarises this point succinctly when she says that, whilst the provision of prescription spectacles is necessary, teachers ought to know that children with albinism have poor vision and they may struggle to read the writing board... A strategic sitting arrangement is therefore required:

> In addition, children with albinism should not be made to share text-books with others, they need their own books so that they can hold them close to their eyes, because they can easily fall behind....*There is no need to confine children with albinism to special schools because that is how isolation begins.* To avoid too much exposure to the sun, persons with albinism ought to wear long sleeved shirts, trousers, skirts, sunglasses and wide brimmed hats to protect their skin and eyes. Some school rules do not permit the wearing of long sleeves during summer, but there is need for educational staff to make exceptions for students with albinism.[16]

Again, there is the need for an establishment that is now completely absent in African societies but is crucial for the understanding of albinism and the improvement of the well-being of persons with albinism in the African continent. It is the establishment, by African nations jointly or separately — preferably jointly by the African Union — of an institute or centre for the research on, or study of, albinism in Africa. The establishment of such an institute or research centre would provide a research platform on albinism in (sub-Sahara) Africa because managing the albinism situation is largely dependent on gaining accurate knowledge and information about the condition through consistent research effort, including, for instance,

Overcoming violent othering of albinism 127

gene therapy, which we shall turn to shortly. To be sure, improving the well-being of persons with albinism depends largely on the outcome of committed research on the subject matter. Such an institute would, for instance, organise regular conferences on the subject matter, have a series of publications including information pamphlets on the subject matter, provide research grants for, and encourage research on, albinism at the postgraduate level of study in different fields of inquiry, and collaborate with related bodies and organisation to see to the well-being of persons with albinism and the proliferation of facts and accurate information about albinism on the African continent. I have developed a comprehensive blueprint for such a research centre or institute, but I have been unable to get the needed audience and resources to implement it. The gap in the efforts to deal with the albinism dilemma remains unfilled, and it needs to be dealt with as quickly as possible if the well-being of persons with albinism is of priority to concerned stakeholders.

It is also important that African states and interested non-governmental organisations and corporate bodies provide social welfare tailored to the needs of persons with albinism. Many persons with albinism are unable to afford education, healthcare products such as sunscreen and lenses and other life necessities. A majority of the primary caregivers such as parents struggle to provide the needs of the persons with albinism they care for. This accounts for the increasing rates of persons with albinism who drop out from school or die of skin cancer. As unfortunate as it may be, it is a fact that at least ninety percent of persons with albinism do not live for more than forty years. The lack of social support and welfare contributes greatly to this precarious situation. As far as I am aware, all African states do not have specific social welfare plan for persons with albinism. This could have included free medical care and free education. In this way persons with albinism are encouraged to go for regular medical check-ups and to attend schools. There is therefore an urgent need for a social welfare system for persons with albinism if they are to be properly catered for.

Beyond these needs for the establishment and sustenance of key structures in existing institutions in African societies or the establishment and sustenance of new institutions such as the research institute, there is also need to improve on the effectiveness of existing institutions in improving the well-being of persons with albinism. Currently, the justice system and the security system in many African societies are failing in their protection of persons with albinism. Personnel in these key institutions need to be properly trained and enlightened about the matters involved in order to operate properly. It is difficult to expect a police man who believes that persons with albinism are ghosts to effectively combat other persons who share in his beliefs and thus hunt for persons with albinism. The enlightenment project is key to adequately equip these already existing institutions to live up to expectations.

Gene research and therapy: Implications and prospects for albinism

In recent times, there has been increasing interest in research on genes, both human and animal, that is, an increasing research on the part of the cell that controls human and animal physical appearance, growth, strength and other attributes. My focal point here is on genetic research on human beings. There have been two main aspects of this research: research on gene therapy in humans and research on gene enhancement in humans. Gene therapy is an experimental technology that uses genes to treat or prevent disease. The research in gene therapy is done with the hope that it will provide insights on how to cure and prevent various forms of illnesses and disorders by simply inserting the appropriate gene into the right cell of a patient instead of using drugs and surgery. Currently, researchers in gene therapy are conducting several tests including: (i.) replacing a mutated gene that causes disease with a healthy copy of the gene; (ii.) inactivating a mutated gene that is not working properly; and (iii.) introducing a new gene into the body to help fight disease.[17] Substantial progress has been made in recent times in using gene therapy in curing various forms of cancer. In fact, more than sixty percent of all ongoing gene therapy research target various forms of cancer. Currently, two cancer-gene therapy products have received market approval in China, which show that the research is yielding results.[18]

Gene enhancement, on the other hand, consists of an attempt to increase or enhance the normal status of a biological organism, and it is not necessarily or largely for the sake of treatment. In other words, 'gene enhancement refers to the transfer of genetic material intended to modify nonpathological human traits... to make someone not just well, but better than well, by optimising attitudes or capabilities — perhaps by raising an individual from standard to peak levels of performance.'[19] Gene enhancement is, for instance, meant to make a person run faster than normal, grow faster and bigger than normal, process information faster than normal. It is physically being a superhuman.[20] This of course raises immediate moral problems and challenges that gene therapy may escape — although gene therapy has its own moral dilemma. What justification does anyone have to want to be superior in physical/biological attitude than other fellow human beings? If supermen were created would it not result to anarchy and chaos in the human society? These are legitimate concerns and questions that cannot be ignored when doing research on gene therapy. Hence, most government has actually prevented any gene enhancement research. Hence, our focus here for albinism is gene therapy and not gene enhancement. The questions precisely are: What is the importance of gene therapy for understanding of albinism? Are the prospective effects of gene therapy on albinism desired results?

Albinism is caused by a mutated gene, and one of the central concerns of gene therapy is the replacement of a mutated gene with a healthy copy of

Overcoming violent othering of albinism   129

the gene. I am in no way a scientist in the lab researching gene therapy, but assuming that it is possible to replace the muted gene that causes albinism with a healthy copy of the gene, and thereby prevent albinism, would it not be a welcomed idea? If this process is possible, it would imply that before or after a person with albinism is born, the anomaly would be correctable by using gene therapy. And if this practice of therapy works, albinism would become a treatable condition. Now, this is not just logic reasoning about the prospects of treating albinism with gene therapy; this possibility is already being tested with positive results by gene therapy researchers, although there is not yet a market-approved treatment. As far back as 2000, a group of scientists successfully used gene therapy to correct albinism in hair follicles.[21] There have been a series of successful and positive research studies recently that show albinism can be treated by using gene therapy. For instance, a group of scientists published a paper in 2007 showing the possibility of correcting vision problems caused by albinism using AAV-mediated gene therapy.[22] In 2011, Prashiela Manga and Seth J. Orlow published their research on the subject matter which *Science Daily* summarises as follows:

> Individuals with oculocutaneous albinism, type 1 (OCA1) have white hair, very pale skin, and light-colored irises. Affected individuals have impaired eyesight and a substantially increased risk of skin cancer. Current treatment options are limited to attempts to correct eyesight and counselling to promote the use of sun protective measures. However, researchers have now generated data in mice that provide hope for a new treatment for a subset of patients with OCA1.[23]

More recently, in 2014, a team led by Brown University biologists discovered a way in which a specific genetic mutation appears to lead to the lack of melanin production in OCA2.[24] John Kariuki, who was a postgraduate student of the Department of Biochemistry at the University of Nairobi, did an amazing research study, giving detailed discussions and analysis of current gene therapy research in albinism in his dissertation *Albinism and Gene Therapy*. In his summary, he says that:

> Until up to late 2011 no potential treatment or permanent cure existed for albinism, no one device can serve the needs of all patients in all situations. The conventional interventions for management of albinism include the use of glasses for young children with low vision, while older children may require bifocals. Occasionally, telescopic lenses mounted glasses (biopticals) are prescribed for close up walk and distant vision. Tinted glasses may be used to reduce photophobia but some patients prefer wearing a cap or visor when outdoors. It also includes the use of sunscreen and sun glasses for light sensitivity. Gene therapy is a technique used to correct a defective gene. A foreign gene is

130 *Overcoming violent othering of albinism*

inserted by use of viral or nonviral vectors, to correct or replace the mutant gene sequence. The objective of this dissertation was to review on some of the modern ways for the treatment of albinism. One of the most recent and ongoing scientific way is by use of gene therapy. For instance, Adeno-associated virus (AAV)-mediated Tyrosinase gene transfer that can restore melanogenesis and retinal function in a model of Oculocutaneous albinism type 1 (OCA1).[25]

These are amazing discoveries for researchers in genetics, because prior to the twenty-first century, it was widely thought that albinism could not be treated but only managed. In fact, much literature on albinism today still tells the same story for the obvious reason that these experiments and research are still in progress and that no solutions have been formally approved for treating persons with albinism.

But the second important moral question is: Is this the desired approach to albinism? Must persons with albinism in African culture, for instance, be normalised into blackness before they become human beings? It is possible to be given birth to as infants with albinism and yet still live a normal, successful life, as long as the recommendations mentioned above are followed. So, is it necessary to provide means of helping such persons develop melanin and become like their coloured neighbours? To approach this problem from an ethical perspective is to enter into a steep and radical terrain of perennial philosophical and moral debates and arguments revolving around otherness, alterity and normalised bodies, one that I deliberately wish to avoid. However, the need to sustain and support research on the use of gene therapy for treatment of albinism, particularly in African contexts, can be understood from the perspective of its utility, viewed from the angle of persons with albinism in Africa. If a person with albinism in an African community is offered a treatment that helps her body generate melanin such that her skin becomes a bit tanned and she is able to go about her normal life without the usual experience of stigmatisation, discrimination, name calling, sunburn, visual impairment and other problems, she is likely going to grab the offer with both hands. Such a treatment would add meaning to her life and reduce the burden she faces on a daily basis as well as the burden the caregivers face. Hence it is the right thing to do to provide gene therapy treatment as an option of care for persons with albinism to choose from.

However, making gene therapy treatment available as an option of care for persons with albinism in Africa, for instance, is only possible if current ongoing researches are supported and sustained and treatment approval is received. Unfortunately, there is not much of such research going on in Africa today. It is therefore important to bring this option to the table in different forums of discourse and deliberation on albinism and to encourage it. Governments and nongovernmental organisation can provide funds and other forms of support to encourage scientists to take up such research. The

Overcoming violent othering of albinism 131

much needed centre for research on albinism in Africa discussed above can play a key role in pushing research in this direction.

Notes

1. The First Pan-African Albino Conference. Global Disability Watch. Accessed on May 14, 2017 from: http://globaldisability.org/2016/01/02/the-first-pan-african-albino-conference.
2. Regional Action Plan on Albinism. United Nations Human Rights: Office of the High Commissioner. Accessed May 14, 2017 from: http://www.ohchr.org/EN/Issues/Albinism/Pages/AlbinismInAfrica.aspx.
3. 'Kenya Holds World's First Albino Beauty Pageant'. *The Guardian*, October 31, 2016. Accessed May 14, 2017 from https://www.theguardian.com/world/2016/oct/31/kenya-hosts-worlds-first-albino-beauty-pageant.
4. 'Tanzania Bans Witchdoctors to Deter Albino Killings'. Thomson Reuters Foundation, Jan 14, 2015. Accessed May 13, 2017: http://www.reuters.com/article/us-tanzania-albinos-idUSKBN0KN16B20150114.
5. See David Edward Diehl. (2005). 'Adoption of Ornstein and Olivia's Educational Philosophies. In A Study of Faculty-Related Variables and Competence in Integrating Instructional Technologies into Pedagogical Practices', PhD Dissertation (Texas: Texas Southern University). 18–22.
6. David Edward Diehl, 'Adoption of Ornstein and Olivia's Educational Philosophies'.19–20.
7. See M. Horkheimer (1993). 'Between philosophy and social science: selected early writings' (Cambridge: MIT Press). Chap. 1.
8. J. G. Finlayson (2005). *Habermas: A Very Short Introduction* (Oxford: Oxford University Press). 3–5.
9. See J. Habermas (1973). *Theory and practice* (Boston: Beacon Press).
10. S. Tong (2006). "Critique" immanent in "practice": new Frankfurt school and American pragmatism. Frontiers of Philosophy in China 1.2: 296.
11. J. G. Finlayson, 4.
12. Paulo Freire (1970). *Pedagogy of the Oppressed* (New York: Continuum).
13. Aislinn Laing (2015). 'The Albino Children Locked Away to be kept Safe from Witchdoctors'. *The Telegraph*, June 5, 2015. Accessed on April 20, 2017 from: http://www.telegraph.co.uk/news/worldnews/africaandindianocean/tanzania/11718452/The-Albino-children-locked-away-to-be-kept-safe-from-witch-doctors.html.
14. Aislinn Laing, 'The Albino Children Locked Away to be kept Safe from Witchdoctors'.
15. Aislinn Laing, 'The Albino Children Locked Away to be kept Safe from Witchdoctors.
16. Christine Peto (2017). 'Myths Surrounding Albinism'. In *Sunday Mail*, April 30, 2017. Accessed on June 12, 2017 from: http://www.sundaymail.co.zw/myths-surrounding-albinism/.
17. 'What is gene Therapy?' *Genetic Hope Reference*. Accessed on May 12, 2017 from: https://ghr.nlm.nih.gov/primer/therapy/genetherapy.
18. Thomas Wirth and Seppo Yla-Herttuala (2014). 'Gene Therapy Used in Cancer Treatment'. *Biomedicines*, 2: 149.
19. 'Genetic Enhancement'. National Human Genome Research Institute. Accessed May 13, 2017 from: https://www.genome.gov/10004767/genetic-enhancement/.
20. Nick Bostrom (2003). 'Human Genetic Enhancement: A Transhumanist Perspective'. *Journal of Value Inquiry*, 37.4: 493–506.

132   *Overcoming violent othering of albinism*

21. See M. Zhao (2000). 'A Novel Approach to Gene Therapy of Albino Hair in Histoculture with a retroviral Streptomyces Tyrosinase Gene'. *Pigment Cell Research*, 13.5: 345–351.
22. Ciro Bonetti, et al. (2007). 'AAV-Mediated Gene Therapy of Albinism'. *Molecular Therapy*, 15.1: S286.
23. 'A Treatment for One Form of Albinism?' *Science Daily*, September 26, 2011. Accessed on June 4, 2017 from: https://www.sciencedaily.com/releases/2011/09/110926131748.htm. For the full paper summarized by *Science Daily*, see Prashiela Manga and Seth J. Orlow (2011). 'Informed Reasoning: Repositioning of Nitisinone to treat Oculocutaneous Albinism'. *The Journal of Clinical Investigation*, 121.10: 3828–3831.
24. 'New Research Unlocks a Mystery of Albinism'. *News from Brown*: Brown University News, December 16, 2014. Accessed on June 4, 2017 from https://news.brown.edu/articles/2014/12/albinism.
25. John Kariuki (2014). *Albinism and Gene Therapy*, Unpublished Dissertation (Kenya: University of Nairobi).

Bibliography

A Treatment for One Form of Albinism? *Science Daily*, September 26, 2011. Accessed June 04, 2017 from: https://www.sciencedaily.com/releases/2011/09/110926131748. htm.

Abberly, P. (1987). The Concept of Oppression and the Development of a Social Theory of Disability. *Disability, Handicap and Society*, 2.1.

Achebe, C. (1969). *Things Fall Apart*. New York: Ballantine Press.

Adeofe, L. (2004). Personal Identity in African Metaphysics. Lee M. Brown, Ed. *African Philosophy: New and Traditional Perspectives*. Oxford: Oxford University Press.

Africa: Myth of Magical AIDS cure fuels Sexual Assaults on Albino Women. BreitBart: the Official BreitBart Store. Accessed on April 12, 2017 from: http://www.breitbart.com/faith/2016/06/08/witchcraft-fueled-albino-killings-reaching-record-levels-africa/.

Aigbodioh, J. A. (2011). Stigmatization in African Communalistic Societies and Habermas' Theory of Rationality. *Cultura: International Journal of Philosophy of Culture and Axiology*. 8.1.

Alcoff, L. M. (2007). Epistemologies of Ignorance: Three Types. In S. Sullivan and T. Nancy (Eds.), *Race and Epistemologies of Ignorance*. Albany: State University of New York Press.

Ali, P. (2006). *Esan Traditional Values and the Roman Catholic Church. A Comparative Discourse*. Lagos: Decraft Communications.

Amadi, E. (1982). *Ethics in Nigerian Culture*. Ibadan: Heinemann Educational Books Ltd.

Andolsen, B. A. (1993). Justice, Gender and the Frail Elderly: Reexamining the Ethic of Care. *Journal of Feminist Studies in Religion*, 9.1.

Appiah, K. A. (2005). African Studies and the Concept of Knowledge. In Bert Hamminga Ed., *Knowledge Cultures: Comparative Western and African Epistemology* (Amsterdam: Rodopi).

Ardener, E. W. (1954). Some Ibo Attitude to Skin Pigmentation. *Man*, 54.

Ashcroft, R. (2005). Making Sense of Dignity. *Journal of Medical Ethics*, 31.11.

Baker, C. Lund, P., Nyathi, R. and Taylor, J. (2010). The Myth Surrounding People with Albinism in South Africa and Zimbabwe, *Journal of African Cultural Studies*, 22.2.

Baker, C. *Representing the tribe of ghosts: Stereotypes of albinism emerging from reports of recent attacks in Tanzania and Burundi*. Accessed 09/09/2015 from: www. inter-disciplinary.net>bakerwpaper.

134 *Bibliography*

Barnes, E. (2009). Disability, Minority and Difference. *Journal of Applied Philosophy*, 26.4.

Baskerville, S. (2009). Freedom of the Family: The Family Crisis and the Future of Western Civilization. *Humanitas* XXII.1&2.

Bay, M. (2000). The Historical Origin of Afrocentrism. *American Studies*, 45.4.

Bonetti, C. et al. (2007). AAV-Mediated Gene Therapy of Albinism. *Molecular Therapy*, 15.1.

Bonzon, R. (2009). Thick Aesthetic Concepts. *The Journal of Aesthetic and Art Criticism*, 67.2.

Bostrom, N. (2003). Human Genetic Enhancement: A Transhumanist Perspective. Journal of Value Inquiry 37.4.

Brown, L. M. (2004). Understanding and Ontology in African Traditional Thought. Lee M. Brown, (Ed). *African Philosophy: New and Traditional Perspectives*. Oxford: Oxford University Press.

Bryceson, D. F., Jonsson, J. B. and Sherrington, R. (2010). Miners' Magic Artisanal Mining: The Albino Fetish and Murder in Tanzania, *The Journal of Modern African Studies*, 48.3.

Bujo, B. (1998). *The Ethical Dimension of Community: The African Model and the Dialogue between North and South*. Nairobi: Paulines Publications.

Bujo, B. (2003). *Foundations of an African Ethic*. Kenya: Paulines Publications Africa.

Bunnin, N. and Yu, J. (2004). *The Blackwell Dictionary of Western Philosophy*. (Malden MA: Blackwell Publishing.

Chidothe, I. A. And Masamba, L. (2014). Neoadjuvant Chemotherapy in Albinos with Locally Advanced Skin Cancer at a Blantyre Hospital – Case Series. *Malawi Medical Journal*, 26.3.

Curran, A. (2009). Rethinking Race History: The Role of the Albino in French Enlightenment Life Science. *History and Theory*, 48.3.

Diehl, D. E. (2005). *Adoption of Ornstein and Olivia's Educational Philosophies. In A Study of Faculty-Related Variables and Competence in Integrating Instructional Technologies into Pedagogical Practices*, PhD Dissertation (Texas: Texas Southern University).

Driberg, J. H. (1936). The Secular Aspect of Ancestor Worship in Africa. *Supplement to the Journal of the Royal African Society*, XXXV.

Drury, F. (2015). Hunted Down like Animals and Sold by their own Families for $75,000: Tanzania's Albinos hacked Apart by Witchdoctors who believe their body parts 'bring luck' in Sick Trade Fuelled by the Country's Elite. In *The Daily Mail Online*. Accessed from: http://www.dailymail.co.uk/news/article-2922243/Hunted-like-animals-sold-families-75-000-Tanzania-s-albinos-hacked-apart-witchdoctors-believe-body-parts-bring-luck-sick-trade-fuelled-country-s-elite.html.

Dyer, R. (1993). *The Matter of Images: Essays on Representations*. London: Routledge.

Ebongue, S. Albinism in Africa: Interview with Stephane Ebongue, Freedom from Fear Magazine. Accessed on April 13, 2017 from: http://f3magazine.unicri.it/?p=609#

Ehiakhamen, J. O. (2013). Beyond Culpability: Approaching Male Impotency through Legitimated Adultery in Esan Metaphysics. In Elvis Imafidon and John A. I. Bewaji Eds., *Ontologized Ethics: New Essays in African Meta-ethics* (Lanham: Lexington Books).

Ekanola, A. B. (2006). Metaphysical Issues in African Philosophy. Oladipo O. Ed. *Core Issues in African Philosophy*. Ibadan: Hope Publications.

Bibliography 135

Eklund, M. (2011). What are Think Concepts? *Canadian Journal of Philosophy*, 41.1.

Elebuibon, Y. (2008). *Invisible Powers of the Metaphysical World: A Peep into the World of Witches*. Ibadan: Creative Books.

Ero, I. Women with Albinism: Intersecting Social and Gender based Discrimination. (Inputs from the Special Rapporteur on Albinism - Mandate of the Independent Expert on the enjoyment of human rights by persons with albinism, Human Rights Council Resolution, Special Procedures Branch. Accessed May 20, 2017 from: www. ohchr.org/Documents/Issues/Women/WRGS/Report/.../albinism.docx. 2

Evans-Pritchard, E. E. (1973). *Witchcraft, Oracles and Magic among the Azande* (Oxford: Clarendon Press).

FederKittay, E. (2011). The Ethics of Care, Dependence and Disability. *Ratio Juris: An International Journal of Jurisprudence and Philosophy of Law*, 24.1.

Finlayson, J. G. (2005). *Habermas: A Very Short Introduction* (Oxford: Oxford University Press)

Freid, G. and Polt, R (2000). Translators' Introduction to Martin Heidegger, Introduction to Metaphysics (New York: Yale University Press).

Freire, P. (1970). *Pedagogy of the Oppressed*. New York: Continuum.

Frequency of Albinism. In *Under the Same Sun* website. Accessed 12/03/2017 from: http://www.underthesamesun.com/sites/default/files/Frequency%20of%20Albinism.pdf.

Gallie, W. B. (1955/56). Essentially Contested Concepts. *Proceedings of the Aristotelian Society*, 56.

Gbadagesin, S. (1998). Yoruba Philosophy: Individuality, Community and the Moral Order. Eze, E. C. Ed. *African Philosophy: An Anthology*. Oxford: Blackwell Publishing.

Gbadegensin, S. (2004). An Outline of a Theory of Destiny. Lee M. Brown Ed. *African Philosophy: New and Traditional Perspectives*. Oxford: Oxford University Press.

Genetic Enhancement. National Human Genome Research Institute. Accessed May 13, 2017 from: https://www.genome.gov/10004767/genetic-enhancement/.

Genetic Hope Reference. What is Gene Therapy? Accessed 12/05/2017 from: https:// ghr.nlm.nih.gov/primer/therapy/genetherapy.

Global Disability Watch. The First Pan-African Albino Conference. Accessed on May 14, 2017 from: http://globaldisability.org/2016/01/02/the-first-pan-african-albino-conference.

Gray, G. G. (1952). Heidegger's Being. *The Journal of Philosophy* 49.12.

Guignon, C. B. (Ed.) (1996). Introduction to *The Cambridge Companion to Heidegger*. Cambridge: Cambridge University Press.

Gyekye, K. (1987). *An Essay on African Philosophical Thought*. Cambridge: Cambridge University Press.

Gyekye, K. (1992). Person and Community in African Thought. In Kwasi Wiredu and Kwame Gyekye Eds., *Person and Community: Ghanaian Philosophical Studies* (Washington DC: The Council for Research in Values and Philosophy).

Gyekye, K. (1996). *African Cultural Values: An Introduction*. Accra: Sankafa Publishing Company.

Habermas, J. (1973). Theory and practice. Boston: Beacon Press.

Hallen, B. (2004). Yoruba Moral Epistemology. In Kwasi Wiredu Ed., *A Companion to African Philosophy* (Malden MA: Blackwell Publishing).

Hallen, B. and Sodipo, J. O. (1997). *Knowledge, Belief and Witchcraft: Analytic Experiments in African Philosophy*. Stanford: Stanford University Press.

136   *Bibliography*

Hamminga, B. (2005). Epistemology from the African Point of View. In Bert Hamminga Ed., *Knowledge Cultures: Comparative Western and African Epistemology* (Amsterdam: Rodopi).

Heidegger, M. (1962). *Being and Time*, trans. J. Macquarie and E. Robinson (Oxford: Basil Blackwell, 1962).

Ho, L. (2011). What is Social Justice: Occasional Paper #1 *National Pro Bono Resource Centre Occasional Papers* (Australia: The University of New South Wales).

Horkheimer, M. (1993). Between philosophy and social science: selected early writings. Cambridge: MIT Press.

Hospers, J. (1973) *An Introduction to Philosophical Analysis* (London: Routledge and Kegan Paul Ltd).

Hursthouse, R. (1999). Virtue Ethics and Human Nature. *Hume Studies*, 25.1&2.

Idoniboye, D. E. (1973). The Idea of African Philosophy: The Concept of Spirits in African Metaphysics. *Second Order* 11.1.

Idowu, B. (1966). *Olodumare: God in Yoruba Belief*. New Jersey: Prentice Hall Press.

Ikuenobe, P. (2006). *Philosophical Perspective on Communalism and Morality in African Traditions*. London: Lexington Books.

Ikuomola, A. D. (2015). 'We Thought we would be Safe Here': Tanzanian Albinos in Kenya and South Africa, *African Research Review: An International Multidisciplinary Journal*, 9.4.

Ikuomola, A.D. (2015). Socio-Cultural Conception of Albinism and Sexuality: Challenges among Persons with Albinism (PWA) in South West, Nigeria. *International Journal of Arts and Humanities*, 4.2.

Imafidon, E. (2011). Rethinking the Individual's Place in an African (Esan) Ontology. *Cultura: International Journal of Philosophy of Culture and Axiology* 8.1.

Iwelomen, P. O. (2008). Burial Rites and Inheritance Laws in Esanland. P. O. Iwelomen, Ed. *Who is Who in Esan Land* (Ekpoma: Esan Magazine Publication.

Jaspers, k. (1957). *Man in the Modern Age* (London: Anchor Books).

Jost, J. T. and Kay, A. C. (2010). Social Justice: History, Theory and Research. In S. Fiske and D. Gilbert (Eds.), *Handbook of Social Psychology* (New Jersey: John Wiley and Sons).

Kagame, K. (1976) *La Philosophie Bantu Comparee*. Paris.

Kaphagawani, D. N. (2004), African Conceptions of a Person: A Critical Survey. Kwasi Wiredu (Ed.) *A Companion to African Philosophy*. Malden, MA: Blackwell Publishing.

Kariuki, J. (2014). *Albinism and Gene Therapy*, Unpublished Dissertation (Kenya: University of Nairobi).

Kenya holds World's First Albino Beauty Pageant. The Guardian, October 31, 2016. Accessed May 14, 2017 from https://www.theguardian.com/world/2016/oct/31/kenya-hosts-worlds-first-albino-beauty-pageant.

Krappe, A. (2012). Albinos and Albinism in Iranian Tradition. *Folklore*, 55.4.

Kuhn, T. (1996). *The Structure of Scientific Revolution* (Chicago: University of Chicago Press).

Laing, A. (2015). The Albino Children Locked Away to be kept Safe from Witchdoctors. *The Telegraph* 5/6/15. Accessed on April 20, 2017 from: http://www.telegraph.co.uk/news/worldnews/africaandindianocean/tanzania/11718452/The-Albino-children-locked-away-to-be-kept-safe-from-witch-doctors.html.

Livingston, J. (2008). Disgust, Bodily Aesthetics and the Ethic of being Human in Botswana. Africa: *The Journal of the International African Institute*, 78.2.

Bibliography 137

Macklin, R. (2003). Dignity is a Useless Concept: it means no more than Respect for Persons or Their Autonomy. *British Medical Journal*, 327.7429.

Makinde, A. (1988). *African Philosophy, Culture and Traditional Medicine*. Ohio: Ohio University Press.

Malawi Albino Attack Survivor: 'I am too Scared to Sleep. Interview by Patience Atuhaire, BBC News Africa, February 21, 2017. http://www.bbc.com/news/world-africa-39026482.

Malawi24 News. Albino Lady Commits Suicide. Malawi24 News. Accessed on April 14, 2017 from: https://malawi24.com/2016/11/02/albino-lady-commits-suicide/.

Manga, P. and Orlow, S.J. (2011). Informed Reasoning: Repositioning of Nitisinone to treat Oculocutaneous Albinism. *The Journal of Clinical Investigation*, 121.10.

Martinez, M. E. (2001). The Process of Knowing: A Biocognitive Epistemology. *The Journal of Mind and Behaviour*, 22.4.

Mattson, D. J. and Clark, S. G. (2011). Human Dignity in Concept and in Practice. *Policy Sciences*, 44.4.

Mazama, M. A. (2002). Afrocentricity and African Spirituality. *Journal of Black Studies* 33.2.

Mbiti, J. S. (1969). *African Religion and Philosophy*. London: Heinemann Publisher.

McCall, J. C. (1996). Rethinking Ancestors in Africa. *African Journal of the International African Institute* 65.2.

Menkiti, I. A. (2004). On the Normative Conception of a Person. K. Wiredu, Ed. *A Companion to African Philosophy*. Malden, MA: Blackwell Publishing.

Metz, T. (2007). Toward an African Moral Theory. *The Journal of Political Philosophy*. 15.3.

Moloisane, M. L., Liebenberg, W., Lotter, A. P. and De Villiers, M. (2004). Formulation of a Topical Sun Protection Cream for People with Albinism. *East and Central African Journal for Pharmaceutical Sciences*, 7.3.

Mswela, M. and Nothling-Slabbert, M. (2013). Colour Discrimination against Persons with Albinism in South Africa. *South African Journal of Bioethics and Law*, 6.1.

Mudimbe, V. Y. (1988). *The Invention of Africa: Philosophy and the Order of Knowledge*. London: James Currey.

Ndubuisi, F. N. (2004). A Conception of Man in African Communalism. In Jim I. Unah (Ed.). *Metaphysics, Phenomenology and African Philosophy*. Lagos: FADEC Publishers.

Nel, P. J. (2008). Morality and Religion in African Thought. *ActaTheologica* 2.

[1]New Research Unlocks a Mystery of Albinism. News from Brown: Brown University News, December 16, 2014. Accessed June 04, 2017 from https://news.brown.edu/articles/2014/12/albinism.

Ntinda, R. N. (2009). Customary Practices and Children with Albinism in Namibia: A Constitutional Challenge. In liver C. Ruppel (Ed., *Children's Rights in Namibia*. Windhoek, Namibia: Macmillan Education.

Ocular Albinism. In *Vision of Children Foundation* website. Accessed on 07/01/2017 from: http://www.visionofchildren.org/what-is-ocular-albinism/.

Okafor, S. O. (1982). Bantu Philosophy: Placide Tempels Revisited. *Journal of Religion in Africa* 13.2.

Okojie, C. G. (2005). *Esan Dictionary*. Lagos: Perfect Printers Ltd.

Oladipo, O. (1996). *Philosophy and the African Experience: The Contributions of KwasiWiredu*. Ibadan: Hope Publications.

138 *Bibliography*

Oladipo, O. (2004). Religion in African Culture: Some Conceptual Issues. Wiredu, K. Ed. *A Companion to African Philosophy*. Malden, MA: Blackwell Publishing.

Oladipo, O. (2008). *Thinking about Philosophy: A General Guide*. Ibadan: Hope Publications, 2008.

Olafson, F. A. (1996). The Unity of Heidegger's Thought. In Charles B. Guignon Ed., *The Cambridge Companion to Heidegger*. Cambridge: Cambridge University Press.

Olagunju, O. S. (2012). Toward a Biblical Response to Myth and Discrimination against the Human Rights of Albinos in Yorubaland. *Journal of Studies in Social Science*, 1.1.

Onobhayedo, A. (2007). Western Education and Social Change in Esan Land. *IRORO: A Journal of Arts* 7.1 & 2.

Oyeshile, O. A. (2006). The Individual-Community Relationship as an Issue in Social and Political Philosophy. In Olusegun Oladipo Ed., *Core Issue in African Philosophy* (Ibadan: Hope Publications).

Ozumba, G. O. (2004). African Traditional Metaphysics. *Quadlibet Online Journal of Christian Theology and Philosophy*. 6.3: Accessed 01/15/2005 from http://www.Quadlibet.net.

Parker, J. N. and Parker, P. M. (Ed.) (2007). *Oculocutaneous Albinism: A Bibliography and Dictionary for Physicians, Patients and Genome Researchers*. San Diego: ICON Health Publications.

Pearson, K., Nettleship, E. and Usher, G. H. (1911). *A Monograph on Albinism in Man*. London: Dulau and Co Ltd.

Peto, C. (2017). Myths Surrounding Albinism. In *Sunday Mail* 30/04.17. Accessed June 12, 2017 from: http://www.sundaymail.co.zw/myths-surrounding-albinism/.

Plumey, J. M. (1975). The Cosmology of Ancient Egypt. C. Blacker, and M. Lowe (Eds.), *Ancient Cosmologies*. London: George Allen & Unwin.

Probert, T. (Ed.) (2014), *Unlawful Killings in Africa: a Study prepared for the UN Special Rapporteur on Extrajudicial, Summary or Arbitrary Executions*. Cambridge: Centre of Governance and Human Rights, University of Cambridge.

Proctor, R. N. and Londa, S. (Eds.) (2008). *Introduction to Agnotology* (Stanford: Stanford University Press).

Quine, W. V. O. (1953). On What There Is. *The Review of Metaphysics*, 2 (1).

Ralston, D. R. (2011). *The Concept of Disability: A Philosophical Analysis*. Texas: Rice University Unpublished Doctor of Philosophy Thesis.

Richardson, W. J. (1963). Heidegger through Phenomenology to Thought (New York: Fordham University Press).

Salamanca, A. *25 Facts about People with Albinism that we Need to be Aware of*. Accessed on 11/03/2017 from: www.list25.com.

Sartre, J-P. (1957). *Being and Nothingness* (New York: Philosophical Library Press).

Schalow, F and Denker, A. (2010). Historical Dictionary of Heidegger's Philosophy, 2nd Ed. (Lanham: The Scarecrow Press).

Setiloane, G. (1998). Towards a Biocentric Theology and Ethics – via Africa. Du-Toit, C. W. Ed. *Faith, Science, and African Culture: African Cosmology and Africa's Contribution to Science*. Pretoria: UNISA Press.

Shaoping, G. and Lin, Z (2009). Human Dignity as a Right. *Frontiers of Philosophy in China*, 4.3.

Sinari, R. (1970). The problem of human alienation. *Philosophy and Phenomenological Research*, 31.1.

Bibliography 139

Sogolo, G. (1993). *Foundations of African Philosophy: A Definitive Analysis of Conceptual; Issues in African Thought.* Ibadan: Ibadan University Press.

Sullivan, S. And Nancy, T. (Eds.) (2007), Introduction to *Race and Epistemologies of Ignorance.* (Albany: State University of New York Press).

Tanzania Bans Witchdoctors to deter albino killings. Thomson Reuters Foundation, Jan 14, 2015. Accessed May 13, 2017: http://www.reuters.com/article/us-tanzania-albinos-idUSKBN0KN16B20150114.

Tempels, P. (1959), *Bantu Philosophy.* Paris: Presence Africaine.

The Equal Rights Trust in partnership with the Kenya Human Rights Commission (2012). *In the Spirit of Harambee.* London: The Equal Right Trust.

Thuka, M. (2011), Myth, Discrimination and the Call for Special Rights for Persons with Albinism in Sub-Saharan Africa. Accessed 13/03/2017 from: http://www.underthesamesun.com/sites/default/files/MYTHS.Final_pdf.

Titchkosky, T. (2000). Disability Studies: Old and New. *The Canadian Journal of Disability,* 25.2.

Tong, S. (2006). "Critique" immanent in "practice": new Frankfurt school and American pragmatism. Frontiers of Philosophy in China 1.2.

Tutu, D. (1999). *No Future without Forgiveness.* New York: Random House.

Ukhun, C. E. and Inegbedion, N. A. (2007). Ontological Validation of Land Tenureship in Esan Tradition. *Studies in Tribes and Tribals* 5.1.

Ukhun, C.E. (2006). Metaphysical Authoritarianism and the Moral Agent in Esan Traditional Thought. *Uma: Journal of Philosophy and Religious Studies* 1.1.

Ukpong, J. S. (1983). The Problem of God and Sacrifice in African Traditional Religion. *Journal of Religion in Africa* 14.3.

Unah, J. I. (2004). The Nature of African Metaphysics. In Jim I. Unah (Ed.) *Metaphysics, Phenomenology and African Philosophy.* Lagos: FADEC Publishers.

UNHCHR (2013). Persons with Albinism, Report of the Office of the United Nations High Commissioner for Human Rights to the Twenty-Fourth Session of the Human Rights Council of the United Nations' General Assembly. Accessed 13/03/2017 from: www.ohchr.org>A_HRC_24_57_ENG.

United Nations Human Rights: Office of the High Commissioner. Regional Action Plan on Albinism. Accessed May 14, 2017 from: http://www.ohchr.org/EN/Issues/Albinism/Pages/AlbinismInAfrica.aspx.

Usman, E. and Onyegbulam, E. (2015). 23-yr-old Albino Commits Suicide over Condition, Vanguard Newspaper. Accessed April 14, 2017 from: http://www.vanguardngr.com/2015/08/23-yr-old-albino-commits-suicide-over-condition/.

van Heerden, D. (2016). Hunting for Humans: Malawian Albinos Murdered for their Bones. CNN. Accessed May 20, 2017 from: http://edition.cnn.com/2016/06/07/africa/africa-albino-hunted-bones-malawi/

Welshing, F. C. (1991). *The Isis Paper: The Key to the Colours.* Chicago: Third Word Press.

Williams, B, (1985). *Ethics and the Limits of Philosophy.* Cambridge: Harvard University Press.

Wiredu, K. (1980). *Philosophy and an African Culture.* Cambridge: Cambridge University Press.

Wiredu, K. (1992). Death and After Life in African Culture. K. Wiredu and K. Gyekye Eds. *Person and Community: Ghanaian Philosophical Studies.* Washington D.C: The Council for Research in Values and Philosophy.

140 *Bibliography*

Wirth, T. and Yla-Herttuala, S. (2014). Gene Therapy Used in Cancer Treatment. *Biomedicines*, 2.

Wolfe, A. W. (1959). Man's Relation to Man in Africa. *American Anthropologist* 61.4.

World Health Organisation (2011). *World Report on Disability*. Malta: World Health Organisation.

Zhao, M. et al. (2000). A Novel Approach to Gene Therapy of Albino Hair in Histoculture with a retroviral Streptomyces Tyrosinase Gene. *Pigment Cell Research*, 13.5.

Index

ableism 6, 46–48
ableist terms 47, 48
abnormal 19, 23, 70
abnormality xiv, xv, 19
abstraction 5
abuse 84, 88
Achebe, Chinua 42, 51, 133
actinic keratoses 26
activism 111
adages 65
addiction 67
adeno-associated virus 130
adultery 36, 56, 57, 68, 71, 108, 134
Aesthetics 26, 136
afin 19, 47, 53
African belief 30
African body 3
African communalism 49, 87, 137
African cosmology 92, 138
African elite 70
African epistemology ix, 29, 71,
    133, 136
African ethics ix, 29, 75, 76, 82
African metaphysics 49, 51, 133,
    136, 139
African ontology 23, 29–34, 37–9,
    44–6
African representation x
African traditions 6, 38, 40, 44, 55, 63,
    78, 91, 95
afterlife 73
Akan ontology 29, 37
albinism, African peculiarities 23–5
albinism as disability 14–17
albinism, biological understanding
    9–14
albinism, thick concept 17–23
alienation 111, 112, 105, 110, 138
alterity ix, 1, 44, 130

anarchy 128
anatomy 14, 16
Anaximenes 4
ancestors 20, 33–7, 39–41, 43, 46, 50, 56,
    57, 61, 81, 91, 137
ancestral cult 35, 37, 44
angst 97–100
angular kyphosis 38
animals 31, 33, 37, 38, 42, 73, 83, 98,
    99, 134
anti-albinism 24
Appiah, Kwame Anthony 58, 67, 71,
    72, 133
authentic life 99, 105, 107
authoritarianism 49, 139
awareness education 6, 113, 115, 119,
    120, 133
Axiology 50, 93, 133, 136
Azande 42, 72, 135

bad-faith 105
Bantu thought 31
Beauvoir ix, 1
being-in-the-world 102
beingness 4
being-to-herself 102
being-with-fear 98
being-with-others 102
bi-dimensional community 41
bio-psycho-social model 15
black-community 2
bodily aesthetics 26, 136
bodily colour 2
bodily norm 3
bodily normalisation 2
bodily other 3
bullying 14, 15
burden of care 6, 85, 87, 113
burial 35, 40, 50, 136

142　*Index*

Cameroon 103
cancer-gene 128
caregiver 83–7, 89, 106, 122, 124
care-giving 84
causal agency 42, 44
causal explanation 69
causality 42
Chemotherapy 27, 134
children with albinism 27, 86, 90, 91,
　107, 109, 117, 124, 126, 137
civilization 12, 71, 134
co-dependency ethos 77
coexistence 76, 103
cognition 54
cognitive abilities 63
cognitive development 63, 66
cognitive ideal 58, 59
cognitive process 69
cognitive theory 63
colonial masters 115
coming-to-be 45, 52
commensality 41
commodification i, 53, 80
communalism 49, 51, 72, 74, 77, 92, 93,
　136, 137
community-accepted lifestyle 64, 81
communo-cognitive theory 63
compassion 22, 78
Congo 30
corporealities 2
courtship 75
craftsmen 75
crime 22, 108
cultural contexts 15, 17, 29
cultural differences 2
cultural forms 16–18
cursed 14, 47, 83, 104

dark-skinned people 11
deeply entrenched ideologies
　6, 86, 90
deformity 38
deity 19, 78
Deleuze, Gilles ix, 1
dermatologists 24, 124
Derrida, Jacques, ix, 1
Descartes, Rene 59
difference ix–xi, xiii, xiv, 1–3, 6, 19,
　23–6, 39, 45, 111, 116, 120, 134
dignity 6, 48, 75, 77, 78, 87, 88, 90–2, 94,
　106, 112, 121, 123, 133, 137, 138
disabilities 15, 83, 96, 116, 125, 126
discrimination ix, 17, 26, 27, 46–8, 74,
　80, 88, 90, 92, 97, 102, 104–6, 108,

110–2, 115, 118, 121–3, 125, 130, 135,
　137–9
disease 14, 22, 41, 42, 128
disgust 26, 122, 136
dismembering 13, 44, 71, 112
disorder 10, 13, 14, 16
divinities 19, 33, 34, 36, 37, 39, 41, 43,
　46, 56, 61
domination 12, 114
dread x, 6, 97, 98, 100
duty x, 6, 48, 66, 76, 79, 83, 85–7, 89
dwelling 34, 40, 46, 96
Dyer, Richard 16–18, 26, 134

Eastern African 21, 103
easy-to-read pamphlets 123
eclecticism 113
education system 89, 115, 117,
　124–6
elder 56, 64–6, 91, 103, 119
elite 63, 65, 66, 70, 72, 91, 92, 117, 119,
　120, 134
elite-virtue ethics 74
elitism 65, 66
emancipation 114, 120, 121, 123
embodiment ix
encounter 47, 95, 116, 118
energy 30–2, 36–8, 48, 61
enlightenment 26, 46, 113, 114, 116, 117,
　119–21, 123, 127, 134
entities 4, 28, 30–3, 36, 38, 39, 43, 46, 56,
　60, 79, 80, 82, 112
environment xii, 1, 15, 24, 87, 118
epistemic competence 53, 56, 60, 63–5
epistemic framework x, 1, 5, 53
epistemic virtue 55
epistemological modesty 57
equality 84, 85
equal opportunities 118
equal reciprocity 84
equal rights 27, 139
Esan ontology 30
essence xv, 30–2, 44, 45, 60, 84, 109
ethical principles x, 73
ethics 73–6, 78, 80–2, 91–4,
　133–6, 138, 139
ethos 78, 71, 72, 85
Eurocentrics xii
eventing 81
evil 34, 36–9, 45, 37, 57, 68, 82, 83,
　90, 119
existentialism xv, 102
experimental technology 128
eyesight 13, 16, 129

Index   143

facticity 103, 106, 107, 109
fact-norm distinction 45
fairness 92
fair skin 10
falsehood 52, 53, 69–71, 122
families 15, 19, 64, 69, 71, 84, 96, 99, 124, 125, 134
fear x, 2, 6, 21, 22, 70, 96–100, 106, 108, 110, 121, 134
females x, 6, 92, 97, 107, 108
feminine experience 106, 107
feminine figure 2
feminist critique 84
feminist ethicists 85
feminist studies 93, 133
fingers 48, 82
first-hand information 52–6
fishermen 103
Foucault, Michel ix, 1
fragile skin 82, 86
frail 84, 93, 133
freedom 25, 37, 72, 95, 110, 134
frustration 96, 97
functional explanation 67, 69, 71

gender 1, 35, 93, 110, 133, 135
gene enhancement 128
gene research 128
gene therapy x, 113, 127–32, 134–6, 140
gene transfer 130
ghost 14, 21, 46, 47
girl 21, 61, 82, 91, 102, 106–8, 113
glasses 11, 16, 99, 129
gruesome death 98
guardian 37, 38, 131, 136

hacked 72, 134
Hallen, Barry 136, 50, 54, 55, 71, 135
Hamminga, Bert 60–2, 71, 72, 133, 136
harassment 17
harm i, 6, 21, 37, 80–3, 99, 112, 119
harmful beliefs ix, x, 5
haunting 35
health challenges 122, 124
Heidegger 46, 47, 49, 51, 97, 102, 105, 109, 110, 135, 136, 138
herbalist 32
heuristic xvi, 115, 117, 118
hierarchy 33, 37, 38, 66
honey 24, 94, 122
honour 19, 35, 97
hospitality 8, 73, 78
human action 5, 73
human alienation 111, 110, 138

human being 4, 15, 22, 33, 34, 54, 40, 43–5, 57, 75, 82, 90, 95–7, 103, 104, 109
humanism 77, 88, 81, 82
human rights x, xiii, 3, 26, 27, 90, 107, 109–112, 131, 135, 138, 139
human sacrifices 104
hunt 42, 99, 127
husband 40, 56, 57, 83, 85, 107
hygiene 86, 121
hypopigmentation 13

Ibo 20, 27, 30, 37, 133
identity ix, xv, 23, 51, 75, 120, 133
ideological commitments x, 5
ideology 80
idiosyncrasies 55
ignorance x, xiv, 6, 46, 52, 53, 69–72, 86, 94, 113, 116, 117, 122, 133, 139
Ikuenobe, Polycarp xiii, xvi, 31, 42, 49, 51, 72, 74, 77, 92, 93, 136
illness 32, 36, 56, 69
ill-treatment ix, 3, 5, 74, 82, 102, 106, 116
impotency 21, 71, 134
inauthentic existence 105
inauthenticity 102
incantation 19
individual interests 60, 77
infant with albinism 43, 55, 57, 82, 107
infidelity 107, 108
inhuman 21
injustice i, 71
invisible agencies 56, 58
invisible forces 68, 69
isolation 6, 45, 46, 60, 64, 97, 101, 102, 104, 107, 109, 121, 122, 125, 136

job 16, 68, 98, 119, 122, 123
justice ix, 8, 36, 78, 87, 88, 90, 92–4, 127, 133, 136
justification x, 53, 74, 76, 77, 81, 128

Kagame, Alexis 49, 136
Kenya 8, 21, 22, 27, 92, 111–3, 131, 132, 134, 136, 139
kidnapping 100, 108
killings ix, 23, 27, 44, 131, 138, 139
kin 35, 40, 41, 43, 56, 76, 81, 83, 107, 119
kindness 73, 78
kinship 63
knowledge xiv, 48–50, 52–66, 68–72, 86, 87, 89, 93, 95, 100, 107, 113–5
Kwame, Gyekye 50, 58, 71, 72, 78, 79, 92, 93, 135

labour 83, 84, 86, 87, 126
Lacan, Jacques ix, 1
language 28, 29, 46–8, 54, 116, 123
lenses xi, 11, 122, 124, 127, 129
lentigines 8
light-colored irises 129
light-sensitive tissue 10
limbs 76, 82
literacy 65, 114
living-dead 51

machetes 22
magic 27, 36, 37, 72, 134, 135
maiming 25, 80
Malawi 27, 98, 99, 107, 109, 110,
   134, 137
male 71, 106, 107, 134
Mali 49
maltreatment x, 3, 15, 21, 49, 71, 91,
   111, 119
manipular forces 33, 36, 37, 44, 56
marginalization 108
marriage 21, 23, 25, 64, 71, 91, 92, 107
meaningfulness 95
meaninglessness 95
medical-scientific theories 68
melanin 10, 13, 14, 24, 58, 120, 129, 130
menstruation 20
Metz 74–6, 92, 93, 137
misfortune 36, 83
modernity 43, 53
moneymaking rituals 23
monism 5
moral agent 49, 75, 76, 139
moral authority 66, 92
moral code 4, 79, 80
moral humanism 61, 62, 65, 66
moral responsibility 44, 68
moral values 79, 91
murder 22, 27, 36, 71, 76, 134
muscular dystrophy 85
muscular dystrophy 119
mutations 26
myths 20, 27, 96, 131, 138, 139

Nairobi 22, 50, 129, 132, 134, 136
name-calling 102, 105, 121
natural remedies 122
Nollywood 20, 119
non-disabled people 15
non-entity 30
non-European 62, 60
non-governmental organisations 119,
   111, 120, 121, 123, 124, 127

normalcy 14, 64
normalisation 2, 3, 25
normalised bodies 130
norms xv, 2, 23, 45, 60, 65, 73, 74,
   78–80, 83, 88, 105
Nothingness 110, 138
ntu 30
nystagmus 10, 11, 13, 16

object–inhabiting spirits 34
obligations 45, 83, 87
oculocutaneous albinism 10, 11, 13, 16,
   25, 26, 129, 130, 132, 137, 138
ontic 38, 61, 81
ontological commitment 28
ontological differences 39
ontological essence 60
ontological exclusion 44, 45
ontological fact 95, 96
ontological principle 6, 30, 44
ontological relativity 28, 29
ontological representation 45
ontological structure 40, 41
ontological supremacy 33
ontological unity 16
openness 97, 102
ostracism 108
othering x, xv, 2, 44, 111, 112
otherness ix, 1, 12, 46, 130

Pan-African Albino Conference 111,
   131, 135
Paralympian 106
Parmenides 28
partiality 71
peculiarities x, 6, 9, 23, 109
Pedagogy 114, 131, 135
perennialism 113
permissibility 74, 81, 91
persecution 14
perseverance 100, 105
personal hygiene 86
personal identity 23, 51, 133
personhood xv, 6, 66, 74, 75, 102,
   112, 113
phenomena 23, 32, 42, 69
phenomenon-aura 32
photophobia 13, 16, 129
physicalistic representation 5
pigmentation 9–11, 13, 16, 20, 25, 27,
   39, 107, 133
pink-coloured skin 10
polycentric 53
polygamy 81

Index   145

poverty 109, 114
power 18, 21, 13, 30, 34, 36, 53, 61, 65, 103
prejudice 88, 92, 119
primitive whiteness 12
primordial 33, 34, 38
privileges 41, 112
progressivism 113
proliferation 127
psychological trauma 22
punishment 19–21, 35, 39, 56, 57, 82

quadruplets 38
qualities 5, 38, 40, 96
quantity 84, 86
quasi-material substance 37
queerness 23, 39, 44, 96
Quine, Willard V. O. 28, 49

race ix, 1, 12, 26, 72, 73, 133, 134, 139
racism 8, 25
radical communitarian theory 62
rape 6, 36, 97, 108
rationality 8, 68, 93, 33
Rawls, John 87, 94
ready-made patterns of beliefs 67
realist ontology 6
reconstructionism 114
relational value 84
relatives 15, 41, 64, 69
relativism 73
religiously garnished ideologies 70
repugnant 19, 20
repulsive 20
retina 10
revenge 44, 77
reverence 33, 65
rites 35, 40, 50, 80, 136
rituals 19, 21, 23, 33, 37, 56, 80–2, 112

sacred 32, 42, 44
sacrifices 104, 112
sad 102, 125
salt 24, 86, 93, 94
Sartre, Jean-Paul 105, 110, 138
second-hand information 54
security 84, 100, 121, 125, 127
self-actualization process 37, 51
self-esteem 121
self-estrangement 101
self-preservation 82
self-realization 75, 76, 82
self-removal 107
self-respect 87, 90

self-scrutiny 48
self-worth 92, 106
senicide 80, 83
sensitivity 10, 11, 13, 16, 66, 122, 126, 129
sensory perception 54
sex 21, 23, 73, 108
sexual assaults 110, 133
sexual intercourse 20, 108
sexuality 27, 136
sexual relations 61, 81, 82, 107
sexual violence 108
shame 64, 65, 81
shared-knowledge 68
shrines 19, 34, 35
singleness 06
skin-care 122, 123
solidarity 32, 75
solipsism 55
sope 47
sorcery 31, 36, 37
sores 94
spirits 30, 34, 36, 47, 59, 68, 136
sports 11, 16
stigmatisation 6, 90, 102, 104, 106, 118, 119, 122, 125, 130
storytelling 65
sub-Saharan Africa 14, 20, 21, 23, 27, 39, 81, 90, 99, 124, 139
suffering 43, 88, 95, 97, 98, 104
suicide x, 6, 22, 35, 92, 97, 101, 104, 105, 110, 137, 139
sunburn 24, 94, 122, 124, 130
sunlight 16, 24
sunscreen 24, 122, 127, 129
supernatural 23, 36, 39, 43, 45, 46, 53, 79, 80, 83, 104
superstitious beliefs 21
supremacy 12, 33
systemically produced falsehood 69, 70

taboos 56
tanned 130
Tanzania 11, 14, 21, 22, 27, 44, 47, 97, 99, 107, 108, 111, 113, 118, 125, 131, 133, 134, 136, 139
teachers 89, 90, 117, 126
technology 13, 90, 114, 128
Thales 4
therapy x, 113, 127–32, 134–6, 140
thrownness 95, 96
togetherness 60, 62, 77
trauma 22

146 *Index*

triplets 38, 39, 45
twins 38, 39, 45

Ubuntu 75, 76
universalism 73
unlawful killings 27, 138
utilitarianism 5
utility 52, 53, 67, 68, 82, 83, 130

victim 36, 83
village 21, 47, 69, 81, 113, 120
violence 20, 77, 108, 115, 119
virtue x, 54, 55, 83, 85–7, 91, 92, 94, 106, 109, 136
vision 10, 11, 25, 26, 57, 83, 88, 99, 122–4, 126, 129, 137
vision-sensitive duties 16
visual acuity 11
visual gadgets 88
visual impairment 16, 130
vitality 30, 32, 36, 38, 62
vitiligo 13
volition 84
vulnerability 109

weather 126
welfare 74, 75, 77, 78, 123, 124, 127
wellbeing 3, 16, 82
whiteness 12
witchcraft 21, 23, 31, 36, 37, 50, 61, 67, 72, 135
Witchdoctors 72, 131, 134, 136, 139
witches 36, 38, 50, 80, 81, 135
wizards 36, 80, 81
woman 20, 22, 56–8, 78, 69, 71, 103, 107–9, 113
worldviews 43, 62
wrinkles 24

Yoruba 19, 20, 29, 30, 36, 37, 39, 43, 47, 50, 53, 54, 71, 93, 135, 136
youth 21

Zande 67
zeruzeru 47
Zimbabwe 21, 22, 27, 47, 133
Zulu ontology 29
Zulu people 75